Marriage, Divorce, and the Abandoned Wife in Jewish Law

A CONCEPTUAL UNDERSTANDING OF THE AGUNAH PROBLEMS IN AMERICA

Marriage, Divorce, and the Abandoned Wife in Jewish Law

A CONCEPTUAL UNDERSTANDING OF THE AGUNAH PROBLEMS IN AMERICA

by

Michael J. Broyde

KTAV Publishing House, Inc.
2001

Library of Congress Cataloging-in-Publication Data

Broyde, Michael J.
   Marriage, divorce and the abandoned wife in Jewish Law : a conceptual understanding
of the agunah problems in America / Michael J. Broyde.
   p. cm.
 ISBN 0-88125-678-1
 1. Divorce--Law and legislation--United States. 2. Divorce (Jewish law) 3.
 Agunahs--United States. I. Title.

KF536.B76 2000
296.4'444--dc21

                                                          00-060751

                              Distributed by
                       Ktav Publishing House, Inc.
                          900 Jefferson Street
                          Hoboken, NJ 07030
                       201-963-9524 FAX 201-963-0102
                          Email ktav@compuserve.com

לכבוד מ.ע.ר.

חותמו של הקדוש ברוך הוא אמת.
כתב ראש הפילסופים היוני: אהוב סקראט אהוב אפלטון רק האמת אהוב יותר.
שו״ת חוות יאיר סימן ט (גם ראה הקדמת הרז״ה לספר המאור)

The seal of God is Truth.

So says the great philosopher:
"Love Socrates, love Plato; love truth more."

*This book is dedicated to the one who taught me to live by these rules,
and to accept truth as the guiding light.*

Contents

Foreword
The Purpose of This Book   xi

Preface
A Restatement of the Agunah Problem   xv

Chapter One
Jewish Marriage: A Conceptual Review
    of Marriages in the Jewish Tradition   1
        The Fault Exception   3
        Historical Agunah Problems and Solutions   3
        The Talmudic Agunah Problem   3
        The Levirate Marriage Problem and the Case of Agunah   5
        Summary   7
        The Modern Agunah Problem   7
        Solved Cases   7
        The American Agunah Problem   8
        Proposed Solutions to the American Agunah Problem   10
        Annulments   11
        Conditional Marriages   12
        Conditional Promises to Give a *Get*   12
        State Intervention in the Jewish Divorce Process   12
        Support Agreements   13

Chapter Two
Paradigms for Marriage as Grounds for Divorce in
    the Jewish Law Tradition: An Historical Review   15
        The Image of Divorce in the Torah   17
        The Rabbinic Period   17

Post-Talmudic Jewish Law I: The Geonim   19
Post-Talmudic Jewish Law II   20
Option I: Unilateral No-Fault Divorce   20
Option II: Mutual Consent or Hard Fault   21
Option III: Return to Contractual Rules   22
Option IV: Marital Abode as the Norm   23
Gender Equality as the Issue?   23
Modern Developments and Summary   25

Chart 2.1:
Views of Marriage, Divorce, and *Igun* in the Era of the *Rishonim*   28

Chapter Three
Dual System and Divorce: The Impact on the Agunah
  Problem of the American Legal System   29
    Introduction   29
    The Dual System and the Problem of the Agunah   30
    Two Legal Systems   32
    A Comparison of Private and Public Law Models   33
    The New York Experience   35
    Creating the Right to Be Divorced   36
    One Solution: Ignore the Dual System Problem   37
    A Critique of This Approach   38
    The Issue of Commercial Custom   38
    Another Solution: Follow Secular Law   39
    Summary of the Dual System Problems   40

Chapter Four
The Role of Bet Din: How Does a Jewish
  Court Prevent Abandonment of Spouses?   43
    Introduction: Theory and History   43
    The Modern Reality   43
    Jewish Law and Its Role in Marriage   45
    Modern Jewish Law and Marriage in America   46
    Modern Jewish Law and Marriage in Israel   49
    Comparison of Modern Jewish Law and
       Marriage in Israel and America   52
    The Bet Din Issue in America   54
    The Relationship Between the Bet Din System
       and the Secular System   55
    Conclusion   57

Chapter Five
The Multitextured Agunah Problem
    and Proposed Modern Solutions: A Conceptual Critique   59
    Unilateral No-Fault Divorce as the Solution   60
    Abandoning Marriage as a Solution   63
    Contractarian Solutions and Their Problems   63
    Rabbinical Tribunals as a Solution   65
    Prenuptial Agreements as Marriage Contracts   66
    Secular Intervention as a Model for Divorce   68
    Summary of the Modern Solutions and Their Problems   70

Chart 5.1:
Views of Marriage, Divorce, and Igun in the Modern Era   71

Chapter Six
Summary: A Conceptualization of
    the Agunah Problem   73
    The Nature of the Agunah Problem   73
    Preconditions to Successful Solutions   75

Chapter Seven
Summary: A Conceptualization of Solutions
    to the Agunah Problem   79
    The Nature of the Solutions   79
    Pluralistic Images of Marriage and Divorce   81
    Multiple Types of Prenuptial Agreements: A Real Solution
        to the Root Problem of Multiple Images of Divorce   82
    The Bet Din System   82

Chapter Eight
Conclusion: What Can Be Done?   85

Appendix A
A Brief Historical Introduction to Jewish Law   87

Appendix B
Error in the Creation of Jewish Marriages:
    Under What Circumstances Can Error Void
        the Marriage Without Requiring a *Get*   89
    Preface   89
    Introduction   91

Marriage as Contract   92
Defects in the Man   97
Continuing Marriages Which Started with a Defect   100
Conclusion   102

Appendix C
The 1992 New York *Get* Law: A Less than
   Ideal Solution that Creates Halachic Problems   **103**
Introduction   103
Halachic Considerations   105
The Reality of Divorce   113
Conclusion   115

Appendix D
Brief History of Secular Marriage and Divorce Law   **119**

Appendix E
Civil Death as a Concept in Public Marriage Jurisdictions
   Including American Law and Islamic Law   **125**

Appendix F
Sample Arbitration and Prenuptial Agreements   **127**
Memorandum of Agreement   128
Model A   128
Model B   129
Model C   129
Model D   129
Model E   130
Additional Paragraph Governing Fault   130
Model F: The Prenuptial Agreement Authorized
   by the Orthodox Caucus   132

Notes   137

Table of References   187

Subject Index   193

About the Author   197

FOREWORD

The Purpose of This Book

This book is about the relationship between the institution of marriage and the process for ending that institution in the Jewish tradition. The Jewish tradition contains a number of different views of what the "ground rules" are for when divorce is proper, and these rules affect and effect when and how divorce happens. This book is not primarily about devising a mechanism to force the giving or receiving of a *get* in any particular case or set of cases; rather it aims to understand properly what we mean when we speak about the "agunah problem." There are a number of different types of agunah problems (from soldiers lost at war to recalcitrant husbands) that are conceptually quite different from one another. We should not allow the use of a common term to confuse us into thinking that we have a single or united problem.

Essentially, the modern American agunah problem relates to the inability of people to come to an agreement about the terms and conditions for ending their marriage, and thus the marriage does not end.

The theoretical solutions to this problem are not difficult; four solutions come readily to mind, though not all of them are consistent with normative halachah.[1]

1. Judaism can change the rules of divorce so as to allow and encourage divorce anytime either side wishes to be divorced. Disagreements about procedure become secondary, as mar-

riage is viewed as a partnership, with either side able to leave
whenever he or she wishes. (Annulment, then, becomes a
mechanism to achieve this goal; conditional marriage or
conditional divorce can be used similarly as well.)[2]

2. Judaism can follow the secular legal system and announce
   that whenever secular law rules the couple divorced, they
   should be divorced according to Jewish law too. Some prenuptial agreements state this, creating an enforceable right to
   give or receive a *get*.

3. Judaism can revive and empower the Jewish court system so
   as to allow it to adjudicate when Jews should or should not
   be divorced, and to rule on the respective rights of the parties concerning marital assets and children.

4. Judaism can abandon Jewish marriages and allow adherents
   of Jewish law to marry civilly if they wish.

Any one of these four solutions will accomplish the goal of eliminating the agunah problem, but each in very different ways in terms
of what marriages, and thus community and family, will look like.
Option 1 weakens the bonds of marriage and makes people view
marriage as a less stable institution. Option 2 continues the post-
emancipation emasculation of Jewish law; ceding jurisdiction to the
secular legal system rarely strengthens Judaism in either the long or
the short run. Option 3 is not appealing since the bet din system
lacks a track record for solving problems in America. Indeed, some
claim that the system is close to non-functional generally. Option 4
changes the community in incalculable ways; the decision to abandon marriage to solve the agunah problem would lead to the
destruction of the Jewish marriage, and would produce dire consequences. As a matter of public policy, I am convinced that options 1
and 4 are disasters in the making for the Jewish community, having
within them the ability to destroy the central features of the Orthodox Jewish community. (In addition, many of these proposals
nakedly violate Jewish law.)

In sum, I want not to write a book on how to solve the agunah
problem; many different mechanisms have been proposed, each

with its own strengths and weaknesses. Instead, my intention is to note that each of these possible solutions points the Jewish family in different directions, takes the Jewish community and its family structures down different paths, and produces a different type of Jewish family structure. This problem has not previously been explained, possibly because the agunah problems have not been well understood and explained. Doing so is a major purpose of this book.

As a final, and intensely personal note, the reader of this book will see that I do not view the general secular community's solutions to the problems of marriage and divorce as fundamentally successful. I am much less bothered by the perceived irrelevance of the Jewish model to the secular community as a whole, something which I have noticed bothers others intensely. I think the secular community has undergone a vast and systemic decline in interpersonal sexual and marital ethics, particularly in the area of family structures and marital integrity. Rome has fallen. We must make sure that Jerusalem does not fall, too.

★ ★ ★ ★ ★

Many people assisted me in my thinking about the agunah problem. Emory University graciously granted me leave for a year to pursue my interests in Jewish family law, for which I am very grateful. Professor John Witte, Jr., of the Law and Religion Program, and Dean Howard Hunter of the Law School deserve much thanks for arranging leave, and for assisting me in many different ways throughout my career at Emory. The Beth Din of America (founded by and affiliated with the Rabbinical Council of America, and jointly sponsored by the Union of Orthodox Jewish Congregations of America) graciously allowed me to serve as the Director of the Beth Din for a year and continues to allow me to serve as a *dayan* (judge) in that court. It is in that rabbinical court where theory meets practice on a daily basis. Rabbi Gedalia Schwartz, Rabbi Mordechai Willig, and Mr. Sheldon Rudoff are all to be thanked for the help they gave me during that year. Rabbi Willig, particularly, was always willing to assist me in my thinking about this topic. My colleague at Emory,

Rabbi Dr. Michael Berger, was instrumental in pushing me to write
this book, and we collaborated intensely in studying many of these
topics. I look forward to his work in the area and feel a deep sense of
gratitude to him for his assistance in many different matters. Rabbi
Jonathan Reiss, the current director of the Beth Din of America,
served as a sounding board for many of these ideas. I would also like
to thank my research assistants, Jason Caplan and Angela Riccetti.
All errors, however, remain my own.

Finally, my wife, Channah Sageev Broyde, has been an incredi-
ble source of patience, stability, inspiration, joy, and (most significantly) intense intellectual stimulation for this and almost every
other project I have worked on. Without her, none of this would be.
Besides being the mother of our children, and a respected labor lawyer in her own right, she has contributed in many ways to this work.
In truth, this book should be dedicated to her, but who wants to
dedicate a book about divorce to one's wife? Rather, as I have told
many others, the talmudic phrase is more appropriate: *shèli
veshelachem, shela hu.*

Michael J. Broyde

PREFACE

A Restatement of the Agunah Problem

Solving the agunah problem seems to be on everyone's agenda in the Jewish community. Even the popular press writes about it as "a burning issue." Comprehending the agunah problem, however, seems to be an issue that few have worked on, and even fewer have prospered in the work that they have done. The theme of this work is that the contours of the agunah problems are widely misunderstood and that this conceptual misunderstanding vastly exacerbates the difficulty both of determining which problems can be solved and of actually solving them.

This work aims to provide some intellectual coherence and order to the issues of defining what a case of an abandoned wife is, such that the Jewish community ought to consider sanction against one who declines to receive or give a *get* (Jewish divorce rite). As a general matter, this work will not consider what *form* of sanction is permitted by halachah; that is a separate topic that has been extremely well addressed by Rabbi Irving Breitowitz in his excellent work, *Between Civil and Religious Law: The Plight of the Agunah in American Society.*

This work opens with a review of the historical and current agunah problems as well as an introductory survey of proposed solutions and their weaknesses. It then provides an overview of different conceptions of marriage in the rabbinic tradition, as well as different conceptions of divorce. Differing theories of marriage provide a variety of theories of divorce. No less than five different mod-

els of marriage and divorce are noted in the rabbinic tradition. Each
of these models creates certain parameters in which the right to
receive a divorce ought to be supported by the Jewish community.
On the other hand, each of these models also defines certain cases,
different for each model, where there is no right to be divorced
according to Jewish law and thus there would appear to be no right
to receive a *get*. This section notes the ways in which the modern
American agunah problem is unique.

The next section analyzes a uniquely American (and Canadian)
feature of the modern agunah problem, which is the presence of a
mandatory system of secular marriage and divorce. This means, in
essence, that everyone who wishes to be married and divorced
according to Jewish law must really be married and divorced according to two legal systems, Jewish law and American law. This section
also examines the sad state of the Jewish law courts in America, and
how that weakness compounds some agunah problems and makes
others simply unsolvable.

In light of this classification system related to marriage and
divorce, this presentation systematically analyzes different types of
agunot so as to clarify by what right or claim the person seeking a *get*
is "entitled" to one. Presenting the duty to give or receive a *get* in
light of this classification system leads to the conclusion that who is
defined as an agunah/agun (one who is entitled to a *get* and whose
spouse is being improperly recalcitrant) depends on one's conceptual framework of marriage and divorce. Therefore, the book next
systematically analyzes different types of agunot that flow from each
model. Indeed, a woman defined as an agunah in one conception of
marriage and divorce need not be defined as an agunah in all other
models, since each model generates its own particular entitlement to
divorce. With no duty to issue or receive a *get,* one cannot define a
person as an agunah/agun, because that status is logically defined as
a person who is entitled to be divorced but cannot be divorced.[1]

Next, the book notes that of the different categories of agunah
that can be identified, there is a genuine dispute among the viable
definitions of marriage and divorce found in the Jewish tradition as
to whether, in a number of cases, the woman is entitled to a *get* and

is thus an agunah if she does not receive one. Nearly all proposed solutions to the agunah problem do not recognize that their solution is inconsistent with some of the normative images of marriage and divorce found in the Jewish tradition. A rejection by those who adhere to such models has nothing to do with the technical requirement of Jewish law, but is grounded in an image of marriage and divorce as institutions.

This work recognizes the fact that there are significant differences found in the various Jewish communities as to when a woman is entitled to a *get* and thus when a divorce is proper. The book concludes by noting both the theoretical and the practical futility of trying to resolve cases of agunah in a community which does not recognize the halachic right of the woman to receive a *get* regardless of the particular case. Furthermore, an inherently unethical solution to the agunah problem occurs when one group seeks a resolution through secular legislation designed to force the adoption of its image of marriage and divorce on the Jewish community as a whole through the coercive authority of the secular government.

Finally, it must be observed that the legitimate diversity found in the various Jewish communities renders the search for a uniform solution theoretically impossible if that diversity is to be preserved. One cannot force a person to give or receive a *get* in a community that maintains that withholding a *get* is proper. Moreover, to deliberately suppress that diversity is halachically problematic. It forces us to reexamine seriously the propriety of supporting secular coercive legislation that imposes only one particular model of marriage on other segments of the halachic community that subscribe to alternate conceptions.[2]

The final sections of this work propose a conceptual solution to the agunah problem that recognizes this duality of definition and notes one step that can be taken to minimize the modern end of marriage problems in the Jewish community.

Finally, there are six appendices to this work. The first offers a brief history of Jewish law. The second discusses errors in the creation of a marriage, to demonstrate the inapplicability of that principle to mainstream Jewish law of divorce. The third discusses the two

New York *Get* Laws in detail. The fourth reviews the history of secular marriage and divorce law briefly; the fifth examines the legal issue of "civil death" and how it affects marriage in American and Islamic law, and the sixth consists of a series of sample prenuptial and binding arbitration agreements.

CHAPTER ONE

Jewish Marriage: A Conceptual Review of Marriages in the Jewish Tradition

Introduction

The nature of marriage and divorce in the Jewish legal tradition is different from that of any other mainstream legal or religious system in that marriage and divorce are private neo-contractual rights rather than public rights. Thus, in the Jewish view one does not need a "license" or permission to marry or divorce. Private marriages are fundamentally proper, and governmental or even hierarchical (within the faith) regulation of marriage or divorce is the exception rather than the rule. This view stands in sharp contrast to the historical Anglo-American common law view, which treats a private contract to marry or divorce as classical examples of an illegal and void contract; the Catholic view, which treats marriage and annulment (divorce) as sacraments requiring ecclesiastical cooperation; or the European view, which has treated marriage and divorce as an area of public law.[1]

Talmudic Views of Marriage and Divorce

This view of entry into and exit from marriage as contractual doctrines is basic and obvious to those familiar with the rudiments of Jewish law. While the Talmud imposes some limitations on the private right to marry (such as castigating one who marries through a

1

sexual act alone, without any public ceremony)[2] and the later codes impose other requirements (such as insisting that there be an engagement period),[3] basic Jewish law treats marriage as a private contract requiring the consent of both parties. Marriages entered into without consent, with consent predicated on fraud or duress, or grounded in other classical defects that modern law might find more applicable to commercial agreements are all void in the Jewish tradition.[4]

The talmudic view of divorce as contractarian is a bit more complex, in that under biblical law it is possible to claim the husband had an unfettered right to divorce his wife without her consent. It was merely required that she know she was being divorced. Thus, from the view of the wife, this cannot be called contractarian.[5]

From ancient times,[6] however, the husband's unrestricted right to divorce was curtailed through contractarian means, the *ketubah*. The *ketubah* was a premarital contract, agreed to by the husband and wife,[7] that contained terms regulating the conduct of each party in the marriage and discussing the financial terms should the marriage dissolve through divorce or death. While the *ketubah* did not explicitly restrict the unilateral right of the husband to divorce, it did impose a significant financial obligation on the husband should he do so without cause.[8] In addition, and more significantly, the Talmud mandates that the couple may not commence a marital (sexual) relationship unless both the husband and wife have agreed on the provisions of the *ketubah* and one has been executed. There is considerable evidence that the presence of such a mandatory prenuptial agreement provided leverage for women to add provisions to their prenuptial agreements regulating other aspects of their marriage. Indeed, there are prenuptial agreements in the archives (*genizot*) that are 2,000 years old that condition the marriage on the husband's waiver of his right to marry another at some future date, contractually limiting the husband's biblical right to be polygamous.[9]

Certainly, after the decrees of Rabbenu Gershom, of approximately 1,000 years ago, which granted women the right to refuse to accept a writ of divorce and required the consent of both parties to

be divorced in all but case of fault, the Jewish tradition had moved
to a fuller contractarian model.[10]

The Fault Exception

The one exception to the contractarian model has always been the
case of fault. However fault is defined,[11] the Jewish legal tradition
always recognized that in cases of fault either side has the right to
seek unilateral divorce without the consent of the spouse who committed the fault. To this day that remains the view of Jewish law.[12]

Historical Agunah Problems and Solutions

The problem of the agunah, the woman (or man) who is chained to
a marriage and unable to free herself from this marriage, is not a
new one. Indeed, the theoretical problem flows directly from the
very nature of Jewish marriage and divorce. If marriage and divorce
are contractual, what should one do when one party does not wish,
or is unable, to enter into or exit from the contract? Indeed, a historical survey reveals that this overarching issue has been pressing the
Jewish legal system since talmudic (or earlier) times.

The Talmudic Agunah Problem

The Talmud uses the term *agunah* to refer to a woman whose husband has disappeared, leaving her "chained" to a marriage that
exists in name only, since the absent husband is unable to consent to
the divorce. More broadly, this paradigm of a case does not really
involve the genuine desire on the part of the woman or man to be
divorced. This is consistent with the general data extant that divorce
was extremely rare in premodern times, and divorce initiated by the
woman even rarer.[13] Rather, what this woman desired was one of
three options, in descending order. Preferably, she would like her
missing husband to return; absent such, she would like his absence
to be evidence of his death, thus granting her rights of widowhood;
if that alternative is not possible, she would like to be divorced. The
same is true to a lesser extent for the secondary talmudic case of

igun, the spouse who lacks the mental capacity to be divorced. In such a case, the chained spouse does not really want a divorce; rather divorce is merely the best of all the reasonable options.

In response to the problem of the disappearing husband the talmudic Sages elaborated on and liberalized the rules and type of evidence needed to announce that a person who had disappeared was actually dead. This solution allowed a chained woman to free herself from her chains through widowhood. However, it entailed certain risks, because if there was some error and her husband who was thought dead returned, her status as a widow would be in error. If she had subsequently remarried on the basis of that status, her second marriage would be void, resulting in children who were illegitimate and leaving her with the status of either an intentional or unintentional adulteress. It was and is beyond the power of the rabbis to declare the husband dead if he is not, and thereby nullify his marriage.[14]

The second solution advanced by the Sages was one of conditional divorce, whereby a man, before going off on a hazardous journey, would authorize (or even write) a bill of divorce conditional upon his not returning in a certain number of days, weeks, months or years. If the husband did not return within that specified time, the bill of divorce would be delivered (or effectuated, if it was previously conditionally delivered), and the woman would be freed from this marriage.[15] Even if her husband returned, she was no longer married to him if the preconditions for delivery of the Jewish divorce were met. They could remarry, if both of them wished to do so. This solution, while effective in wartime when there were expected risks, was generally thought to be ineffective if the husband and wife were regularly residing in a single domicile unaware of any risk, for reasons that relate to technical Jewish law of intentionality.[16]

It is worth noting that while the Talmud repeatedly discusses the problems of disappearing husbands, and proposes a number of leniencies in different areas of evidence law,[17] the Talmud never proposes that annulment be a solution to cases of spousal abandonment, nor do any of the later codes. Indeed, even in the very troubling talmudic case where two witnesses come forward and attest that a woman's husband is dead, and a Jewish court accepts that testimony and grants the woman the right to remarry upon which she acts, the Talmud cannot find any recourse for this woman or her children from the second marriage if the testimony was incorrect and her first husband returns. The best that the Talmud can provide is that she can return to her first husband, since her adultery was predicated upon a rabbinical error.[18] Annulment, if possible, would be a proper solution, since this is a case of judicial error. Yet the absence of this proposal is itself important evidence of the inability of Jewish law to end marriages through annulment.[19]

The Medieval Agunah Problem

In addition to the ongoing problem of disappearing husbands, post-talmudic Jewish law confronted a different type of agunah problem: the husband who converted to another faith. That faith did not recognize the validity of his prior marriage to a Jewess, allowing him to remarry without divorcing his first wife. She remained "chained" to her husband, with whom she could not live as they were of different faiths. (Such cases of *igun* were common after conversion to Islam and Christianity.)

No solution was ever found that systemically resolved this problem; rather the rabbinical authorities sought to make it easier and easier for a man who had apostatized to another faith to authorize a Jewish divorce for his wife; these liberalizations[20] made it easier to resolve any individual case but never presented a global solution to this problem.[21]

The Levirate Marriage Problem and the Case of Agunah

One agunah problem that repeatedly occurred in this era and that produced a generalized global solution was the case of the levirate marriage to an apostate. (In Jewish law, when a man dies without children, the man's brother may marry his widow; this is called a levirate marriage [*yibum,* in Hebrew]. If he will not engage in a levirate marriage, he must perform a levirate divorce [*chalitza*].)

A common problem of *igun* at that time was the case of a man whose brother had apostatized from Judaism to another faith. Experience had taught that were the husband to die without a child, it would prove very difficult to convince the apostate to perform the requisite levirate divorce; if he were willing to perform it, he might demand considerable payment. Since the couple was readily aware of this contigency at the time of the marriage, the custom developed that at the time of the marriage ceremony the marriage would be made conditionally if there was an apostatized brother. The condition would be that if the woman fell to this brother in a levirate marriage or divorce, this initial marriage should be void.[22] In essence, this condition eliminated the problem.[23]

The Problems of Immigration

With the movement of large segments of the Jewish community from Eastern Europe to America, a new form of agunah problem arose. A husband would efmigrate to America, promising to send for his wife when he accumulated enough money to support her, and would then disappear in America. As with the talmudic case discussed previously, there were only two solutions. As a general proposition, the cases where there might be a basis for declaring the husband to be dead were few and far between. Thus the rabbinical authorities began to encourage men who embarked on the journey to America to either write out a bill of divorce prior to leaving, or to write out an authorization for the Jewish law court in the area to do so. Unlike previous cases of immigration from one location where there was a Jewish community to another such location, in this case there was no Jewish community in America that could facilitate the writing of a Jewish divorce, nor see that it was to be delivered to the wife who awaited her divorce or her ticket to America. (This solution worked when implemented, since the husband and wife were apart during the period where the *get* was pending.)

Summary

Since in the Jewish view marriage and divorce are contractual and not governmental, the problem of spouses who unexpectedly abandon their marital abode and refuse to participate in a divorce proved unsolvable as a matter of theory in the many different premodern agunah cases. Essentially, Jewish law does not allow for divorces that do not have the participation of the husband, and no amount of thought or analysis could create any mechanism that changed this view of the Jewish tradition. It was only in the case of levirate agunah, because that problem could be anticipated by the couple at the time of their marriage and contractual provisions could be taken to minimize or eliminate it, that a global solution was found (and the marriage was over already because of the death of the husband). In all other cases, while the system did the best it could to resolve any given case justly, the high-level principles of private marriages and divorces prevented any successful solution to this problem.

The Modern Agunah Problem

Modern life in America has produced a number of changes in Jewish family law and life; from the view of the agunah problem, a number of these changes are of great significance. As shall be explained, some cases that could not be solved by Jewish law of 500 years ago have been solved by changes in technology or sociology. So too, however, cases that would not have existed 500 years ago because of the structure of the community are now troubling us.

Solved Cases

Technology has effectively eliminated one category of the agunah problem: the involuntarily disappearing husband. Modern technology has made it easy to communicate. People who wish to be found are found. Death is much more easily verifiable, and facts are generally clearer. Thus, while the talmudic and medieval literature is filled with discussion of what to do when a person goes on a boat trip and simply disappears (perhaps the boat sank and the person swam to safety in another country, unable to return or communicate),[24] we now have very few cases where individuals actually disappear without confirmation that they are either alive and locatable or dead. These same advances in technology allow Jewish law to ascertain that a corpse really does belong to a particular person, and thus allow his wife to remarry as a widow when a body is found.

Along the same lines, advances in technology have made communication easier, allowing Jewish divorces to be written in cases where they could not be written a century ago.[25] Even the problematic cases in which one party fled the marriage and was in hiding have been greatly aided by advances in technology and changes in sociology. It grows increasingly difficult to hide one's place of residence, telephone number and bank accounts. Since authorizing the writing of a *get* is relatively easy now,[26] few people, even those who care nothing about Jewish divorce, will avoid giving or receiving one when one is requested merely because of the technical burdens associated with writing or receiving a *get*. It is a rare case when both parties wish to be divorced according to Jewish law and external impediments prevent that.

The American Agunah Problem

The modern American agunah problem is substantively different from the historical agunah problem in that it involves a husband (or on rare occasion a wife) who is available to give a *get* and refuses to do so because he desires something from his wife, such as money or increased access to the children or the like. The husband has not disappeared, nor is he technically incapable—rather, he is recalcitrant. Aware of the fact that his wife cannot, as a matter of religious consciousness or self-imposed Jewish law, consider herself divorced absent a *get*, he will not give her that *get* unless she gives him something in return.

Why did this problem not exist in previous years? After all, if marriage is contractual in nature, surely husbands in other eras should have been aware of this available leverage. This type of agunah problem should be thousands of years old. The answer can be found in substantive Jewish law. When a husband and a wife separate, he is generally obligated to support her according to Jewish law as explained in the *ketubah*; this obligation runs until the marriage is over.[27] Thus when a man refused to give his wife a *get* in times of old, the Jewish law courts imposed support obligations on him to encourage him to give a *get* and exempt himself from these payments. Indeed, even when he was under no obligation according to technical Jewish law to support her, such as when she had committed adultery or the like, the Jewish law courts generally eventually imposed an obligation of support on him.[28] Why is this procedure no longer employed in America? The single most significant reason is that Jewish law has been emasculated since the emancipation. Jewish law courts have been deprived of juridical authority and are powerless to impose obligations on individuals. They have only moral and ethical authority. This situation makes the emasculated Jewish law courts impotent, and vastly exacerbates the modern agunah problem in America.[29]

The Israeli Agunah Problem

The agunah problem in Israel is vastly different from that in America, and much smaller in scope. In Israel the rabbinical courts continue to have jurisdiction over many family law matters; they are courts of the state with many powerful, coercive tools at their disposal to compel compliance with the wishes of the rabbinical courts. Furthermore, the Israeli rabbinical courts have jurisdiction over the marriages and divorces of the entire Israeli Jewish population, including large numbers of individuals who have no fidelity to Jewish law. (This is much less true in America, where those who do not wish to have a Jewish marriage do not have one; in Israel, Jews have no choice.)

Essentially, in Israel the agunah problem revolves around the decision of the rabbinical courts to not impose sanctions encouraging or mandating divorce except where it is absolutely clear that the marriage is irreconcilably over, or where there is clearly demonstrable hard fault present. Thus they rarely order the use of coercion to compel the giving or receiving of a *get,* and only slightly more frequently order support payments as a means to encourage the giving of a *get.* The rabbinical courts discourage unilateral no-fault divorce and very much hesitate to compel a *get* in such circumstances. They are inclined to require counseling, therapy, mediation, and other techniques of reconciliation as alternatives to divorce, particularly when there are children in the marriage.

This is not, in the classical sense, a case of *igun,* if one defines *igun* as a case where a woman is entitled to be divorced according to Jewish law and is not receiving her divorce. Rather the "agunah" in this case is a person whose marriage has, in fact, ended in her (or sometimes his) view, and who feels that she should be out of the marriage de jure that has ended de facto. The understanding of Jewish law found in the Israeli rabbinical courts (which will be elaborated on in Chapter 2) does not agree with her view.

Proposed Solutions to the American Agunah Problem

In the last 70 years there have been many proposed global solutions to the modern American agunah problem described above. These solutions fall into six basic categories: annulments, conditional marriages, conditional promises to give a *get,* state intervention, support agreements, and submission to rabbinical jurisdiction. Some of these solutions are faulty as a matter of normative halachah; others fly in the face of the historical Jewish view of marriage. Others present technical problems in the area of coerced divorce (*get meuseh*), and still others are technically viable but will not be widely implemented because they misunderstand the underpinnings of marriage found in many segments of the Jewish community. The next sections will explain these proposals, and elucidate any fundamental flaws.[30]

It is worth emphasizing that there is another approach to the agunah problem which is commonly employed: to seek a case-by-case resolution based on whichever tool at hand produces a satisfactory resolution of the issue. Sometimes this approach focuses on finding an error in the marriage[31] (thus eliminating the need for a *get*), conducting a din torah to address the parties' concerns, paying money for the *get*, using persuasion or social pressure, or using force or the threat of force. This work will not address these personalized solutions, meritorious or detrimental as they may be, since the very nature of our discussion involves the search for a principled and global solution.

Annulments

The use of annulments to resolve the agunah problem has been proposed with some regularity by a variety of authors. While there is a small amount of literature about annulments from the view of technical Jewish law (the concept is discussed in the talmudic literature in five specific cases), normative Jewish law limits annulments to cases where either the marriage was not yet consummated or there was a gross impropriety in the enactment of the marriage. This is the technical view of Jewish law adhered to by the overwhelming majority of scholars.[32] Those who disagree with this view argue that it is conceivable to permit annulments when there is a communal decree permitting them (even post-consummation), and even then only for marriages contracted after the decree.[33]

The essential problem with annulment as a solution is elaborated on in Chapter 4, but should be noted here. Annulment is predicated on a view (common in modern American law) that marriage and divorce are governmentally regulated activities that are part of the public legal system. Jewish law essentially does not view marriage and divorce as public law, and thus does not, on a systemic level, give the Jewish law courts the ability to end marriages without the participation of the parties. Annulment, like all court-granted divorce systems, presupposes that the public law system is supposed to "grant" divorces. However, in Jewish law the community cannot enact legislation that restricts a person's ability to marry without the consent of the community as a whole, or without the presence of a larger quorum than required.[34]

Conditional Marriages

The use of conditional marriages as a solution to the agunah problem is quite old and has a considerable amount of support. Essentially, the technical halachic problem here has to do with the well-established view in normative Jewish law that conditions imposed on a marriage that involve the participants themselves are generally waived by the parties in the course of the marriage, and in the face of an ongoing sexual relationship between the parties.

Conditional Promises to Give a Get

Another version of the conditional marriage is the signing of a conditional obligation or authorization to give a Jewish divorce upon a set of specific circumstances. The same objections are raised to this solution as to conditional marriages. As a general proposition, according to technical Jewish law, one cannot authorize the writing of a Jewish divorce and yet continue to live together as husband and wife.

State Intervention in the Jewish Divorce Process

State intervention in the Jewish divorce process actually involves two completely different types of intervention, which will be explained at great length in Chapter 3. Suffice it to review here the two New York State *Get* Laws as prototypes of the two kinds of interference. The 1984 *Get* Law prevents New York State from granting a civil divorce until a Jewish divorce is forthcoming in cases where an Orthodox rabbi performed the marriage and one who filed for divorce is withholding the *get*; it never encourages a Jewish divorce, and it insists that the civil divorce system will wait for the Jewish divorce. The 1992 New York *Get* Law, on the other hand, encourages the giving of a Jewish divorce in those cases where a civil divorce will be granted. (The same can be said about the occasional tort award issued against a husband for the intentional infliction of emotional distress when he withholds a *get*.)[35]

These two models of secular interference are very different; the first is nearly without controversy within Jewish law, while the second creates vast technical problems as well as significant ideological ones. In short, the second type of secular law attempts to solve the agunah problem by directing that a *get* should be given at times determined by the State of New York, whereas the first *Get* Law merely deprives one of a civil privilege (civil divorce) until a Jewish divorce is issued. On the other hand, the first type of law is frequently ineffective, because the party withholding the *get* is willing or happy not to be civilly divorced too.[36] This same criticism can be directed at tort law judgments that aim to direct the giving of a *get* as well. This type of civil court judgment to give a *get* creates a host of technical problems in the area of coerced divorce (*get me'useh*) and also involves the wholesale abandonment of the autonomy of Jewish law. In this model, a *get* is proper when a civil divorce is proper. For reasons that will be explained in Chapter 3, that image of Jewish law will never be accepted by the breadth and depth of the Jewish community.

Support Agreements

Support agreements are the oldest proposed solution to the problem of recalcitrant husbands, having their origins in a proposal of the author of the *Nachlat Shiva* nearly 300 years ago. These agreements elaborate on the fact that Jewish law directs that a husband support his wife while they are married; such agreements generally require that the husband turn the inchoate obligation to support (which is in place while the couple shares bed and board) into a concrete financial obligation should they separate. The term "divorce" is never mentioned. This type of agreement directs that so long as husband and wife are married according to Jewish law, husband shall support wife. If they are not sharing bed and board, such support

shall be a sum specified (which must reasonably correlate to the true
cost of living). Unstated in this agreement is that the husband may
end his ongoing obligation to support by divorcing his wife according to Jewish law.[37]

These agreements are without serious technical obstacles
according to Jewish law. However, as will be explained in Chapter 2,
they are predicated on the model of unilateral exit rights from a
marriage, which is not the model of marriage and divorce extant in
many communities.[38]

Submission to Rabbinical Arbitration

Another type of solution is to have the couple sign a binding arbitration agreement that directs that all disputes, or merely disputes
about the giving or receiving of a Jewish divorce, shall be resolved by
a rabbinical tribunal. In the United States, after proper notice and
compliance with statutes that govern form rather than substance,
every state in the Union will enforce the order of a rabbinical tribunal.

What is unclear about this solution is whether it will solve the
problem of recalcitrant husbands. As will be explained at the beginning of the next chapter, there are a considerable number of models
of marriage and divorce that are not predicated on the right of each
party to be divorced when he or she wishes to be. If this solution is
widely implemented, the agunah problem in America will resemble
the agunah problem in Israel.

Conclusion

This chapter serves as an introduction to the problems related to
end-of-marriage issues in Jewish law, and the many proposed developments or changes that have been put forward to alleviate the
plight of the abandoned wife in Jewish law, both historically and
currently. The next chapter is a more conceptual analysis of the
abandoned spouse problem, focusing on conceptualizations of the
status of marriage and the proper role of divorce in Jewish tradition.

CHAPTER TWO

Paradigms for Marriage as Grounds for Divorce in the Jewish Law Tradition: An Historical Review

Introduction

In the Jewish tradition, marriages are ideally entered into with the view that they are permanent relationships. Divorce is not the ideal. That having been said, it is clear that within the halachic traditions, the matter of why and when divorce is frowned upon has different meaning for different decisors. Jewish law defines an agunah as a woman who wants to be divorced, is entitled to a *get,* but is not receiving one. The question of when a divorce is encouraged, mandated, permitted, desired, or deserved varies among the Jewish law traditions and has changed since biblical times. A review of these changes within Jewish family law concerning the grounds for divorce offer a fascinating review of the possible options available in end-of-marriage problems. The normative rules of Jewish law have undergone a number of deeply significant changes.

Consider certain basic Jewish doctrines about entry into and exit from marriage. In general, marriage requires the mutual consent of both parties. Not only must this consent be unconditionally given, but as a matter of legal and religious theory one is under no ethical or religious duty to give that consent merely because one person wishes to marry him or her, even if he or she wishes to marry that person very much. One can, fully consistent with Jewish law and ethics, decline to marry a person because the person lacks financial resources, the person will not commit to a larger dowry, or because one simply does not love the person. Marriage is a discretionary act in almost all cases, and consent to marry, freely given and freely withheld, is required for almost all marriages.

Suppose for example, someone owns a painting that another likes. The fair market value of this painting is $100. For how much must this owner of the painting sell the painting to the one who wishes to buy it? The answer is that Jewish law does not provide a price. The seller need sell it only at a price at which he or she is comfortable selling it, and the buyer need buy it only at a price at which the buyer is comfortable buying it (so long as they are both aware of the fact that the fair market value is $100). The same is true for a marriage; neither party needs to consent to marriage unless he or she genuinely wishes to do so.[1]

What, then, according to Jewish legal theory, is the rule for exit from the marriage? When is divorce proper or required?

This section will not discuss how Jewish law or ethics punishes violators of the duty to divorce, since that is a secondary, mechanistic question, albeit an important one. Rather it will seek to answer a more fundamental question relating to the agunah problem: In an ideal society where everyone obeys Jewish law (either because they have to or because they want to), when does divorce occur according to the Jewish tradition?

One note on terminology: We will refer to marriages with unilateral exit rights as partnerships, in that the essential characteristic of a partnership is the unfettered exit rights of each partner. When the exit rights are severely restricted, by either mutual consent requirements or other requirements, the marriage is referred to as a domestic corporation, since the essence of a corporation is that one cannot exit merely by deciding to leave.

The Image of Divorce in the Torah

While the Torah has a number of stories and incidents concerning marriage,[2] in terms of divorce law little is known other than the talmudic description of biblical law and the brief verses that incidentally mention divorce in the course of describing remarriage of one's divorcee. According to the talmudic understanding of Torah law, there was a unilateral (and apparently unrestricted) right to divorce by the husband, with no right to divorce by the wife except in cases of hard fault.

The majority opinion within Jewish law maintains that there is no right to dower (*ketubah*) according to biblical law. The minority opinion is that under biblical law there was a right to dower, which was restricted to first marriages for virgin brides, and the amount of the dower was two hundred zuz: no more than one hundred pounds of silver.[3] Thus, the biblical rules appeared as follows:

1. The husband had a unilateral right to divorce (and perhaps in some marriages had to pay dower absent fault).

In addition, marriages could be polygamous, although polyandry was never permitted in the Jewish tradition.

Thus, according to Torah law, exit from marriage was drastically different from entry into marriage. It did not require the consent of both parties. The marriage could end when the husband alone wished to end it. Marriage was imbalanced in other ways as well; a man could be married to more than one wife, any of whom he could divorce at will, whereas a woman could be married to only one man at a time, and she had no clearly defined right of exit, perhaps other than for fault.[4]

The Rabbinic Period

As soon as codified Jewish law was recorded, there was the development (which might have biblical origins) of the notion of dower (*ketubah*) for all brides, and this became, by rabbinic decree, a precondition to any marriage (first or not, virgin bride or not). Thus while the right to divorce remained unilateral for the husband, with no right of consent by the wife, it was now restricted by a clear financial obligation imposed on the husband to compensate his wife if he exercised his right to engage in unilateral divorce absent judicially declared fault on her part. The Talmud even records views that if the husband cannot pay the financial obligation, he is prohibited from divorcing his wife.[5]

Indeed, the wife, as a precondition to entry into the marriage, could insist on a dower higher than the minimum promulgated by the rabbis. In the case of divorce for provable fault by the wife, the obligation to pay dower was removed. In addition, there is the clear enunciation of the wife's right to sue for divorce where there is fault by the husband, including such grounds as provable repugnancy, impotence, and other such grounds. In such a case, the husband must divorce his wife (and in most cases pay the dower too). Of course, divorce could be by mutual consent, subject to whatever agreement the parties wished.

Thus the talmudic rules were as follows:

1. The husband had a unilateral right to divorce and had to pay dower absent fault.
2. There was divorce by mutual consent with dower to be determined by the parties.
3. There was a right to divorce through a judicial declaration of "hard" fault: if by the woman, with no dower; if by the man, with dower.

Marriages could still be polygamous for the man. Thus, in a case where the husband and wife no longer wished to live together, the husband could marry another and continue to support his first wife. She could not under such circumstances sue for divorce[6] as a general rule, although she could perhaps restrict his rights through a *ketubah* provision.[7] Marriage remained fundamentally a partnership for the husband, in that he could leave whenever he wished. However, such unilateral no-fault exit was expensive for him. To the wife, marriage was corporate, except in cases of fault. A significant imbalance remained between the husband and the wife on the rights of exit from their marriage.

Soon after the close of the talmudic period, the rabbis of that time (called *geonim*) changed or reinterpreted[8] the substantive understanding of Jewish law to vastly increase the right of a woman to sue for divorce. According to the *geonim* all the woman had to do was leave the household for a period of time and she had an automatic right to divorce, according to most opinions, with a full or partial right to dower. The husband too had this right, as he always did deriving from pre-talmudic times.

Thus during the last two hundred years of the Jewish community's existence in Babylonia, Jewish divorce law appeared as follows:

1. The husband had a unilateral right to divorce and had to pay dower absent fault.
2. The woman had a unilateral right to divorce, and if she exercised it, she received dower.
3. There was divorce by mutual consent with dower to be determined by the parties.

Marriages could still be polygamous for the husband.

These two changes in talmudic law were profound; they fundamentally equalized the rights of exit from a marriage. In the view of the *geonim*, marriage, like all partnerships, requires the consent of all the partners to continue to function; when either partner desires to leave, the marriage should end. Indeed, the *geonim* devised a mechanism to ensure that it did end: this appears to be annulment, or coercion to divorce even in the absence of fault.[9]

There is considerable evidence that the era of the *geonim* was the only one in which the annulment process (mentioned in only a very few cases in the Talmud, and always either pre-consummation or involving bad faith marriages or divorces) was actually used with any consistency and frequency by rabbinic authorities. Based on considerable evidence from the responsa literature (response to a question on a specific matter by a Jewish legal scholar), it appears that in cases where a divorce needed to be given by a husband who would not provide one, the *geonim* of that era annulled these marriages (under the *dina de'metivta* decree). Thus, there was a fourth ground:

> 4. There was divorce through a judicial declaration: if by the woman, with no dower; if by the man, with dower.

It cannot be emphasized enough that whether the *geonim* used this power or not, regardless of rubric, such annulments remain a dead letter in modern Jewish law.[10]

Post-Talmudic Jewish Law II

Within a hundred years of the Jewish expulsion from Babylonia, there was full abandonment of the rules used by the latter-generation Babylonian rabbis (*geonim*), in favor of a number of different alternatives:

Option I: Unilateral No-Fault Divorce

Maimonides (Rambam) ruled that Jewish law did not possess any annulment power, but that the obligation upon a husband to divorce his wife for fault included her assertion (even if unproven) that "he was repugnant to her." In such a circumstance, the husband must divorce his wife, and a Jewish law court should compel such a divorce under the threat of court sanction, including physical coercion if the husband would not give the *get* of his own free will.

Thus according to Maimonides, both husband and wife had a unilateral right to divorce, with no dower paid when the woman initiated divorce absent cause, and dower paid when the husband initiated divorce without cause. Marriages could still be polygamous.

This is a no-fault divorce system and remains to this day the normative rule of law in only small portions of the Jewish community (such as Yemen). This model, like the model of the *geonim*, achieved equality between husband and wife by granting to the woman the same right that the man had: the right to seek

unilateral no-fault divorce. Marriage was, in the view of Maimonides, a partnership. When either side wanted out, Jewish law
allowed him or her to leave.[11]

Option II: Mutual Consent or Hard Fault

European Jewry, too, ruled that Jewish law did not possess any
annulment power and the broad sweeping rule of the *geonim* was not
to be followed. More significantly, through the efforts of a sage,
Rabbenu Gershom, a decree was enacted which significantly
changed the whole model of marriage. The view of Rabbenu Gershom was that in order to equalize the rights of the husband and
wife to divorce, it was necessary to restrict the rights of the husband
and prohibit unilateral no-fault divorce by either husband or wife.
Divorce was limited to cases of provable fault or mutual consent. In
addition, fault was vastly redefined to exclude cases of soft fault
such as repugnancy, and in only a few cases of serious fault could
the husband be actually forced to divorce his wife or the reverse.[12]

Equally significant, this decree prohibited polygamy, thus placing considerable pressure on the man in a marriage that was ending
to actually divorce his wife, since not only would she not be allowed
to remarry, but neither would he. (Absent the prohibition on polygamy, the decree restricting the right to divorce would not work, as
the husband who could not divorce would simply remarry and
abandon his first wife.) According to this approach, Jewish law permitted divorce only through mutual consent or very significant
fault. When there was no finding of fault, little (perhaps other than
imposition of a support obligation) could be done to encourage the
couple to be divorced.

Essentially, there are two theoretical solutions to the power
imbalance between the husband and wife. The *geonim* and Rambam
attempted to solve the problem by increasing the power of the wife.
R. Gershom, and nearly all *rishonim* after him (with the exception of
Rambam), adopted a completely contrary solution, attempting to
solve this problem by restricting the power of the husband.

According to R. Gershom, this solution to the problem of equality in right to exit is corporate in nature. Neither party may exit the marriage without the consent of another. Marriage requires the consent of both parties to enter into it, and according to the view of Rabbenu Gershom, both parties to exit it. It is only in the case of hard fault that consent is not needed.[13]

Option III: Return to Contractual Rules

Even Oriental Jewry rejected Maimonides' and the *geonim's* views of Jewish law. It ruled that Jewish law did not possess any annulment power and that fault was limited to hard fault when the woman alleged it against the man. However, Oriental Jewry rejected the decrees promulgated in Europe prohibiting unilateral divorce by the husband and prohibiting polygamy. Thus it returned to the classical talmudic rules of regulation and restriction of the husband's right to unilateral divorce by dower contract; women, in this view, should protect themselves by insisting on their rights at the time of entry into marriage. If they wished to restrict the husband's entry rights, they could do so by imposing a high dower payment. So too, if they wished to curtail his right to take a second wife, they could impose that obligation in the *ketubah*. Most decisors ruled that absent fault, it was prohibited to divorce one's wife unilaterally unless one was financially able to pay the dower contract.

The woman had a right to sue for divorce only on the basis of hard fault (such as leprosy), and she could use the waiver of her rights under the dower contract as an inducement to be given a unilateral divorce. Polygamy was permitted, and the husband still had his right to unilateral divorce even without fault, although he would be required to pay the amount agreed on by the parties in the *ketubah*. In this view, marriage was a partnership for him, albeit one whose exit costs were contractually delineated, and perhaps even restricted. Marriage for her was corporate in nature; she could exit only with his consent or in a case of judicially determined fault.

Option IV: Marital Abode as the Norm

A second view within European Jewry agreed with the rule that Jewish law did not possess any annulment power and the broad sweeping rule of the *geonim* was not to be followed. It also agreed with the decrees of the sage Rabbenu Gershom, that to equalize the rights of the husband and wife to divorce, it was necessary to restrict the rights of the husband and prohibit unilateral no-fault divorce by either husband or wife. This was true under all circumstances except where the marital estate had ceased to exist and the couple had de facto ended all marital relations. This approach modified Option II to include the failure of the marriage as itself ground for coercing the giving or receiving of a *get*. Rabbenu Chaim Or Zarua was the authority who clearly elaborated on this approach in his responsa. In modern times this ruling resonates in the writings of Rabbi Yosef Eliyahu Henkin[14] and Rabbi Moshe Feinstein.[15]

According to this approach, Jewish law permitted divorce only through mutual consent, failure of the marriage through the end of a marital residence, or very significant fault. This approach accepted as correct the decree of Rabbenu Gershom, which prohibited polygamy, thus placing considerable pressure on the man in a marriage that was ending to actually divorce his wife, since not only would she not be allowed to remarry, but neither would he.

This solution to the problem of equality in right to exit was somewhat corporate and somewhat partnership in nature. Neither party could exit the marriage without the consent of the other or the de facto end of the marriage. When the corporation is running, neither could end it; once the marital corporation ended de facto, it had to end de jure. Marriage was a state of existence in which the two parties were required to coexist in a marital state. Absent that marital state, either party had a right to exit, which the other could not refuse.

Gender Equality as the Issue?

Some have asserted that the fundamental problem with the Jewish tradition has nothing to do with when one can be divorced, but with the inherent inequality in rights between the husband and wife to seek divorce. This "equality of rights" view argues that it does not matter when divorce is permitted (or even if it is never permitted), so long as both husbands and wives have the same rights and the same access to divorce. The failure in Jewish law, claims this view, relates to the imbalance in options: men can divorce their wives, and women cannot divorce their husbands. Indeed, privately a number of people have argued that it hardly matters whether Jewish law adopts the "no fault divorce" view of Maimonides or the "no divorce absent consent or hard fault" view of Rabbenu Tam, so long as both partners have the same rights.[16]

While there is something to this view in the Jewish tradition, since the theoretical inequality is vast according to biblical law, the inequality is immensely overstated on a practical level. It also profoundly misunderstands the reality of Jewish divorce since the decrees of Rabbenu Gershom prohibiting polygamy and unilateral no-fault divorce by the husband,[17] which nearly all of world Jewry (all Jews in America, Israel and Europe) accept as binding.

As explained above, under the rules of Rabbenu Tam and Rabbenu Gershom, or the rules of Rabbenu Chaim Or Zarua and Rabbenu Gershom, the gender inequity is extremely small; it is limited to cases of hard fault, where the woman will not or cannot accept a *get* and the husband is prepared to undergo the process of receiving permission from 100 rabbis located in various places to take a second wife, after issuing his first wife a bill of divorce. This process is rare, accounting for a very small portion of the cases under discussion, since this leniency is applicable in only a few cases. Statistics demonstrate that the problem of inequality created by the 100 rabbis procedure cannot be the agunah problem on everyone's mind. In 1996, when there were a large (perhaps even too large) number of *heter meah rabbanim*[18] issued by the Israeli chief rabbinate (the only organization authorized to issue such documentation in Israel), there were 4,700,000 Jews living in Israel, of whom 37,000 contracted to marry in the state of Israel, 9,680 were divorced with a *get,* and 12 were issued 100 rabbi documents permitting remarriage of the husband without the divorce of the wife.[19]

One in every 3,083 marriages entered into in Israel ended in this process, and one in every 850 marriages that ended in any way ended with the 100 rabbis rite. This is an astonishingly small number. Indeed, if one were to extrapolate from the Israeli experience to the American-Jewish experience, I would guess that there are no more than two or three such cases per year in the United States, since there are fewer than 750,000 people who seek to be governed by Jewish law in America, in contrast to 4,700,000 such people in Israel. This number (two or three *heter meah rabbanim* per year) is consistent with the number this writer hears about as a *dayan* in a bet din.

In sum, while the system is not grounded in equality of biblical rights, the purpose of the decrees of Rabbenu Gershom were to create equality in fact, and such is generally the norm. The agunah problem is not caused by inequality of rights.[20]

There is, without a doubt, a secondary problem associated with the 100 rabbis rite which waives the man's prohibition on polygamy. It has been alleged (and it appears to be true) that there are less-than-ethical Jewish law courts in America that will issue "one hundred rabbi letters" in circumstances not permitted according to Jewish law or even when the whole document is forged. This failing (which could be quite serious) reflects not a theoretical failing of the structure of Jewish law, but structural problems with the bet din system in America. Serious as this question is, and much as it affects the plight of men and women who adhere to Jewish law in matters of family law, it is not really a family law problem. This issue is addressed at some length in Chapter 4.

Modern Developments and Summary

For reasons that are beyond the scope of this work,[21] neither Maimonides' view[22] nor Rabbi Karo's view[23] are currently in use in any parts of the normative Jewish world (with perhaps the small exception of the tiny remaining Jewish communities in Iran, Iraq, Egypt, and Yemen). Israeli Orthodox Jewry, at a national rabbinic conference called by the chief rabbis of Israel, in 1950 passed an enactment generally making monogamy binding upon all Jews irrespective of their communal affiliations.[24]

The two remaining models differ profoundly in a conceptual way, which greatly affects how one views the agunah problem. According to one model, the exact decree to equalize the power of the man and the woman, enacted through Rabbenu Gershom and Rabbenu Tam, created a situation in which neither side can seek divorce without the consent of the other. The "solution" to the problem of the husband's right to divorce his wife unilaterally, in this view, is to prohibit such a divorce. Neither side may divorce the other without consent, or without an order from a bet din announcing a determination of fault. If one wished to be divorced and the other did not, one had to persuade the other to acquiesce. One such method of persuasion is money.

According to the second view, the "death" of the marriage de facto is itself grounds to end the marriage de jure through a *get*; once the marriage is really over, the marriage should end and a divorce should be given. The "solution" to the problem of the husband's right to divorce his wife unilaterally, in this view, is to allow for divorce any time the marriage has functionally ended, whether it be by husband or wife. Either side may seek to divorce the other without consent, or without an order from a bet din announcing a determination of fault, when the marriage is dead de facto.

Maimonides' view, since rejected by normative Jewish law, also is an attempt to address the problem of the husband's right to divorce his wife unilaterally; in this view the solution is to allow the woman (or the man) to seek unilateral no fault divorce for herself (or himself) as well. Either side may seek to divorce the other without mutual consent, or without an order from a bet din announcing a determination of fault, whenever they wish.

In sum, the talmudic period left the woman at a disadvantage in the area of divorce. Husband could unilaterally seek to divorce wife, but wife could seek to divorce husband only upon a finding of fault, or with his consent. Three solutions were put forward to address this problem. Each made marriage "fairer," albeit in vastly different ways.

1. Unilateral no-fault divorce should be allowed to women as well (Rambam).
2. Unilateral no-fault divorce should never be allowed to either party (R. Gershom and R. Tam).
3. Unilateral no-fault divorce should only be permitted when the marriage is factually over (Or Zarua).

Each category created some form of equality, albeit very different kinds from one another. Chart 2.1 elaborates upon and summarizes these different views (p. 28).

Chart 2.1:

Views of Marriage, Divorce, and *Igun* in the Era of the *Rishonim*

Implications → / Models of Divorce ↓	Authorities Supporting Such	Conceptual Model of Marriage	Role of Bet Din	When a *Get* Is to Be Issued	Sources on the Duty to Divorce
Unilateral No Fault	Early: *Geonim* and Rambam; Late: Yemen	Partnership (polygamous)	Procedural (arranges *get*)	Upon request of either party	*Takanat ha-Geonim*, pp. 11–12; *Teshuvot ha-Rosh* 43:8; Rambam, *Ishut* 14:8
Mutual Consent or Fault	Early: R. Gershom and R. Tam; Modern: Rama	Domestic corporation (monogamous)	Substantive (determines fault, which permits unilateral divorce or nominal polygamy) or procedural in the case of mutual consent divorce	Fault or mutual consent to issue the *get* (acknowledged end of marital state not sufficient)	Tosafot, Ketubot 63a s.v. *aval*; *Shulchan Aruch*, Even ha-Ezer 1:9, 77:2 (Rama, writing for an Ashkenazic audience)
Unilateral for Him, Fault for Her	Early: R. Joseph Karo (Shulchan Aruch); Modern: Egypt	Partnership for him, corporate for her (polygamous)	Substantive (determines fault which permits unilateral divorce or nominal polygamy) or procedural in the case of mutual or divorce initiated by husband	Fault or husband's consent; (acknowledged end of marital state not sufficient)	Shulchan Aruch, Even ha-Ezer 1:9, 77:2 (R. Karo, writing for a Sefardic audience, accepts R. Tam, but does not accept R. Gershom)
Mutually Agreed End of Marital State; Fault	Early: R. Chaim, Or Zarua; Modern: R. Moshe Feinstein	Functioning marital state (monogamous)	Substantive in two different modalities: determines end of marital state even absent fault, or fault which permits unilateral divorce or nominal polygamy; or procedural in the case of divorce by mutual consent	Fault or mutual absence of marital state	R. Chaim, Or Zarua, Teshuva 126; *Kol Kitvei ha-Rav Henkin* 1:115a–b; *Iggrot Moshe*, Even ha-Ezer 3:44 and Yoreh Deah 4:15; *Tzitz Eliezer* 18:58; *Peskai Din Rabaniyin* 1:238, 9:171

CHAPTER THREE

Dual System and Divorce: The Impact on the Agunah Problem of the American Legal System

Introduction

One of the issues unique to the American modern agunah problem is the presence of a secular civil divorce law that governs the process of divorce for all members of society. Unlike the norm of civil law throughout the world a hundred years ago, where matters of family law were left to religious authorities within each community and where "secular" marriage and divorce were, at best, reserved for those who were not a member of any religious community, modern American divorce law (and to a lesser extent, marriage law) mandates being married and divorced in accordance with the neutral, secular principles of law established by society.[1] Thus, each person who marries in America, even with the intent that the marriage be governed exclusively by Jewish law, must be divorced by the secular legal authorities and secular law.[2]

Secular law can and will impose its own values on divorce, from its ethical perception of the proper place for children to reside, to its understanding of the respective rights of spouses in cases of divorce, to the tax ramifications of divorce. On some of these issues the state will impose its values even against the wishes of both spouses, and in others it will do so at the request of one spouse. Absent a prenuptial agreement, it is rare that the state will not seek to adjudicate every

area of a divorce, even if the parties would not have wanted that at
the time of their marriage.

This overarching civil divorce system is nearly unique historically. Never before the twentieth century has the Jewish community
been subject to a system of compulsory civil marriage and divorce
law, and this requirement has had a major impact on both the contours of the agunah problem and contours of solutions to it.[3]

The Dual System and the Problem of the Agunah

The presence of the civil divorce system is not only relevant to the
question of withholding a *get,* but also to the determination of the
division of assets, and other "tangential" matters related to divorce.
Consider the differences in the following four cases:

1. Husband withholds *get* until the civil divorce is final and
   then gives *get.*
2. Husband withholds *get* until settlement of financial matters
   relating to divorce are settled.
3. Husband withholds *get* until wife agrees to go to bet din to
   resolve financial disputes related to end of marriage.
4. Husband withholds *get* until financial disputes are resolved
   in his favor.

The reason case 4 is viewed (correctly so) as illegitimate and
improper is that the husband is using the withholding of the *get* as
leverage to receive something that he is not entitled to receive; this is
extortion in its simplest form. However, it is crucial to understand
what makes this extortion. The husband withholds the *get* is in order
to receive an *illicit* benefit: money to which he is not entitled.[4] What
makes this conduct less problematic in case 1 is that when there is a
genuine commitment to giving and receiving a Jewish divorce at the
time of the civil divorce, no illicit benefit is sought in most people's
minds, even though the woman is having her Jewish divorce held
captive, albeit to the just resolution of her civil divorce.

There are those who assert that the withholding of a *get* in
any circumstance (even a case 1 situation) is improper, and a man

should give a *get* whenever his wife requests it. This approach too does not solve the problem of dual system issues; quite to the contrary, the only way one can advance this approach is with the belief that the secular system is the primary one that will resolve all disputes, and that the giving of a *get* is a mere ritual that should not be of use in the dispute.

Consider the identical situation in a civil context. Surely one would not adopt the posture that it is unethical to contest a spouse's filing for divorce in civil law. Rather, each party in a civil case litigates the matter to the degree to which he or she is comfortable. Thus the question is: why is it proper to litigate a civil divorce and not a religious one? The answer is that the mindset of those who adopt this posture portrays the system of Jewish law as a mere handmaiden to the civil legal system, and the use of substantive Jewish law to reach a result contrary to civil law is simply wrong in this view.[5]

The presence of the American divorce courts has become so accepted culturally that some in our society recognize no real "right" to a *get* until there is a "divorce," which this group understands to mean a civil divorce. What makes a husband's demand in case 3 appear unreasonable to some is that Orthodox society has not generally accepted that a bet din ought to settle end-of-marriage disputes and that it is reasonable and proper to insist that this be done. The husband is in case 3 essentially seeking something illegitimate according to this group: adjudication in a bet din. What makes case 1 and 2 proper is the implicit understanding that the civil divorce system will settle these disputes properly, and then a *get* will be given.

This approach has within it the distinct possibility of creating yet another model of Jewish marriage and divorce: couples that marry in accordance with the common commercial customs of the time and expect that the Jewish legal tradition will accommodate that expectation. This approach is consistent with none of the models explicitly developed in Chapter 2, although its underpinnings have their origins in some contractual theory model of marriage, since that is the only way such a model can be incorporated in Jewish law, as will be explained in the section on contractarian solutions in Chapter 5.

Two Legal Systems

In essence, unlike the situation under the halachic system of only a short time ago, when observant Jews wish to be divorced they now must effectuate a divorce in a manner that is valid according to both halachah and secular law.[6] (In the alternative, they can choose not to marry according to secular law and thus not be bothered by secular divorce law at all.) The interaction of these two systems, and the complexity associated with having to fulfill the demands of both, are the theme of the rest of this chapter.

Every system of law that ponders divorce and marriage recognizes that there are two basic models for marriage and divorce law:[7] the public law model and the private law model. In the public law model, marriage and divorce are governed by societal or governmental rules and not exclusively by private contract or right. There is no "right" to marry and no "right" to divorce.[8] Both are governed by the rules promulgated by society. One needs a license to be married and one must seek legal permission (typically through the court system in America) to be divorced. Were society to rule that divorce was prohibited, divorce would cease to be legal.[9] Indeed, there were vast periods of time when divorce essentially never happened in the Western legal world.[10] The American legal tradition exemplifies the public law model.

In the private law model, marriage and divorce are fundamentally private activities. Couples marry by choosing to be married and divorce by deciding to be divorced; no government role is needed. Law is needed only to regulate the process to the extent that there is a dispute between the parties, or to adjudicate whether the proper procedure was followed. Government is not a necessary party in either a marriage or divorce.

Jewish law in its basic outline and contours adheres to the private law model for both marriage and divorce, and it recognizes that divorce in its essential form requires private conduct and not court supervision. Thus, private marriages and private divorces are valid in the Jewish tradition, so long as the requisite number of witnesses (two) are present.[11] Indeed, the Jewish tradition does not mandate the participation of a rabbi in any manner in either the marriage or divorce rite.[12]

A Comparison of Private and Public Law Models

A private law system creates a model for a court system that is fundamentally different from a public law system. Spelling out these differences clarifies the scope of the Jewish court.

1. In a public law system, agents of government (courts, typically) create valid marriages and valid divorces.[13] In a private law system participants in the marriage create valid marriages and valid divorces.[14]
2. In a public law system, agents of government (courts, typically) adjudicate disputes about the *res* of marriage because it is a creation of public law. In a private law system, agents of government adjudicate disputes in a marriage in a manner similar to that for any private law dispute.
3. In a public law system, participants in a marriage or divorce may not engage in private agreements ordering their arrangements. In a private law system such ordering is permissible and is the norm.

It is important to realize that some incidents of tragedy are inevitable in either system, although a public law system creates a different set of problems than a private law system. Consider the simple (talmudic) case of the person who disappears with no evidence of death. A public law system could create a procedure in which that person is declared "dead" or divorced after a certain period of time, and free the abandoned spouse to remarry; a private law system cannot do that. Whether that solves the problem of abandonment in wartime really depends on whether the one who disappears eventually returns. If that person returns, the public law system seems to have done more harm than good, since its ability to end a marriage without the participation of one of the parties has created a tragic situation. If that person never returns, the inability of the private law system to act creates serious problems in that it chains a person to a nonfunctional marriage.

The same is true for cases of recalcitrance; while the difficulties of abandonment within the Jewish tradition are clear and well documented, it is also quite clear that the system of public divorce creates certain intractable problems.[15] Indeed, while little has been written in defense of the private marriage approach generally, it is quite clear that the system of governmental regulation of the details of marriage and divorce has within it the possibility of significant abuse from overreaching, the exact opposite of the Jewish problem, which is caused by the lack of authority to end marriages. Consider the fact that many states have curtailed the ability of one to marry as punishment for criminal activity.[16] Abuses can occur in all systems.

Besides these two models, there is the hybrid model of mixed public and private divorce. Currently a number of Arab countries have incorporated Islamic law into the civil system to create such a model, in which either one can privately divorce, or a court can grant a divorce.[17] Indeed, the problems of public divorce are well explained in reference to the actions of the Islamic law courts of Egypt, which have used their authority over divorce as a way of ending marriages between people who are heretics or infidels who wish to remain married to their spouses.[18]

End of marriage creates certain unanswerable dilemmas that go to the very heart of the role of law, and the legal conception of divorce. *Does Jewish law, Canon law, common law, or any other legal system create marriages and end marriages or does law merely recognize marriages and divorces that have been created?*[19]

Jewish law and American law answer this question differently. Jewish law is a private law system; American law is a public law system. Thus the dual system issues related to divorce are twofold: there are two legal systems with which one has to comply if one wishes to obey both Jewish law and function in secular society as a married couple, and these two legal systems view marriage and divorce in a different jurisprudential light.

The New York Experience

Consider the two New York *Get* Laws[20] and the controversy they engendered; such controversy acknowledges the ultimate power of the secular divorce law.[21] The 1984 New York *Get* Law[22] recognized that a fundamental wrong was occurring when secular society allowed a person to be civilly divorced who had been religiously married and a couple that had been religiously married considered themselves to remain so until a religious divorce was executed. How did the 1984 New York *Get* Law fix this problem? It prevented the civil authorities from exercising their authority to divorce a couple civilly who still needed a religious divorce. *The law prevented a splitting of the civil and religious statuses by preventing the civil authorities from acting, absent the religious authorities.*[23] This law harmonizes civil law with Jewish law, in that Jewish law maintains that the couple is married until a *get* is issued, and New York commits itself to not issuing a civil divorce in such cases until a *get* is issued. It contains no incentive for a person actually to issue a Jewish divorce unless that person is genuinely desirous of being divorced.

The 1992 New York *Get* Law has a completely different approach. While the problem it confronted remains the same (individuals were refusing to participate in religious divorces when their spouse was desirous of one) the solution advanced by the Law is different. It allows the secular divorce law to impose penalties on the recalcitrant spouse in order to encourage participation in the religious divorce by basing the division of the assets on whether the *get* has been issued. The law seeks to prevent the splitting of the religious and civil status by encouraging the issuing of the religious divorce when a civil divorce is to be issued. This law harmonizes Jewish law with secular law, by commiting itself to a policy of encouraging a *get* to be issued. A woman is an agunah in such a model when the man refuses to give her a *get* although she has been given a civil divorce.

Creating the Right to Be Divorced

Secular law at some level forms part of the agunah problem in that it creates a situation in which there is a reasonable expectation of a "right" to be divorced, predicated on the existence of that right in secular law. The presence of secular law allows for a reasonable adjudicative process that creates a "fair" resolution of the issues involved with no reference to Jewish law. If one were to define an agunah as a woman "entitled" to a *get* who is being denied one, the civil legal system is the source of the entitlement in many cases. Indeed, to a great extent this situation is at the heart of the recent controversy related to the 1992 New York *Get* Law. Consider the following case:

> A couple has separated. The husband genuinely wishes to remain married and desires his wife to return to the marital abode. The wife files for divorce, alleging irreconcilable differences and not fault.

New York divorce law currently permits the granting of a civil divorce in those circumstances, and almost indubitably the judge will grant such a divorce based on the 40-year-old public policy perspective of New York that marriages should end whenever *either* spouse wishes to end them. Under the most recent New York *Get* Law, there is little doubt that the judge will impose a financial penalty on the husband if he refuses to cooperate in the issuing of a *get*. The question is: why is the husband's conduct perceived as improper? The answer appears to be that the civil determination that the woman ought to be divorced gives rise to a right to be divorced which is recognized by normative Jewish society. Hence, a woman is socially classified as an "agunah" because her Jewish divorce is being withheld and *her civil divorce is not.*

This right to divorce was not recognized by secular society three or four decades ago, not because the substantive Jewish law has changed in that time (it has not), but rather because the substantive American law has. If a woman had filed a divorce action under this same circumstance in 1950, civil law would have denied her the right to her divorce, and the secular legal system would have told her that she had to seek (purchase) the cooperation of her husband if she wished to be divorced absent fault. Jewish society would no more have called this woman an agunah in 1950 than secular society would, since *both her civil and her religious divorce would have been withheld.* It is precisely because secular society is prepared to allow unilateral no-fault divorce that women with such divorces believe they are entitled to a *get* and are thus agunot if they do not receive one. In essence, the dual system has created an implicit secular right to be divorced, which has created a considerable portion of the agunah problem in America.[24]

One Solution: Ignore the Dual System Problem

One approach to addressing this issue is simply to deny the presence of the problem. A simple example can be found in the writings of Rabbi Chaim Malinowitz, a *dayan* (judge) in one of the Jewish law courts in New York, who writes in the course of an exchange:

> A secular, contested civil divorce requires a court verdict; surely a contested *get* deserves no less, and in a halachic forum.[25]

He also states:

> Without th[e] halachic process, no one is justified in assuming that a *get* is obligatory or even appropriate. . . . The [*Get*] law helps women obtain a *get* when there has been no finding whatsoever by any halachic body that a *get* is either warranted or appropriate.[26]

In Rabbi Malinowitz's opinion, where there are no halachic grounds for bet din to order (or rule a *mitzvah*) a divorce or there has been no ruling by a bet din at all, there can be no agunah problem, since there is no halachic "right" for the woman to be divorced and receive a *get* (and thus there is no "wrong" for the husband to seek enrichment from his wife as a price for writing a *get*).

Essentially, this solution to the dual system problem denies the impact of the secular legal system and culture on the realities of Jewish divorce in America. What makes a woman an agunah, claims R. Malinowitz, is a determination by a bet din that she is. Absent a determination, she is not. Secular law never impacts on this decision.

A Critique of This Approach

This writer suspects that the above approach misunderstands the fundamental nature of a variety of "realities" that the presence of a dual system has inculcated into normative Jewish law, such that they have become implicitly part of many marriages.

As modern American culture has become more and more enmeshed in the correctness of unilateral no-fault divorce, that concept has become normative within the culture of some Jewish marriages, such that one can recognize the impropriety of coercing participation in a marriage of which one person wishes to be freed. As was demonstrated in Chapter 2 of this work, such an approach has considerable grounding in Jewish law, even if it is not the normative one.[27] Even if it is not incorporated formally into Jewish law in this process, Jewish law recognizes the ability of the Jewish community to incorporate the law of the land into Jewish financial dealings through common commercial custom (*minhag hasochrim*); this incorporation of secular law and norms into Jewish law could include such matters as the finances related to divorce.

The Issue of Commercial Custom

This point needs to be elaborated upon, because it is possible that at the heart of the dual system dispute is a disagreement about money and the propriety of the modern American asset division system. I believe that the custom of the Orthodox Jewish community (or vast portions of it) is to accept as part of our customary financial law the concept of alimony, post-divorce payments, and very likely equitable distribution. This fact is reflected in the American custom of *not* negotiating the dollar amounts in the *ketubah,* in terms of either how much money the woman brings into the marriage or how much the husband will pay her upon divorce or his death, as is done in Israel or as was the custom in Europe centuries ago. Indeed, the standard *ketubah* used in Israel leaves these amounts blank to be filled in for each couple, and the standard American *ketubah* fills in the amount of "200 silver coins," an amount worth considerably less than $10,000. The simple fact is that the community has accepted some sort of equitable distribution and alimony as the *minhag hamakom* to determine the financial rights of each party in a divorce.[28]

The Shulchan Aruch makes it clear that common commercial practices override many Jewish law default rules that would otherwise govern a transaction.[29] Moreover, these customs are valid even if the majority of the business people establishing them are not Jewish. Rabbi Moshe Feinstein explains:

> It is clear that these rules which depend on custom . . . need not be customs . . . established by Torah scholars or even by Jews. Even if these customs were established by Gentiles, if the Gentiles are a majority of the inhabitants of the city, Jewish law incorporates the custom. It is as if the parties conditioned their agreement in accordance with the custom of the city.[30]

In addition, many authorities rule that such customs are valid under Jewish law even if they were established because the particular conduct in question was required by secular law.[31]

Another Solution: Follow Secular Law

Another possible solution to the dual system problem is more nuanced and recognizes that when the parties have a common communal practice, accepting the norms of the secular society as the basis for their interactions, it is as if they had explicitly agreed to such an arrangement. As Rabbi Avigdor Nevetzal, Rabbi of the Jewish Quarter in Jerusalem, simply states:

> In the laws of oaths, vows, sales and rentals, the intent of most people when they speak nowadays is that the term "day," "month," and "year" follow the Christian calendar. . . So too, in many activities that are dependent on the state of mind of a person, their state of mind follows the secular law and not the Torah law.[32]

This approach recognizes the possibility that the dual system problem can be resolved in accordance with the norms of secular law rather than normative Jewish law, if such is the intent of the parties at the time of entry into the marriage. Thus it is my view that there are Jewish communities, functioning in accordance with halachah, whose members properly adjudicate their end of marriage disputes in accordance with secular law or custom, albeit in a bet din.[33]

Summary of the Dual System Problems

The dual system problem of the agunah is compounded by the sense that because of the different understandings of the nature of secular divorce compared to Jewish divorce, the view of the proper response to the dual system "problem" is, by itself, an unbridgeable problem, which has compounded the agunah problem and made the search for "solutions" problematic.

One view adopts the posture that essentially there should be a unilateral right to a Jewish divorce when there is a right to a secular divorce, and that the current secular model of divorce should be (and indeed is) the normative model within the Jewish community. To this group, the agunah problem is a mechanistic one: Jewish law should search for a technically acceptable way to reach the result of inducing/compelling or otherwise requiring a *get* when either party wants one and when a civil divorce is "in the works" and unstoppable. Whatever halachic mechanism can provide the tools for that goal, if acceptable to normative Jewish law, should be used. Essentially, this is a search for a mere mechanism.

The second view argues that Jewish law should not defer to the secular model of divorce and that there is no agunah problem until such time as Jewish law, not secular law, avers that there should be a divorce in any given case, and that the sole acceptable role for secular law is to mimic Jewish law. This is not merely a search for a mechanism to fix the agunah problem; it is a basic assertion about the contours of the problem and the proper role of secular law.

There is a third group that must also be considered: those who insist that prenuptial agreements which force people to make hard choices solve the problem. This view accepts that there are aspects of end-of-marriage problems that revolve exclusively around neither Jewish law nor secular law. Thus, the agreements allow the parties to choose the legal rules adjudicating their end-of-marriage dispute prior to marriage.[34]

The resolution of the issue has thus divided the Orthodox community into three distinct camps with regard to this matter. There is no bridging this gap. The dual system problem, which flows from the conceptual issues discussed in Chapter 1, but which has a uniquely modern dimension because of the secular law issue, cannot be papered over or harmonized, since it seeks to position secular law as a tool in the agunah problem. Of course, in the reality of life the true problem frequently is that people determine which school of thought they are in depending on which view allows them to emerge victorious. The principles cited sometimes are mere "principles of convenience." Thus, consider the case of the husband who wishes to go to a bet din to adjudicate all matters [financial and *get* related] in a divorce without any reference to common commercial norms of the community, and the wife who wishes to use the secular legal norms to determine asset division and then appear in bet din for the *get*. Who is correct? The answer to this question deeply depends on the prior history of the parties.

CHAPTER FOUR

The Role of Bet Din: How Does a Jewish Court Prevent Abandonment of Spouses?

Introduction: Theory and History

Jewish law, like every other legal system, and most religious systems, has within it not only ethical mandates and religious norms, but legal rules as well. These legal rules are binding assertions of what proper conduct is for adherents of the legal system. Most but not all of these rules call for sanctions against those who violate them. Thus, Jewish law has within it as a matter of theory a variety of punishments available to those who violate Jewish law. The Torah provides for different types of death penalties as well as flogging. Rabbinic jurisprudence adds to this a host of other penalties, from excommunication to corporal punishment to the death penalty. The bet din was the implementer of the judicial system within the Jewish tradition. Until the year 40 C.E. this system functioned like any other court system; there were local district courts and higher courts, with ultimate authority residing in the Sanhedrin, which was located within the walls of the Temple itself. The Sanhedrin was charged with supervising normative Jewish law, and its interpretations and judicial directions were binding on all.

The Modern Reality

Such was, but no longer is, the structure of Jewish law. Since pretalmudic times the Sanhedrin has no longer functioned, and the

Jewish court systems worldwide are not subject to a single supervisory religious authority. However, until the emancipation of the nineteenth century, the local bet din had a jurisdictional mandate to supervise the justiciable aspects of disputes within the Jewish community. The exact scope of this jurisdiction varied from place to place; for example, in Spain 600 years ago it included criminal law and death penalty jurisdiction, while in most places it was limited to financial and family law. Until the emancipation, though, this jurisdiction included supervision of the marriage and divorce process of nearly every Jewish community. Indeed, as is clear to all who have studied Jewish law, the scope of the jurisdiction of a Jewish court is far greater than that of the common law court system in that a bet din serves a supervisory role over a variety of areas of Jewish law independent of whether there is a "case" brought to it. Thus, for example, a Jewish court would not permit a man to marry a woman who could not bear him children if he did not already have children from another, because he would thereby fail to fulfill his obligation to be fruitful and multiply, and thus a Jewish court, as part of its supervisory role in the community, would not permit such a marriage.[1]

Since the emancipation of Jews, the scope of review available to a bet din generally has vastly decreased. Jurisdiction is voluntary, coercive legal authority lacking, and the apparent legal authority of the Jewish court system is vastly diminished. In America, all that one needs to do to nullify the authority of the bet din is ignore it. This chapter notes the implications of that "reality" in America on the situation of the agunah.[2]

One additional point needs to be made. Jewish law insists that, as a general proposition, Jewish law and the Jewish law court system govern the dissolution of the end of marriage. While it recognizes the effectiveness of most secular court financial adjudications after the fact,[3] Jewish law labels the use of the secular court system to adjudicate a dispute between two Jews as violation of Jewish law.[4] Thus Jewish law will encourage the use of the Jewish law court system.

Jewish Law and Its Role in Marriage

As was explained in Chapter 3, Jewish law is a private law system of marriage and divorce, and Jewish law denies that it announces marriages and divorces or that bet din solemnizes marriage; it merely discovers the truth about privately created marriages and divorces. American law creates marriage and divorce and does not merely adjudicate them. Given that understanding of the function and role of a bet din, a review of the role of bet din in family law logically divides the areas into four distinct functions:

1. The bureaucratic function associated with ensuring that religious services, when they are provided, are provided in a manner consistent with the dictates of Jewish law. For example, when a couple decides that they wish to be divorced according to Jewish law, the technical process associated with writing a *get* is sufficiently complex that the services of an expert rabbi (called in Hebrew, a *mesader gittin*) are needed to arrange for the proper writing and delivery of the bill of divorce.

2. The adjudicative function associated with determining whether a couple must be divorced, or may be married. There are a variety of circumstances in which Jewish law directs that divorce is mandatory (such as in cases of adultery) or that divorce is religiously required (*mitzvah*). A corollary is that there are cases where Jewish law directs that a couple not be allowed to marry (even if they wish to do so), and a bet din adjudicates these cases also.

3. The adjudicative function associated with resolving the financial aspects of a divorce. Jewish law recognizes that spouses have financial rights to each other that have to be undone in the course of a divorce. These arrangements can be made by the parties through mutual agreement, but when mutual agreement cannot be forged, Jewish law recognizes that it is the "house of justice" that serves as the adjudicative function.

4. The adjudicative function associated with determining whether one party has raised allegations of misconduct, impropriety, or other violations of the marital bonds that make divorce appropriate in any particular circumstance, and the financial ramifications of such determinations. Unlike function 2, which is directed at situations where the marriage may not continue to function even if both parties wish it to continue, this case involves situations where neither party has raised such significant allegation, but rather "merely" one side wishes to leave the marriage for a variety of reasons, some of which Jewish law rules proper, some permissible, and some improper.

Each of these functions, when all of them are available together, create a system for regulating the institution of divorce as well as marriage. Such is well paralleled in modern American divorce law. In every state in the United States, government controls all four aspects of divorce and regulates them through the adjudicative capacity of the court system. Thus one cannot arrange for a mutual consensual divorce without the family law or divorce courts, even if all of the parties are in complete agreement, because category 1 functions are reserved for the courts in America. So too government adjudicates which people are eligible to be married and, in cases where they are not, will seek to prevent a marriage (or void a pre–existing one[5] entered into in violation of its rules); this is a type 2 case. So too government serves the adjudicative role when there is a dispute about the financial arrangements of a divorce, and in many cases determines whether a divorce is called for at all if one party contests it.[6]

Modern Jewish Law and Marriage in America

Modern Jewish law, which remains a full and complete legal system as a matter of legal theory, is not a complete legal system when it comes to jurisdiction over its adherents. Essentially, in modern America the jurisdiction of bet din is limited to situations in which the parties themselves voluntarily submit themselves to the jurisdiction of the court and promise to obey its rules. In Israel, the compulsory jurisdiction is broader, in that all type 1 cases (the bureaucratic function of arranging a *get*) fall under the jurisdiction of the court, and there is no civil divorce or marriage case; in addition, there are a variety of cases where the Israeli rabbinical courts exercise type 3 jurisdiction as well, depending on who files for divorce and under what circumstances.[7]

The emasculated state of jurisdiction in the rabbinical courts of America is not insignificant in explaining the impotence of the bet din in America, as there are certain models of marriage that rely heavily on the bet din to make substantive determinations of the rights and claims of each of the parties.[8] This situation is potentially a significant contributor to the number of cases in which there is some form of recalcitrance by the husband or wife. The inability of the Jewish law system to adjudicate in any binding way a significant number of cases leads to an increase in the number of cases in which one party denies the obligation to give a *get,* which is the sine qua non for being a modern agunah.

Indeed, consider the following division of situations:

1. The cases in which the structure of Jewish law itself creates the agunah problem. The case of the husband who disappears during war is a situation where the nature of the requirements of halachah, that a man divorce his wife of his own free will, creates the problem. While a more powerful bet din might help resolve these problems at the margins, in fact almost all of them are "solved" on a case-by-case basis by the responsa writing process which develops a consensus around a particular result in a particular case.[9]

2. The cases in which Jewish law, were it to be given the full authority that the system thought it should have, would cause the agunah problem to cease. In a case in which Jewish law rules that a divorce is mandatory (*chi'uvi*), Jewish law could never imagine a case of agunah (except a type 1 case above) in which the man who is withholding a *get* is doing so only in direct violation of the ruling of a bet din, something that would result in increasingly heavy sanction.

A fully functioning bet din would presumably curtail such cases.[10]

3. Those cases in which Jewish law recognizes the validity of the right of the spouse to be divorced yet recognizes that Jewish law requires that, absent a clear finding of fault (*chiuv legaresh*), a bet din is incapable of invoking the classical formulation that creates compulsory divorce (beating him until he wishes to divorce his wife) yet does allow for a significant amount of persuasion short of force but more than simply a statement of what the community wishes.

In the classical rabbinic literature this activity (type 3 cases) is referred to as the "distancing of Rabbenu Tam," after the medieval sage who first permitted it.[11] It is important to understand this case. Jewish law mandates that divorces can be given only with the free will of the husband and received with the free will of the wife, after *cherem de Rabbenu Gershom,* yet it also recognizes that there are a variety of cases where the proper thing to do is to encourage divorce; sometimes these are cases in which Jewish law merely classifies the divorce as "good and proper" (*mitzvah legarsha*) and sometimes the reason is even less than that. In those cases, Jewish law and the Jewish court system do considerably more than merely tell the party what it wishes: it also attempts to create a social and religious structure that forces a person to comply with the dictates of Jewish law, short of direct coercion, which is not permitted where there has not been a ruling of mandatory divorce (*chiuv legarsha*).

4. Those cases in which Jewish law is silent about whether halachah permits one to withhold a *get*. Such conduct could be neither consistent nor inconsistent with Jewish law. Indeed, this case is not implausible in any classical sense of the word, and each of the theoretical cases except that predicated on unilateral no-fault divorce has occurred. There are a broad variety of cases in which a bet din would direct neither party to either be divorced or not be divorced or participate in or not participate in a divorce.

The implications for the role of bet din in the agunah situation from these four categories are clear and apparent. They are both limiting and expanding: limiting in that there are a set of cases that appear to be intractable agunah cases which can be resolved only through a profound reorientation of the normative halachah (which is beyond the scope of any particular bet din, and perhaps simply unattainable and indeed undesirable in general); expanding, because many, indeed most, cases of *igun* appear theoretically resolvable were there a functioning bet din system capable of enforcing Jewish law.[12]

A close examination of much of the popular agunah literature reveals that the primary causes of almost all of the agunah cases appears to be either:

1. The decision by the community not to honor the ruling of the bet din in any particular manner, *or*
2. The inability of the bet din system generally throughout the United States to create a Jewish court system that functions with honesty and integrity, such that the community will accept its decisions with regard to suitable punishments and deterrence in cases of *igun,* and will compel observance of its *p'sakim* from community to community.[13]

Modern Jewish Law and Marriage in Israel

The situation is markedly different in Israel, because the rabbinical courts have coercive police power[14] and are capable of enforcing their orders against Israeli citizens who decline to obey their decisions.[15] It could be suggested that the "problem" in Israel is that the vast majority of the Israeli rabbinical courts follow the paradigm of Rabbenu Gershom/Rabbenu Tam and do not perceive a significant problem with requiring negotiations between the couple even after the marriage has broken down, so long as there is no finding of fault.[16] Israel is so much more diligent in preventing flagrant violations of Jewish law in this area that the United States Department of State has issued a travel advisory warning directed to men who are withholding Jewish divorces from their wives that they risk being detained in Israel by the rabbinical courts. The text of the warning issued by the State Department reads:

> Court Jurisdiction: Under Israel's judicial system, the Rabbinical courts exercise jurisdiction over all Jewish citizens and residents of Israel in cases of marriage and divorce and related issues such as support and child custody. Rabbinical courts can also impose sanctions, including jail terms and restrictions against leaving the country, on individuals married in a Jewish religious ceremony who, in case of divorce, refuse to give their spouses a religious divorce (*Get*). In some cases, Jewish Americans, who entered Israel as tourists, have become defendants in divorce cases filed against them in a Rabbinical court in Israel by their American spouses who are seeking a religious divorce that the defendants have refused to give. These Americans have been detained in Israel for prolonged periods while the Israeli courts consider whether such individuals have sufficient ties to Israel to establish Rabbinical court jurisdiction. The Rabbinical courts have also detained in the country a Jewish American tourist who has been sued for support by his spouse in the United States. Jewish American visitors should be aware that they may be subject to involuntary and prolonged stays in Israel if a case is filed against them in a Rabbinical Court. This may occur even when the marriage took place in the U.S., and/or the spouse seeking relief is not present in Israel.[17]

This and other reviews of the literature relating to the functioning of the rabbinical courts leads one to conclude that the rabbinical courts in Israel fundamentally accept as the normative halachic default the position of Rabbenu Tam and Rabbenu Gershom that absent a finding of fault there is no obligation to end the marriage merely in the face of irreconcilable differences, and in such a case the parties must come to an agreement as to the conditions for ending such a marriage.[18]

In a case of irreconcilable differences the rabbinical courts might impose support payments on the husband until he divorces his wife; however, those payments are not designed in any apparent way to coerce divorce. They are imposed because of the requirement that a husband support his wife, by providing either a home or payments instead of these standard support agreements.[19]

Indeed, this policy is noticeably different from the policy of the rabbinical courts in cases where the woman is a *moredet* (a "rebellious wife") and thus, according to most authorities is obligated to be divorced. In the case of a woman who is a *moredet* (such as, in the case Rabbi Waldenberg addresses below, an adulteress), a husband has *no right to* both *decline to support her* and *decline to divorce her.* As Rabbi Eliezer Waldenberg notes:

> [When a woman has improperly abandoned the marital abode (is a *moredet*)], she forfeits her (marital) . . . rights and other financial claims against the husband. However, on the other side, the husband must [*chayav*] divorce her and may not keep her connected to him.[20]

Waldenberg states that the ruling (*psak*) of the Israeli rabbinical courts, with which he agrees, is to require support payments to be paid even to a spouse who improperly abandons the home and is an adulteress, when a reasonable time has elapsed and the husband has not ended the marriage by writing a *get*. Indeed, in the case of a *moredet*, no less an authority than the *Pitchai Teshuva*[21] notes that the accepted practice is to make the husband support his wife (until he gives her a *get*) specifically to encourage him to give a *get* and not to compel a woman to remain in a "dead marriage," even if the marriage "died" because of her misconduct. Similar sentiments can be found in the name of many *poskim*, including such luminaries as the author of the Noda Beyehuda, Rabbi Akiva Eiger, as well as the authors of Chatam Sofer and Beit Meir; this view is the normative halachic posture, even if it is contrary to the assertion of Tosafot.[22] Payments are not designed to support the women, they are designed to encourage the giving of a *get*.

Thus in Israel when the rabbinical courts do decide that a *get* should be compelled, and they have suitable jurisdiction, they have the clear tools to compel fidelity to the rules of the rabbinical courts. It certainly is true that there are a number of cases of recalcitrance that are fundamentally unsolvable under the current model, in that Jewish law allows for only private divorce. However, these cases, such as the man who languished in jail for 32 years rather than give his wife a *get*,[23] represent the basic success of the system, not its failure.[24]

Comparison of Modern Jewish Law and
Marriage in Israel and America

This review of the current state of affairs in Israel puts it in sharp contrast to the problems confronted in America. As Rabbi Yosef Blau (*mashgiach ruchni* of Yeshiva University) states:

> I prefer to focus on the role of the Orthodox rabbinate and its difficulty in criticizing distortions of halachah if they are expressed by other Orthodox rabbis. We are subject to so many external attacks that we have become reluctant to acknowledge any internal problems. A small group of rabbis who see the world from the perspective of men losing control to the onslaught of modern women have attempted in recent years to use halacha to return control to the husbands. Child marriages, concubinage, and this latest manipulation of halacha, permission to enter a polygamous marriage without a *get,* have all come from this group. Uncomfortable with denouncing any position that quotes halachic sources and is said by those claiming to be more religious we remain silent despite the fact that all the leading halachic authorities have rejected these positions. Unfortunately, silence is seen as acquiescence and a new weapon is now in the hands of recalcitrant husbands. It is critical that such second marriages, which invariably follow, be rejected by the Orthodox community. *Much progress is being made in returning Batai Din to their proper role in Jewish life, but unless we can control the unscrupulous* batai din *this will all dissipate.*[25]

Simply put, the recalcitrant spouse problem in America is vastly more complex than in Israel; even when there is a rabbinic will, there might not be any halachic way, since rabbis lack any compulsory authority in America that can form the basis for enforcing their decisions.[26]

When there is rabbinic authority, there is a halachic way to fix the agunah problem. Rabbinic will power without rabbinic authority is insufficient to accomplish the task. For the last two thousand years, rabbinic authority prevented recalcitrant husbands from routinely seeking payment for the delivery of a *get* through the use of mandatory support of one's wife until the divorce. What has changed in America is neither the rabbinic will nor the halachic way, but the absence of rabbinic authority. Rabbis are no less compassionate or concerned now than a hundred or a thousand years ago; rather, they are now powerless in America. Legal systems cannot survive by moral authority alone.

This leads to a very important point, which is one of the fundamental implications for the role of bet din that flows from the characterization of marriage and divorce. Simply put, if there is to be a significant internal solution to those cases of *igun* that Jewish law maintains ought to be solved, even that step will occur only when the community of adherents to Jewish law commit themselves to acceptance of a significant organized bet din process, in which individuals honor and obey the decisions of the bet din on these matters and do not tolerate participation in the community absent such fidelity.

It is very important not to allow "solutions" to the agunah problem that do not address the fundamental problem: a lack of authority by the Jewish law court system. Indeed, a close examination of the rabbinic literature compels one to realize that the bet din system of the last seven hundred years developed a wealth of tools to address cases of *igun* through the imposition of a variety of rebukes, sanctions, and other forms of rabbinic castigation that fall short of compulsion. To wonder why these mechanisms have collapsed while refusing to recognize that the community has forced the abdication of the bet din as the central clearinghouse for practical Jewish law is simply too convenient. There are no legal systems that attempt to govern the conduct of both the faithful and others within the community without some coercive authority. That authority is lacking from the community.[27]

Consider the case of Seymour Klagsbrun, who was accused of improperly chaining his wife by a number of Jewish law courts in New York. At least two major Jewish law courts issued calls for excommunication (*cherem*) or worse against him, with little or no effect, because the American Orthodox community lacks any authority to compel the observance of its directives.[28]

Mr. Klagsbrun continued to function within the community without any apparent sanction. In clear contrast is what happened when Mr. Klagsbrun visited Israel; the Israeli rabbinical courts immediately put him in prison for violation of the bigamy laws and were quite prepared to keep him there until he consented to the writing of a *get*. He was freed only after the apparent interference of the American ambassador, who felt it improper for Israel to be exercising jurisdiction over American tourists when the fundamental dispute was American in nature. Had the rabbinical court had clear jurisdiction, they would have incarcerated him pending divorce. While it is true that there are a number of cases where the rabbinical courts are unable to compel the issuing of a *get* because the husband is willing to be incarcerated rather than divorced, such cases are few and far between, and more significantly are endemic to the private law system that is at the heart of Jewish law.[29]

The Bet Din Issue in America

A candid critique of the problem of the bet din system in America forces one to acknowledge that the issue plaguing rabbinic Judaism in America is not only lack of authority but a lack of communal rabbinic responsibility as well. Secular American models of religious freedom, grounded in important First Amendment principles, allow all individuals unfettered rights to practice their faith in accordance with their religious beliefs, even if their views are far from normative Jewish law, and even if they speak in the name of rabbinic Judaism. Thus individuals can and do establish *batai din* in order to satisfy their own agendas, whether or not their understanding of Jewish law is supported by any significant sources of authority. Indeed, some of these charlatan Jewish law courts are simply organizations that seek to enrich their own members by selling documentation that claims to be permission for a man to remarry, even if he has not divorced his wife according to Jewish law![30]

As a result of the lack of authority in America, the community has abandoned the bet din system as a source of justice and law, and indeed some portions of the system itself have been intensely corrupted, since there is no authority inherent in the system to distinguish between legitimate and illegitimate uses of Jewish law.

Prenuptial agreements and submission agreements are both methods of addressing the failures of the bet din system in America. These agreements compel the parties to choose a specific bet din as the forum for resolving their marital disputes in advance of any such disputes. Thus, the parties can investigate the forum to determine not only whether they agree with its substantive rules but whether it functions ethically and properly. Submission agreements would be much less relevant if the bet din system functioned properly, so that people did not question its integrity.

The Relationship Between the Bet Din System and the Secular System

Once there is a functioning bet din system (and to some extent there is one already), the question then becomes whether a man has the right to use any bet din to (re)litigate financial components of a divorce when the wife does not wish to, and whether he may withhold a *get* to force her to go to bet din. If he may not, when will sanctions be applied to him to compel or encourage the giving of a *get*?

There are four types of cases possible, each with three permutations:

    I. The couple without any prenuptial agreement
   II. The couple with a prenuptial agreement explicitly directing a specified bet din to resolve all disputes
  III. The couple with a prenuptial agreement explicitly directing that the financial side of any dispute will be resolved by the civil courts
  IV. The couple with a prenuptial agreement directing that a specified bet din resolve only matters related to the Jewish divorce

Each of these may have any of the following permutations:

   A. Man requests that bet din adjudicate the financial side of the end of marriage dispute, and no civil litigation has even commenced.
   B. Man requests that the bet din adjudicate the financial side of the end of marriage dispute; civil adjudication has already commenced without his protest.

C. Man requests that the bet din adjudicate the financial side
of the end of marriage dispute after the civil case is over. He
did not request bet din involvement until the civil case was
over or nearly so.

All of the cases in categories II and III are easy. In case II the
man is not in violation of Jewish law and is merely seeking to enforce
his rights according to both Jewish and secular law. The most that
can be said is perhaps in case II:C a waiver has occurred, but that is
unlikely as a matter of American law. Thus sanction of the man is
improper and the parties must appear in front of a bet din. The man
need not authorize a *get* until both parties appear in front of bet din.

In a case II situation the civil courts will compel the parties to
submit to the bet din and prevent the woman from litigating in civil
court. It would be standard practice for many Jewish courts to
require that the husband affirm that he prepared to give the *get* as
soon as the wife agrees to submit to the jurisdiction of the bet din or
he is otherwise ordered by the bet din to give the *get*.[31]

In case III the man has explicitly waived his right to a *din torah*,
which is itself a violation of halachah by both of them but which
would prevent him from claiming that the woman's recourse to
secular court is a form of theft validating his withholding a *get*.
Should he refuse to issue a *get* immediately (or perhaps in some circumstances after the resolution of the matter in civil court), sanctions (in the form of *harchakot shel Rabbenu Tam*) are proper.[32]

Case I:C is also easy, since the man's voluntary participation in
the civil process until he loses waives his right to seek a readjudication in the bet din. If he will not issue a *get*, the bet din would support sanctions (in the form of *harchakot shel Rabbenu Tam*). Case I:B,
absent extenuating circumstances, is halachicly identical to I:C. In
those cases where it is not, it is identical to I:A.

Case I:A is difficult, since halachah recognizes the right and
duty of the parties to go to bet din; the sincere wish of the husband
to do so must be supported in some way. Indeed, a *seruv*[33] might be
issued against the woman in such a case, as a bet din would in any
financial case where one party is duty bound to go to bet din

according to Jewish law and will not.[34] Even in such a case, it would be standard practice for the bet din to require that the husband affirm that he is prepared to give the *get* as soon as the wife agrees to submit to the jurisdiction of the bet din, or he is otherwise ordered by the bet din to give the *get*.[35]

Case IV:C is easy, since the man's voluntary participation in the civil process until he loses waives his right to seek a readjudication in the bet din. If he will not issue a *get*, the bet din would support sanctions (in the form of *harchakot shel Rabbenu Tam*). Case IV:B, absent extenuating circumstances, is halachically identical to IV:C.

Case IV:A is very difficult. Does one understand a prenuptial agreement explicitly designating the bet din as the mandatory forum for adjudicating the giving of the *get* to constitute an implicit condition that all other matters will be adjudicated by civil court (making case IV:A tantamount to III:A), or does one interpret it as tantamount to I:A, where there is no prenuptial agreement? I am unsure. In either case, however, it would be standard practice for the bet din to require that the husband affirm that he is prepared to give the *get* as soon as the wife agrees to submit to the jurisdiction of the bet din or he is otherwise ordered by the bet din to give the *get*.[36]

Conclusion

In sum, one of the central lessons of the agunah problem in America is the need to create a strong, respected bet din system, which hears cases, makes decisions, has rules of reciprocity, and can generally create order within the community so as to prevent people from functioning in defiance of normative halachah while still remaining members in the community. Society has created such a system with regard to the dietary laws; is marriage any less important?

Fixing the bet din system in America will go far toward addressing a number of other problematic issues of communal life that exist only because of a lack of any recognizably centralized (or even reciprocal) form of communal authority. Just as the centralization and communal regulation of kosher supervision restored order and respect to the certification process nearly fifty years ago,[37] the estab-

lishment of communal Jewish law courts will change the process
used to resolve a number of communal quagmires, from divorce
issues to conversion problems to disputes between and within syna-
gogues. Currently the adherents of Jewish law are without a system
of adjudicating Jewish law. When that situation changes, the whole
picture of Jewish law in America will change.

Two concrete solutions can be proposed, one limited to the area
of family law, and the other broader in nature. The narrower solution is that the community of adherents to Jewish law must promul-
gate submission agreements or binding arbitration agreements that
compel divorcing couples to submit their dispute to a specified Jewish law court, which will resolve every aspect of the dispute. These
agreements must be signed prior to marriage, since once a dispute
starts, agreeing on a mechanism for resolution is very difficult.
These submission agreements or binding arbitration agreements
empower the Jewish law courts to resolve disputes responsibly and
fairly.

The broader solution to consider is for the community of Jewish
law adherents to re-create the Jewish law courts' mandatory jurisdiction through the use of submission agreements or binding arbitration agreements in every area of life. In essence, such a document
states that the signer agrees to resolve all disputes in a designated
Jewish law court when the other disputants have signed a similar
agreement.[38] This system would build a community of adherents
with a common court system, legal authority, and the ability to
compel compliance by those who wish to benefit from Jewish law.[39]

CHAPTER FIVE

The Multitextured Agunah Problem and Proposed Modern Solutions: A Conceptual Critique

The Costs and Benefits of a Solution

There is not just a single agunah problem, but rather a multitextured problem of divorce and end-of-marriage issues mixed with a heavy dose of bet din authority problems. Thus it is obvious that there can never be a single solution to the agunah problem that "solves" it without creating a host of profound difficulties in terms of divorce rights and structural issues in the community. Indeed consider the famous, apparently impromptu, remarks delivered by Rabbi Joseph B. Soloveitchik at a convention of the Rabbinical Council of America in response to a suggestion that the organization consider the halachic ramification of some form of annulment of marriages as a solution to the agunah problem. Rabbi Soloveitchik did not focus on the technical halachic issues involved in such a proposal, but instead focused on the implications of such a profound change in the nature of Jewish marriage and divorce law. He stated:

> I also was told that it was recommended that the method of *afkinu rabanan l'kiddushin minei*[1] [annulment of marriage] be reintroduced. If this recommendation is accepted, and I hope it will not be accepted, but if it is accepted, then there will be no need for a *get*. . . . We will be able to cross out this mishnah, that halachah; every rabbi will suspend Jewish marriages. Why should there be this halachah if such a privilege exists?

Why should this privilege be monopolized by the Israeli Chief Rabbinate in Israel? Why couldn't the Rabbinical Council do it just as well.[2]

Rabbi Soloveitchik's point (homiletically made, but made nonetheless) is that systemic change to fix the agunah problem creates systemic problems in and of itself. Rabbi Soloveitchik incisively notes the two profound problems in creating an annulment mechanism:

1. Unilateral and absolute exit rights from marriage destroy the institution of marriage.
2. Authority is so diffuse in the community that if annulments are allowed, every Jewish court will use them in ways that one cannot predict.

This chapter will review the current scope of potential solutions to the agunah problem, inquiring which type of cases each potential solution is aimed at fixing. The analysis will focus not on the precise mechanism used to implement any particular solution, but rather on the categories of cases each seeks to govern.[3] Indeed, mechanisms, and even their ultimate halachic validity, are not of direct concern to this chapter or even this book, since even a halachically acceptable mechanism might be unacceptable to some segments of the community for reasons that have nothing to do with technical halachah, and much to do with images of marriage.

There are five distinct categories of solutions to the agunah problem that have been voiced in the last 50 years. Each needs to be understood as solving certain cases of *igun*, as not solving other cases of *igun*, and as perhaps creating other problems.

Unilateral No-Fault Divorce as the Solution

A small number of authorities have advocated the return of halachah to the normative rules advocated by Rambam and *geonim*, with the revitalization of the model of unilateral no-fault divorce or even annulments. This model would theoretically appear to solve the largest number of agunah cases by creating an unfettered right of divorce in any situation where the couple has separated. Assuming a functioning bet din system (see Chapter 4) or annulments as the mechanism, this model has, in theory, possibilities to end the agunah problem by compelling the giving of a *get* in a variety of cases. The only cases that would not be solved, in this view, are those in which the husband does not submit to the increasing pressure put on him (though annulments could solve those cases too). Conversely, absent a working bet din system capable of applying significant pressure, this solution solves few real problems. However, it does create enormous questions about annulments, since even the most charitable read of the halachic permissibility to do annulments limits that authority to Jewish courts representing, and appointed by, large sections of the community.[4]

Putting aside the nearly insurmountable halachic objections to a return to halachic rules that have not been normative for 800 years, and are not even cited as a possibility by the Shulchan Aruch, there remain two objections to the creation of a unilateral no-fault right of divorce. There are significant downsides, both to the strength of the family unit and the respective rights of spouses in a case of divorce, to the insistence that, even absent fault, each person in a marriage has an unconditional and unfettered right to end the marriage regardless of the consequences. Indeed, few advocates of this proposal even seem willing to discuss this issue substantively. What this will do to halachah, whether annulment is employed to give this teeth or not, is create a structure where the sole criterion for the right to divorce is *to ask to be divorced.*

Just as unilateral no-fault, nonmutual divorce has not proven to be a significant stabilizing force in those states that have adopted it in the last 25 years,[5] so too it will not prove a stable force in Jewish society for the dissolution of marriages. Just as it has not led to a significant decrease in the antagonism associated with secular divorce, so too it will not lead to the reduction of antagonism within the Jewish tradition. Just as it has not led to increased family stability in those states that have adopted it, so too it will not prove to be a stabilizing force in the Jewish family.[6] The same is true for the various proposals that intend to create conditional marriages in Jewish law, that is, marriages that are conditional on their continuing to function. These proposals essentially adopt the view that a *get* ought to be given whenever halachically reasonable, in any circumstance that halachah can imagine a permissible way to give one. The problems of unilateral no-fault divorce are to be ignored, and this solution ignores them.

A modified version of this proposal would limit the cases where halachah would end the marriage to those in which the secular legal system has ordered a civil divorce.[7] While there are certain great advantages to this model, the insistence that the Jewish tradition should simply fall in lockstep with the secular requirements of divorce, whatever they might be, would seem a profound abandonment of the historically autonomous conception of halachah in the area of status determinations. Indeed, it is the inversion of the practice of the British rabbinate, itself abandoned for many years, of insisting that a *get* not be given until a civil divorce is final. The relinquishment of an independent halachic standard for divorce would seem too much for any autonomous legal system. Why should Jewish law accept that whenever New York State, or Alabama or Pakistan, rules divorce proper, that the Jewish tradition will simply affirm that ruling? It is much more logical to assert that the Jewish tradition, which has independent judgments in well nigh every other area of family law, should insist on independent judgment in this area as well.

Indeed, were this approach to be adopted, the Jewish tradition would end the claim that the rules governing marriage and divorce are intrinsically grounded in halachah. Jewish divorce would become a pale ritual, and the Jewish tradition would commit itself to lockstep fidelity to secular law.[8] These types of proposals place more faith in the civil divorce system than it is reasonably entitled to have. There are vast areas of the United States, and certainly other areas worldwide, where there is no apparent reason for the Jewish legal system to abandon its duty to adjudicate marriage and divorce.[9]

So too, and of equal significance, annulments, in which a bet din ends a marriage with or without the consent of either or both parties, violate in a very fundamental way crucial conceptions of Jewish marriage as private rather than public acts. Marriage is, as was explained above, a private contract in the Jewish view; the same is true for divorce. The notion that a Jewish law court can "grant" a divorce without the participation of the parties simply because it wishes to is profoundly contrary to the fundamental view of marriage and divorce as private contracts. There is little doubt that such a dramatic shift in the view of Jewish marriage and divorce is wrong, for reasons that are elaborated on throughout this work.

Abandoning Marriage as a Solution

Other proposals adopt even more far-fetched approaches to the agunah problem. There have been a number of proposals to abolish marriage completely and accept those opinions that *pelagshut*, stable monogamous concubinage,[10] with no requirement of divorce, be instituted. This proposal, having done away with the institution of marriage, does in fact solve the agunah problem. However, as R. Breitowitz notes:

> It would be inconceivable for a religious system to set up the *concubine* as a viable and equal or even preferable mode of relationship. Such a proposal, it was said, degrades the sanctity of marriages and family life, promotes promiscuity, denigrates women and would be a "cure" considerably worse than the illness it seeks to alleviate.[11]

Consider the possibility. To solve a problem affecting a small number of marriages that end with very difficult divorces, one would propose that the very institution of marriage be abandoned. This type of parochial ethical microscope, focusing on just one aspect of a complex legal status (marriage) and evaluating every aspect of every proposal that affects marriage by the litmus test of what it does to agunot (end of marriage problem), is the type of thinking that has to be abandoned if there is to be any hope of significant progress in the area of Jewish end-of-marriage problems.

Contractarian Solutions and Their Problems

Besides the internal halachic suggestions discussed above, a variety of proposed solutions are predicated on contract law (either halachic or secular) to encourage the giving of a *get*. As was explained in Chapter 1, these proposals come in four forms: encouraging the giving of a *get* in set circumstances, encouraging the submission of the dispute governing end of marriage to a particular bet din for resolution, establishing payments as a means of support when there is a separation (to encourage the man to give a *get* in order to avoid these payments), and conditioning the validity of the marriage itself (or the giving of a *get*) upon the occurrence or absence of certain actions.

As has been noted by R. Breitowitz, attempts to create an explicit obligation to give a *get* based on the text of the *ketubah* or some other written document pledging to give a *get* are subject to a variety of significant critiques.[12] From my perspective, the most significant one is that any judicial attempt to derive an obligation to give a *get* in circumstances where Jewish law itself does not require the giving of a *get* is a profound misunderstanding of the nature of Jewish law. Simply put, absent some agreement to define "normative Jewish law," it is impossible to claim that Jewish law requires or even encourages the giving of a *get* in every case where any civil system would mandate civil divorce. That is the essence of a *get me'useh,* a compelled divorce, which is potentially void according to Jewish law.[13] Even in circumstances where such a *get* is not categorically void, it is unwise and deeply contrary to the historic Jewish legal understanding of marriage and divorce to insist that a Jewish divorce should take place merely because either the civil courts or one spouse desires it, where there is no indication that this was the nature of the marriage when the couple first entered into it.[14]

More generally, there are considerable systemic problems with views of the marriage contract that posit unilateral exit from the marriage without any judicial procedure or even any exit rights. Conditional marriages produce a voided marriage when the condition is not met. Neither of the parties were ever married, in the eyes of Jewish law. The *ketubah* is void; neither party has financial claims against the other as they do in a divorce, and neither party has any significant duties toward the other.[15]

Consider the simple suggestion that every Jewish marriage be made conditional on the parties residing together, and that should the parties reside apart for more than two years, the marriage will be void. That condition, even assuming it were valid according to Jewish law,[16] would allow the couple, when they wish to end the marriage, to dispense with the formalism of divorce, or adjudication of their rights toward one another. The one who wishes to divorce simply abandons the marital home, and divorce soon comes automatically.

While one could respond by letting the civil legal system be the backstop for the adjudication of the rights of the parties, such a solution seems deeply unsatisfying within Jewish law, as it fundamentally abandons Jewish divorce law as a substantive field, and allows whatever are the divorce norms within the society that the Jewish community temporarily inhabits to become normative, even when neither party wished for such at the time of their marriage.

Rabbinical Tribunals as a Solution

A second form of this proposal is the binding arbitration agreement in which the parties agree to submit any dispute about the marriage to rabbinical tribunal. This proposal is without controversy as it relates to the laws of marriage and divorce, in that it seeks to establish as the secular legal norm an authority that halachah recognizes as due the rabbinical courts.[17]

However, the same failures discussed earlier apply clearly in this case as well. An agreement to submit a dispute to bet din is not the same as a decision by the bet din to authorize the writing of a *get* or to compel the husband to write such a *get*. All that such an agreement accomplishes is to eliminate the issues addressed in Chapter 4 related to the absence of authority in the bet din system in America. Even if there is authority, there are still a variety of circumstances where the substantive rules of Jewish law either do not compel the writing of a *get* or else allow the bet din to order the writing of the *get* but deny it the authority to impose sanctions.[18] It is clear that there are many different Jewish law courts in the United States, with different standards as to when a divorce is encouraged, demanded, compelled, or even discouraged or prohibited.

Prenuptial Agreements as Marriage Contracts

Jewish prenuptial support agreements come in a variety of forms, with various degrees of complexity. However, all create a situation in which the husband is burdened with financial obligations related to a marriage, from which he can exempt himself only by divorcing through the writing of a *get*. These proposals have a number of advantages, both on a technical and a pastoral level, over any of the other "*get* inducing" proposals. They typically make no mention of divorce; rather they specify that certain duties shall be incumbent on each party while in the marriage (and implicitly admitting that one can exempt oneself from this obligation by divorcing) or until they are lifted by a bet din. This approach eliminates the problem of compulsion, because there is no penalty; rather there is support and maintenance. It addresses many of the pastoral concerns in that divorce is not mentioned in the document.[19]

It is important to understand that the essence of these assumptions of obligation agreements is to create significant incentives to be divorced whenever one side wishes. They are not genuinely aimed at providing for the maintenance of the spouse. Consider for example, the agreement that received the approbation of six eminent Israeli rabbis and is supported as well by Rabbi Mordechai Willig, one of the premier halachic authorities in New York. This agreement states, in part:

> I, the undersigned, husband-to-be, hereby obligate myself to support my wife-to-be, in the manner of Jewish husbands who feed and support their wives loyally. If, God forbid, we do not continue domestic residence together for whatever reason, then I now obligate myself to pay her $____ ____ per day, indexed annually to the Consumer Price Index for all Urban Consumers (CPI-U) as published by the US Department of Labor, Bureau of Labor Statistics, beginning as of December 31st following the date of our marriage, for food and support from the day we no longer continue domestic residence together, and for the duration of our Jewish marriage, which is payable each week during the time due, under any circumstances, even if she has another source of income or earnings. *Furthermore, I waive my halachic rights to my wife's earnings for the period that she is entitled to the above-stipulated sum.* However, this obligation (to provide food and support,) shall terminate if my wife refuses to appear upon due notice before the Bet Din of _____ or any

other bet din specified in writing by that bet din before proceedings commence, for purpose of a hearing concerning any outstanding disputes
between us, or in the event that she fails to abide by the decision or recommendation of such bet din.[20]

While at first read this text appears to be a mere support agreement, upon closer analysis it is in fact a support agreement designed
to encourage the writing of a *get*. Any "normal" halachic agreement
designed merely to provide for the financial support of the wife
because the husband is not fulfilling this duty by providing a joint
residence, would limit this duty to support through the classical offset rule that the income earned by the wife goes to the husband.[21] In
Jewish law, if the husband and wife agree that he will support her,
she agrees that her income from work goes to him. The unilateral
waiver of the right to her income *without the waiver of her right to support*, while clearly permitted according to Jewish law, reflects the fact
that what is really being established is an economic incentive to
divorce or participate in the bet din, albeit one that avoids a host of
technical problems, and thus has received the approbation of a variety of Jewish law scholars.[22] The purpose of this agreement is to
allow for unilateral no-fault divorce, absent the contrary ruling of
the named bet din. This is even truer when this support agreement
is signed after being modified so as to eliminate the ability of a bet
din to halt such payments; such modifications are easy[23] and com-
monplace in prenuptial agreements, even if such was not intended
by the authorizers of this prenuptial.[24]

Thus many prenuptial support agreements, and other similar
agreements,[25] involved a fundamental paradigm shift in terms of the
right to be divorced (see Chapter 2). Essentially these agreements
are technical documents designed to graft a unilateral no-fault right
of divorce onto the technical requirements of the mutual divorce
school of thought. Consider that Rabbenu Tam/Rabbenu Gershom
envision that mutual consent will be the negotiated framework for
every divorce absent fault, whereas these support agreements contemplate that a financial penalty will be imposed as an incentive to
divorce. The incentive is one that the approach of Rabbenu Tam and
Rabbenu Gershom can consider halachically acceptable: it does not

produce a compelled divorce but is fundamentally predicated on the concept that a couple can order their marital relationship in a manner that they see fit, including creating incentives to provide for the unilateral no-fault divorce.[26]

Secular Intervention as a Model for Divorce

Another form of this proposal is to seek secular legislation to govern this process to affect the agunah problem. This coercive secular legislation can take one of three forms, each with its own flavor and problems.

1. Secular government could, as is the law in Israel, delegate the divorce process to the bet din, such that Jews who are married in a Jewish ceremony must be divorced in one too.
2. It could simply withhold the civil divorce process from one who is not religiously divorced.
3. It could use the civil divorce process to penalize individuals who withhold a *get* anytime there is a civil divorce.

All of these techniques are predicated on a specific view of when it is appropriate to be divorced, and that must be clearly understood. Process 1 vastly reduces the agunah problem, since by assigning judicial authority to the rabbinical courts, one accepts that an agunah is a woman who the rabbinical courts feel should be divorced yet is not divorced. As was noted in Chapter 2, a woman's right to divorce differs from model to model in the Jewish tradition. There might well be circumstances where the rabbinical court will not rule a *get* needed; thus the woman would not be an agunah, as the Jewish law agency vested with making that determination has not ruled her entitled to a divorce.[27]

Process 2 works very well, but it does not clearly solve the agunah problem. This process, implemented by New York in its 1984 *Get* Law, accepts that if one is going to religiously withhold a *get,* civil law should not allow the couple to have a secular divorce. The only time this approach works to solve agunah cases is when the one who is withholding a *get* genuinely desires to be free of the marriage and simply wants to be religiously married as a weapon of some sort. When the husband who is withholding a *get* wishes to remain married, both civilly and religiously, this law is of little impact, since its goal is as much to harmonize the civil status with the religious status as it is to encourage the writing of the *get*. In essence, this approach is a commitment by the secular legal authorities not to allow the civil divorce process to be used when the religious divorce process will not be, for couples that clearly intended to have a religious marriage ceremony and a religious divorce.

The third process, using coercive penalties to encourage the writing of a *get* when a civil divorce has been granted, is a decision by the secular legal system to preempt Jewish law. Essentially, in such a system the secular legal system accepts that there is a "right" to receive a Jewish divorce because there is a valid civil divorce. Penalties are imposed to encourage a person to comply with the dictates of the state and give a Jewish divorce, whether or not Jewish law rules that a divorce may or should or must be given. Almost definitionally, Jewish law would view this type of a solution, predicated on the model that secular law determines when a *get* is to be given and that Jewish law merely bureaucratically processes the ritual aspects of the divorce, as contrary to the tradition of independence that Jewish law has had in the area of family law. Indeed, as Jewish law makes clear with its rule that a coerced *get* is void, when the penalties imposed under this system become great enough, Jewish law will view the resulting *get* as void, as it was not given under the required free will standard.[28]

One final type of encouragement can be given in the agunah situation. The civil legal system can provide for awards, either in tort or quasi-contract, to one who has had a *get* improperly withheld. Whether these implied contracts are grounded in the obligation to deal fairly, torts grounded in intentional infliction of emotional distress, or other grounds, awarding them is predicated on the woman's having a right to receive the *get* which is being withheld.[29] These types of awards (putting aside the technical question of whether they lead to a void *get* because of problems related to a compelled *get*) are very difficult to classify in terms of the image of

marriage on which they are predicated. Like all fact-specific determinations made in the American legal system, it is hard to know
why a jury in any particular case insists that a Jewish divorce should
be granted. It is possible that any one of these divorces is proper
under a particular model, although logically a systemic commitment
to letting a jury decide whether the withholding of a *get* is an
improper act worthy of financial punishment would seem most
likely to create a system where popular images of marriage and
divorce predominate, leading to different factors evaluated differently in various cultures. What would be clear, however, is that this
type of an award would be predicated on no right to a divorce in
Jewish law at all.

Summary of the Modern Solutions and Their Problems

Many of the proposed modern solutions to the agunah problems
share a common approach. They are searching for a mechanism that
allows Jewish law to compel unilateral no fault divorce or the functional abolition of marriage, when in fact there is no consensus that
such a solution is a good idea, even if it were possible according to
technical Jewish law.

Chart 5.1 (p. 71) summarizes the type of agunah problems that
exist, various modern solutions, and their underlying view of the
right to divorce.

Chart 5.1: Views of Marriage, Divorce, and *Igun* in the Modern Era

Implications → / Techniques to End the Marriage ↓	Authorities Supporting Such	Conceptual Model of Marriage	Conceptual Model of Divorce	Role of Bet Din	When a *Get* is to Be Issued	Impact on Relevant *Igun* Categories (cf. p. 28)	Sources on the Duty to Divorce
Support Agreement to Encourage Giving of a *Get*	Early: Nachlat Shiva; Late: R. Mordechai Willig	Economic incentives to consent to divorce	Mutual agreement prior to marriage	Determined by parties	Determined by mutual agreement signed before marriage	Encourages the giving of a *get* in cases where the marital residence has ended	R. Mordechai Willig in Herring and Auman, *The Prenuptial Agreement* (Aronson, 1996)
Abolition of Religious Marriage	Early: Rambam Late: R. Moshe Toledano	No marriage exists	None needed	None	Never	Abolishes concept of *igun* or divorce	*Otzar ha-Chayyim*, p. 209, Breitowitz, pp. 68–70
Submission to Rabbinical Arbitration	Early: Implicit norm Late: R. Saul Lieberman	Determined by bet din, which is chosen by parties	Determined by bet din	Adjudicative	When bet din orders	Indeterminate. Different Jewish law courts have different standards	Isaac Klein, *A Guide to Jewish Religious Practices*, p. 293
Conditional Marriage	R. Eliezer Berkovitz	Marriage void when condition unfilled	No divorce needed	None	Never	Ends *igun*	*T'nai be-N'suin ve-Get*
Conditional Divorce	R. Yosef Henkin	Divorce occurs when preset conditions met	Automatic, upon meeting conditions	Procedural	When conditions are met	Ends *igun*	*Perushei Ibra*, pp. 110–117
Prenuptial Agreements	R. Moshe Feinstein	Contractual	Contractual	None	When parties agreed to such in prenuptial	Determined by prenuptial agreement	*Iggrot Moshe*, Even ha-Ezer 4:107
A Secular *Get* Law	Various Jewish women's groups	Secular norms (e.g., mutual desire and monogamy)	Determined by secular law, varies by jurisdiction	Procedural; follows the prenuptial agreement	Upon civil divorce	Depends on status of secular law	Breitowitz, *Between Civil and Religious Law*, pp. 180–238

CHAPTER SIX

Summary: A Conceptualization of the Agunah Problem

The Nature of the Agunah Problem

As is apparent from the review of the developments of Jewish law and the literature concerning the agunah problem, categories of agunah problems can be summarized as follows:

    I. The husband has disappeared; fundamentally the wife desires to remain married to her husband. She is an agunah only until he either returns or is declared dead.[1] Changes in technology and society have basically resolved this problem.

    II. The husband and wife wish to be divorced but lack of communication prevents the delivery of a valid Jewish divorce.[2] Changes in technology and society have basically resolved this problem.

    III. The husband currently does not wish to be divorced and hopes to return to the marriage.[3]

    IV. The husband genuinely wishes to be divorced but wishes to use the *get* as leverage to extract further concessions, proper or improper.[4]

    V. The husband is withholding a *get* out of spite or retaliation and is not seeking anything.[5]

    VI. The *get* is being withheld by the husband because of dual system issues.[6]

VII. The husband decides that no Jewish divorce is needed and
     thus will not cooperate in such.[7]

VIII. The wife is incapable of receiving a Jewish divorce.[8]

In each of these cases (except some of the cases in category I
and all in category VIII) the possibility of recalcitrance is equally
available to the husband and wife, although the penalties for illicit
violation remain different. Notwithstanding that fact, cases of *agun
de-gavra* (withholding of acceptance of the *get* by the wife) remain
rarer than cases of agunah, and thus this section reflects this reality.

The various modern solutions to the American agunah problem
are designed to address cases III, IV, V, VI and VII, since they are the
ones remaining fundamentally unresolved.

As was shown in Chapter 2, there are a vast diversity of models
for Jewish marriages, some of which profoundly recognize the right
of either party to seek divorce at any time, and direct that Jewish law
mandate or encourage a divorce in such circumstances. Other models, equally normative in Jewish law, direct that absent fault, divorce
shall be only through mutual consent: these models cannot accept
the right of either party to seek unilateral no-fault divorce. (Paren-
thetically, it is important to note that both of these models are striving for fairness, in the goal of correcting the imbalance in Jewish law
that allows for unilateral no-fault divorce by the husband; one
model solves this imbalance by striving for unilateral no-fault
divorce by the wife, and the other by stripping the husband of his
right to insist on such a divorce. One seeks fairness by freeing
women from their chains, and one seeks equality by chaining the
men.)

In the end, even solutions that are fully consistent with all
aspects of technical Jewish law (as the consensus perceives some
prenuptial agreements and some rabbinic arbitration agreements),
but that direct that unilateral no-fault divorce shall be the image of
marriage available to the parties, will fail to convince vast segments
of the Jewish community of their usefulness. Such is not the case
because of technical halachic problems, but rather because such an
image of marriage is not the normative one within these segments of

the community. They desire enchaining marriages with vastly reduced exit rights, penalties for improper exit, and other sanctions, including the withholding of a *get*, in cases where exit is sought for no reason. This is even more the case when exit is sought with the aid of the secular legal system, whose values are so different from those in their community. Simply put, these individuals will not sign such a prenuptial agreement, and will discourage others from doing so, because these types of prenuptials reflect values about marriage through its regulation of divorce with which these communities do not agree.

Preconditions to Successful Solutions

As has become apparent throughout this work, my view is that the root source of the agunah problem in America has little to do with whether a mechanism can or cannot be devised that is consistent with Jewish law and is also able to compel a *get* when one party wishes. Rather, the question is this: does the community desire such a form of marriage and divorce? The history and teachings of the Jewish tradition answer that the community as a whole does not wish to allow for unilateral no-fault Jewish divorces. Such universalistic solutions, when imposed on the community by either the civil court system, the secular government, or subgroups within the community, will fail.

Genuinely successful solutions to the agunah problem must recognize the basic truthfulness of this observation and must craft solutions consistent with the diversity of voices within the Jewish tradition. Thus every successful solution either must allow for multiple images of marriage, with some choice mechanism that has to be activated by the couple at the time of their marriage, or must allow for couples to opt out of any proposed solution if that solution is predicated on a model of marriage that does not reflect their view.

An analogy is perhaps helpful. Jewish law desires that Jews keep kosher and maintains that such conduct is religiously obligatory for Jews. Within the community of Jews who do keep kosher, there are a variety of standards, each predicated on a different understanding of some aspect of Jewish law. Frequently it is hard to state with any degree of confidence whose view is correct and whose is not; even when one can make such a claim, such claims are closer to opinion than fact. We all recognize that it is not the role of the secular government to compel Jews to keep kosher, nor is it now perceived as within the purview even of the Jewish community to do so.[9] Should we seek kosher laws that provide rigid definitions of kosher such that there is an appearance of unity in the kosher laws, when in fact what is happening is really suppression of reasonable views of what is and is not kosher? The answer has to be "no." Neither government nor the communal consensus can compel people to abandon their understanding of what is kosher and what is not, whether they be strict or lenient.

What, then, should the Jewish community seek from kosher laws? The New Jersey regulatory model,[10] which does not determine what is kosher, but merely directs that every seller of kosher food disclose its standards so that informed consumers can make their own choices, is the correct approach. What should a consumer do who adheres to a standard different from that employed by the purveyor of the kosher food? The answer is shop elsewhere. Impropriety occurs only when a purveyor of kosher food announces one standard and actually employs another (even if the other standard is also plausibly valid).

The same is true for marriage. We cannot hope to resolve the ancient dispute between halachic authorities as to whether strong or weak marriage bonds are better or worse, and whether the solution to the agunah problem entails shackling the man to promote equality (as Rabbenu Gershom decreed) or unshackling the woman (as Maimonides ruled). We must recognize that the different views exist, and each couple should be encouraged to declare, prior to their marriage, to which view they wish to be contractually bound.

There is no single solution to the agunah problem. Rather, there is a dispute about what the agunah problem even is. Only solutions that correctly comprehend the nature of the problem have any chance of solving it.

A secondary problem, albeit one that vastly exacerbates the issue, is the lack of a functional bet din system that adjudicates fairly and justly according to Jewish law as it is understood within each community. Currently, not only are the scope and nature of the agunah problem misunderstood, but even when they are properly understood, neither party can compel the other to participate in a Jewish-law-based justice system. Each party seeks the adjudicative process that results in his or her victory.

CHAPTER SEVEN

Summary: A Conceptualization of Solutions to the Agunah Problem

The Nature of the Solutions

There is no solution to the agunah problem, because there is no agreement on who is an agunah and on when this status is a problem. Rather the agunah issue is made up of a host of discretely different matters, each with a different solution available. Some groups within the Jewish community do not perceive cases where a couple is left incapable of divorcing according to Jewish law a problem.

In order to craft a remedy, a number of observations concerning potential solutions must be made.

1. Solutions that involve secular law in the workings of Jewish divorce will be successfully implemented only if they are either acceptable to both of the communities outlined above or predicated on some sort of voluntary identification such that those who do not desire benefit of the system need not use it. (A prototype of this type of voluntary identification system is the prenuptial agreement, which can work in a number of ways, all of which, however are predicated on the couple's agreement prior to marriage as to what are the "rules" governing this marriage.)

2. Solutions that involve bringing secular law into the workings of Jewish law in a mandatory way should be sought only if they have the support of vast segments of the Orthodox

community, since it is patently unethical to impose one's understanding of Jewish law on another through the use of secular law. In the alternative, such legislation must have an opt-out clause allowing those who disagree to decline to be governed by it.[1]

3. Given the vastly different conception of the right to divorce found within the Jewish tradition and the resulting disagreements in how to solve the agunah problem, it is likely that the only solution that has the true possibility of "solving" the problem is one that recognizes the diversity of understandings found within Jewish law and that allows each community to adopt whatever solution it deems religiously acceptable. However, to prevent the religious posturing by spouses that comes with acrimonious divorce, such solutions have to be spelled out prior to marriage and agreed upon by the parties. In the absence of such prior agreements as to what the base rules are, Jewish law will not be able to impose a solution.[2]

It is important to understand the impact of these three observations: just as there is diversity in the understanding and application of the Sabbath laws, the family purity laws, the financial laws, and the marriage laws of Judaism, there is diversity in the understanding of the divorce laws. Just as the Sabbath laws, family purity laws, financial laws, and marriage laws of Judaism *never* have most of these disputes resolved in a coercive manner (each community does as it understands the halachah to be, without any coercive direction from other communities), the same is true in the area of divorce law. However, this is harder to do in the area of divorce law. The contest between the spouses in an acrimonious divorce matter causes many individuals to misunderstand the norms of their community, either unintentionally or otherwise, and to seek a rule of Jewish law which, while normative, does not reflect the understanding of the halachah found within his or her community. Thus every person involved in Jewish divorce can recount cases of one spouse or another seeking resolution of a contested Jewish divorce matter, in front of a bet din, that one spouse or the other feels is not representative of the Jewish law traditions of the community in which the *res* of the marriage resided.[3]

Pluralistic Images of Marriage and Divorce

Just as solutions to the problems of kosher food fraud cannot be predicated on the community's agreeing upon a single standard for keeping kosher, the same must be true for rules related to marriage and divorce. Individuals have the right and ability to discuss and agree in a halachicly binding way when and under what circumstances they, and not anyone else, feel that their marriage should end; they can then write a document directing their choice. There are a variety of models that they can choose from, each grounded in the classical Jewish tradition and the sources, or common contemporary practice, or even simply mutual agreement of the parties. Once they reach such an agreement, it is binding on them and controls their end-of-marriage dispute should they have one.

The strength of this approach is that it recognizes that there are vast categories of hard cases where the Jewish tradition cannot claim to speak with one voice about whether a particular woman is entitled to a *get*. So too, experience has taught that the discussion of within what model of marriage a couple should marry cannot be delayed until the couple is contemplating getting divorced, because some individuals will at that time present a biased view of his or her intent at the time of the marriage based on what allows the person to triumph now. Just as we could not imagine the kosher food purveyor being asked to fill out the form concerning what his kosher standards are after a problem is detected, we cannot allow these decisions to be made after the marriage has already collapsed.

As was shown in Chapter 2, there are a number of different images of when divorce is proper that are part of the halachic tradition. In essence, the Orthodox community in America has adherents to each of these five views in its community. Whether any given one of us agrees or disagrees with any one of these views is irrelevant.

Multiple Types of Prenuptial Agreements: A Real Solution to the Root Problem of Multiple Images of Divorce

If society wishes to have prenuptial agreements used all the time, it must write a variety of them and tell people that the single most important thing to do is to use one, any one. If we do not have a variety, many individuals and rabbis will refuse to use such agreements, because they will not reflect "their" view of marriage.

It is my view and hope that when many different prenuptials are available, couples (and perhaps rabbis) will be forced to discuss when they really want marriages to end. Each of these different theories creates a different ending point. When that discussion occurs, and when people grow to see that different prenuptials say different things, I suspect that people will gravitate to a prenuptial agreement that encourages the giving and receiving of a *get* when only one party wishes to be divorced, although such might not happen. That is fine, too, as people will receive justice in the image of marriage that they mutually agreed upon.[4]

If any given community genuinely desires to force its community members to use prenuptial agreements,[5] it must recognize that the single most effective way to encourage their use is to adopt the view that for any marriage conducted after a designated date, if the marriage suffers end of marriage difficulties, the various communal organizations that normally involve themselves as support groups will *not* help, since this harm could have been avoided through a prenuptial agreement. Sometimes people forfeit their right to help when they become "sick," because they decline to use the readily available vaccine prior to the illness.[6]

The Bet Din System

Hand-in-hand with the recognition of the need for prenuptial agreements to lay out the theoretical models is the recognition of the need for a bet din system. The creation of a Jewish law court system that functions in each community to adjudicate fairly disputes that arise in end-of-marriage cases is vital. This system of adjudication has to be capable of discerning truth, adjudicating in a just way within each community, and compelling adherence to this process. A comprehension of the problem without the creation of a justice system to actually adjudicate disputes will not succeed in solving the problem, because people will simply refuse to participate in this system.

CHAPTER EIGHT

Conclusion: What Can Be Done?

The summary of this book is not complicated.

The agunah problem has not been solved in America because there is no consensus about what the agunah problem really is and what is a proper solution to it. Some think that Jewish law created equality in the divorce process by empowering either spouse, when there is no determination of fault, to decline to accept a divorce when unhappy with the terms, be they financial, custodial, or otherwise. In this view, there is no real agunah problem in many cases; rather halachah is working just as it should. Others think that Jewish law created equality by mandating divorce when the marriage has factually collapsed, and that either side is entitled to a divorce when that has happened should they want one. In this view, the solution to the agunah problem is merely a search for a halachicly acceptable mechanism to encourage divorces in those cases while avoiding the technical problems of a coerced *get*. Yet others think that the Jewish divorce rite is a mere ritual that should function in the shadow of secular law, and whenever a secular divorce is to be issued, a *get* should also be issued. Yet other approaches, shades of gray among these three schools of thought, exist in Jewish law in theory and the Jewish community in reality.

All of these schools of thought peacefully co-exist in modern Jewish law, and the intellectual tension between them can never be resolved; "these and those are the words of the living God."

This dispute, which is at the root source of the agunah problem, cannot be "resolved." However, a system can be designed which allows marriage and divorce laws to function according to halachah in a way that fulfills the couple's expectations about their marriage.[1] This can be resolved only by mandating a simple two-step process:

1. Each and every prospective couple must choose the model of marriage within which they wish to live together. They codify their choice through a prenuptial agreement regarding a forum for dispute resolution, or through a set of halachic norms underlining their marriage or through both.
2. Each community creates a bet din system that resolves end-of-marriage disputes in accordance with its understanding of proper halachic norms and values. This bet din system will have the authority to adjudicate such disputes and compel acceptance of its solution within its community, and, through reciprocity principles, in other similar communities.

No other solution will work.

APPENDIX A

A Brief Historical Introduction to Jewish Law

Jewish law, or *halachah,* is used here to denote the entire subject matter of the Jewish legal system, including public, private, and ritual law. A brief historical review will familiarize the reader with its history and development. The Pentateuch (the five books of Moses, the *Torah*) is the historical touchstone document of Jewish law and, according to Jewish legal theory, was revealed to Moses at Mount Sinai around the year 1280 B.C.E. The Prophets and Writings, the other two parts of the Hebrew Bible, were written over the next 700 years, and the Jewish canon was closed about the year 200 before the common era ("B.C.E."). The period from the close of the canon until 250 of the common era ("C.E.") is referred to as the era of the *tannaim,* the redactors of Jewish law, which closed with the editing of the *Mishnah* by Rabbi Judah the Patriarch. The next five centuries was the epoch in which the two Talmuds (Babylonian and Jerusalem) were written and edited by scholars called *amoraim* ("those who recount" Jewish law) and *savoraim* ("those who ponder" Jewish law). The Babylonian Talmud is of greater legal significance than the Jerusalem Talmud and is a more complete work.

The post-talmudic era is conventionally divided into three periods: (1) the era of the *geonim,* scholars who lived in Babylonia until the mid-eleventh century; (2) the era of the *rishonim* (the early authorities), who lived in North Africa, Spain, Franco-Germany, and Egypt until the end of the fourteenth century; and (3) the period of the *achronim* (the latter authorities), which encompasses all scholars of Jewish law from the fifteenth century up to this era. From the mid-fourteenth century until the early seventeenth century, Jewish law underwent a period of codification, which led to the acceptance of the law code format of Rabbi Joseph Karo, called the *Shulchan Aruch,* as the basis for modern Jewish law. The *Shulchan Aruch* (and the *Arba'ah Turim* of Rabbi Jacob ben Asher, which preceded it) divided Jewish law into four areas: *Orach Chayyim* is devoted to daily, Sabbath, and holiday laws; *Even Haezer* addresses family law, including its financial aspects; *Choshen Mishpat* codifies financial law; and *Yoreh Deah* contains dietary laws as well as miscellaneous other legal matter. Many significant scholars, themselves as important as Rabbi Karo in status and authority, wrote annotations to his code which made the work and its surrounding comments the modern touchstone of Jewish law. The most recent complete edition of the *Shulchan Aruch* (Vilna, 1896) contains no less than one hundred and thirteen separate commentaries on the text of Rabbi Karo. In addition, hundreds of other volumes of commentary have been published as self-standing works, a process that continues to this very day. Besides the law codes and commentaries, for the last twelve hundred years Jewish law authorities have addressed specific questions of Jewish law in written *responsa* (in question and answer form). Collections of such *responsa* have been published, providing guidance not only to later authorities, but to the community at large. Finally, since the establishment of the State of Israel in 1948, the rabbinical courts of Israel have published their written opinions deciding cases on a variety of matters, mostly in the area of family, where they have either exclusive or concurrent legal jurisdiction.

(For a more detailed description of Jewish family law generally, read the first four sections of Chapter 2, and the third and fourth sections of Chapter 4.)

APPENDIX B

Error in the Creation of Jewish Marriages: Under What Circumstances Can Error Void the Marriage without Requiring a Get

Preface

This appendix will demonstrate the nature of the halachic response to questions of *kiddushai ta'ut*: errors in the creation of a marriage based on information not being revealed. Essentially, although the grounds upon which women could argue that *kiddushai ta'ut* occurred were extremely narrow in talmudic times, were broader in the era of the *rishonim,* and have grown yet further in America in the last 50 years, this halachic truth was predicated on a social reality regarding marriage. Rabbi Moshe Feinstein recognized this fact, and understood that *kiddushai ta'ut* was a more plausible argument in America in the last 50 years than in other times and other places, and he advanced arguments for *kiddushai ta'ut,* and for what is a significant defect (*mum gadol*), in a much larger number of cases than did other halachic authorities. This sociological response is caused by the recognition that there are more and more cases in America where, had the woman been aware of the full reality of the situation at the time of the marriage, she would not have agreed to marry.

However, the recognition that the change in the status of women both economically and socially leads to an increased possibility of *kiddushai ta'ut* does not and indeed cannot mean that all marriages generally are subject to any form of *kiddushai ta'ut* principles.

Rather, in order for there to be any claim of error in the creation of the marriage, the following four conditions must be met:

1. The woman must discover a serious defect present in her husband after they are married.
2. That defect must have been present in the husband at the time of the marriage.
3. The woman must have been unaware of the defect at the time of marriage.
4. The woman must discontinue marital relations with her husband either immediately or very soon after the discovery of the defect.

Claims of *kiddushai ta'ut* outside of the framework of these four conditions have absolutely no foundation in halachah. No matter how serious the current defect might be, absent proof that the defect was present at the time of the marriage, it is impossible to assert that this marriage is void on the basis of error. Furthermore, there are no *teshuvot* found that permit claims of error unless all four conditions are met. Newly developed conditions or defects can never be grounds for a claim of *kiddushai ta'ut*.

Consider the case of a couple in which, after being married for twenty years, the husband commits adultery with his wife's sister. While the wife would undoubtedly say, "Had I known about this, I would not have married him twenty years ago," such does not state a claim of error in the creation of the marriage, because the condition was not present at the time of the marriage. The same is true if the husband becomes physically abusive after twenty years of marriage. While there is no doubt that the wife would say, "Had I known that he would abuse me after twenty years of marriage, I would not have married him twenty years ago," that demonstrates no error in the creation of the marriage. This case is no different from a case where one spouse becomes blind or lame after many years of marriage.

In contrast, consider the case of a man who is engaged to one woman and, during the engagement, is secretly having an affair with the woman's sister. Here one could argue that the error (fraud, actually) was present at the time of the marriage, and so the marriage

was void. The same is true for a man who is blind or lame or impotent prior to his marriage and hides that fact from his fiancee. If the
three other conditions are present, both of these cases could be
cases of error in the enactment, since the condition was clearly
present at the time of the marriage.

The recent use of the term *kiddushai ta'ut* by the new *bet din
leba'ayot ha-Agunot*[1] is unprecedented in halachah in that this body
is prepared to void every marriage in which the husband or wife
develops a defect in the course of the marriage, even though none of
the other conditions specified above are present.

Introduction

The institution of marriage in the halachic tradition involves a mul-
tiplicity of types of relationships between husband and wife: some
sacramental, some sexual, and some financial. Significant failures in
any one of these areas creates marriages that are far from ideal (and
sometimes void) in the halachic tradition. For example, nonsexual
marriages are frowned upon, spouses have financial obligations one
to another that are immutable, and halachah prohibits people from
marrying each other if they are of certain consanguinities or conditions, no matter how otherwise rewarding the relationship might be.

On the other hand, halachah does recognize a couple's ability to
deviate from the marriage norms of society if both parties desire to
do so. For example, a husband and wife can decline to have a sexual
relationship with each other if that is what both of them wish; a wife
can insist on her right to be self-supporting and self-enriching; and
even some improper marriages, if entered into, are valid and create a
marriage that requires a divorce when the couple separates.[2]

However, most deviations from the norm require the consent of
both parties. Thus error occurs in the creation of a marriage when
one spouse does not inform the other of a highly relevant issue in
any one of the three above-mentioned significant areas. The legal
theory explaining *kiddushai ta'ut*,[3] errors in the creation of a marriage, is fundamentally predicated on the view that the *creation of a
marriage* has significant aspects of a commercial transaction in

which there has to be a meeting of the minds, and a proper *kinyan*,[4] in which each party is aware of what it is he and she are agreeing to. Absent this full meeting of the minds, the marriage is apparently void (there is a failure in the creation of the marriage), and no divorce is actually required, because there is no marriage.[5] In a number of cases the Sages decreed that a *get* is required according to rabbinic law, lest people be confused about when a marriage can end without a *get*. In other circumstances, no *get* is required.[6]

Marriage as Contract

All Jewish marriages are created through an established process made up of four "contract-based" requirements:

1. The intention of the parties must be to marry voluntarily through this ceremony or procedure.[7]
2. The parties must be of suitable age, capacity, and (opposite) gender to marry.[8]
3. A proper method must be used to create a valid marriage, with two witnesses present.[9]
4. The fundamental components of the relationship between the two parties must be agreed upon.[10]

(It is important to understand what is not discussed in this appendix; issues raised by points 1, 2 or 3 are not discussed in this appendix. For example, the issues raised by error in the creation of the marriage due to factual mistake is not the same as the problem of a couple that enters into a marriage ceremony that is not ceremoniously valid according to Jewish law, such as a civil marriage ceremony. The civil marriage problem is a problem related to point 3, in that the issue under discussion is whether a proper method must be used to create a valid marriage, with two witnesses present, whereas problems of *kiddushai ta'ut* involve situations revolving around point 4, whether the fundamental components of the relationship between the two parties has been agreed upon.)[11]

Point 4 is the one that is most dependent on the social norms of the parties, since it goes to the heart of individuals' understanding of what is "created" when steps 1, 2, and 3 are followed. For example, it is generally recognized that marriage establishes the ability to have a licit sexual relationship; while there is nothing intrinsically wrong with a marriage in which a sexual relationship is not medically possible,[12] according to halachah one must inform one's future spouse that this is what he or she is entering into. If one does not, that marriage is possibly void.[13] The same is perhaps true when a sexual relationship is possible but children are not.[14]

Consider an example outside the field of family law. Two individuals meet on an airplane flying from Los Angeles, California, to Sydney, Australia. One looks at the other's wristwatch with great interest and offers to buy it for "one thousand dollars." The other agrees. The one who is wearing the watch takes it off and hands it to the purchaser, who places the watch on his wrist,[15] opens up his wallet, takes out one thousand dollars Australian, and offers full payment. The seller responds by stating, "The purchase price was 'one thousand U.S. dollars.'" The purchaser denies that and states that he would not have purchased the item for U.S. $1,000 and he only offered to purchase it for AU $1,000. The halachah is clear: the purchase is void, because there never really was an agreement. Even though they both agreed to what appears to be a deal, because there was a substantive misunderstanding of what the deal was actually about on a very significant facet, the deal is void. Seller returns AU $1,000 to purchaser and purchaser returns watch to seller. If they want to make a new deal, they certainly can; however, the agreement that they "made" on the plane is void, because it is predicated on *ta'ut*, error.[16]

The same result would be reached even if purchaser had agreed to pay seller "one thousand dollars in 90 days" and the confusion about the terms did not occur until 90 days from purchaser's apparently taking title through the act of wearing the watch (*kinyan meshicha*). This is so because the buyer and seller did not, in fact, have a meeting of the minds on the terms of the deal. Indeed, the talmudic hypothetical "If one sells a cow, and it turns out not to be kosher, the sale is void" (*mocher para, nemtza terefa, mehcho batel*)[17] clearly applies even though neither the buyer nor the seller are, *nor*

even could be, aware of the defect.[18] In the Talmud's case, if it turns
out that there is a significant defect in the animal at the time of the
sale, the sale is void. However, this sale can be voided only by one's
showing the following: (1) that a defect was present at the time of
the sale; (2) that the buyer was unaware of the defect; and (3) that if
the buyer had been aware of the defect, the buyer would not have
completed the sale.[19]

It is important to grasp that the buyer's argument in the talmudic case is not predicated on fraud[20] at all. It is grounded in the fact
that a valid deal requires an agreement about the principal terms
and there was none: the buyer thought he was purchasing an edible
animal, but the animal was not in fact edible.[21] If both parties had
been aware of the facts, they certainly could have made a deal, perhaps at a different price. They were not, however, and no deal was
made. This rule, obviously, is limited to significant components in
the transaction; error in less significant components does not lead to
the deal's being void, but merely to a "reduction in purchase
price."[22]

This same basic principle applies to the marriage arrangement.[23] The Shulchan Aruch, Even Haezer 39 lists many cases that
focus on the problems raised by incomplete revelation by the
woman concerning the physical state of her body, the presence of
constricting vows, and a host of other cases. The basic rule seems
clear: if a man should have been aware of the defect[24] or actually was
aware of the defect,[25] then he cannot claim that the marriage is void
on the basis of its presence. So too, if the "defect" is one that is normally found in many people, even if this man claims he now objects,
he is not to be believed;[26] it is assumed that he was aware of this
defect or the possibility of it being present, and he accepted this
defect or risk of it.[27] However, when there is a hidden defect in the
woman that the man was not aware of and could not have been
aware of, and the defect is serious, the marriage is void or void-
able.[28] (In the reality of practical halachah, this issue of what defect
is sufficiently serious to void the marriage is expressed in the techni-

cal literature as a discussion of what the minimally acceptable attributes of marriage are, given the modern state of marriage and the social and economic reality of the times. These vary from time to time, place to place, and, as Rabbi Moshe Feinstein notes, from level of religious observance to level of religious observance.)[29]

Condition (Tenai) and Error (Ta'ut):
The Conceptual Difference

It is important to grasp the difference between a condition (*tenai*) and an error (*ta'ut*) according to halachah. There is a very significant conceptual difference between a condition in a marriage and an error in enactment of the marriage. Error in enactment is not simply the application of implicit conditions. A condition in a marriage or divorce (and maybe all areas) follows a particular technical formulation and can cover contingencies that cannot ever be predicted by the parties and certainly need not be present.[30] Thus a man may marry a woman and he or she can state under the *chupah* that they are marrying each other only on the condition that neither ever gets cancer or drinks wine (or both). When one makes such a condition in a marriage and that condition is breached, the marriage is void, assuming that both of them never forgave the marital condition.[31]

Thus one can say that a formal *tenai* is a condition and limitation on the status of the marriage and is thus subject to significant procedural restrictions (both in exact formula and in assumed waivability), perhaps for that exact reason. The *tenai* procedure, if correctly followed, works for almost every imaginable contingency, including those currently not present. However, normative halachah assumes that people forgive *tenaim* after the couple commence a sexual relationship, and thus the marriage is valid even if the subsequent conditions are breached, as happily married couples waive otherwise permanent conditions shortly after marriage.[32] However, when a *tenai* is made at the time of marriage, and kept in effect during the sexual relationship and then the *tenai* is breached, the marriage ends without any divorce, as if there never was a marriage. Nevertheless, the marriage is fully valid until such time as the condition is breached.

While it is true that the custom and practice is not to use any conditions in a marriage, since there is a distinct halachic possibility that any such condition is void if the parties live together sexually without explicitly repeating the condition, such is not the categorical halachah; Rabbi Moshe Isserless (Rama) clearly rules that such conditions can and do work, and he proposes one to cover the case of a brother unwilling or unable to do *yibum* (levirate marriage.)[33] Certainly, all agree that a *tenai* can be kept in effect if, for example, the couple repeated the condition to a bet din before each time they engage in a sexual relationship.[34]

In sum, in a *tenai* case, when a condition is used and the procedure for a *tenai* is followed, the marriage is valid but conditional. If the proper procedure is followed, the condition can survive and it can govern many unforeseeable activities. However, in the real world of Jewish marriages, formal conditions are never used, since the procedural requirements to keep them valid once a sexual relationship commences are very onerous in all but the rarest of circumstances.

Such is not the case in *ta'ut*, which functions along a completely different conceptual axis. In an error case, since the marriage is valid only on the basis of mutual agreement, and the mutual agreement was predicated on a mistake of fact so great that, were it known, one party would not have consented to marry (or purchase the watch, in the case discussed above), the marriage (or sale) is void. It always was void and never was valid. The blessings recited under the *chupah* were in vain and no marriage ever took hold. While it is true that a subsequent marriage can take place between the parties,[35] that is possible only if the parties are actually aware of the facts and still desire to be married in light of them, just as the parties in the watch case could agree, once aware of the misunderstanding, to sell the watch for $1,000 (Australian). So too, in a case of error the parties could agree not to continue the relationship and could seek to contract with others. Obviously, this type of error can be present and apply to facts present only at the time of marriage.[36]

Defects in the Man

There is no discussion in the Shulchan Aruch itself concerning defects in the man, although there is a lengthy and detailed discussion of defects in the woman found throughout Even Haezer 39.[37] However, such a discussion does appear quite clearly in the Beit Shmuel[38] and can be implied from the talmudic discussion, found in Bava Kama 110b/111a, concerning the woman who marries a man whose brother is diseased.[39] In that talmudic case the Gemara clearly states that Jewish law does *not* assume that a woman would decline to marry a man who is right for her merely because she *might* fall to her future husband's brother as a *yevamah* and he might not wish to do *chalitzah* so she might have to marry him. Indeed, the *rishonim* split about what exactly is the proper limit to this presumption: Does it apply when the brother is an apostate? A heretic? A eunuch? All of these cases present troubling hypotheticals and the *rishonim* disagree over what exactly is the correct line to draw.[40] However, it is important to understand the nature of the disagreement: at what point is the defect in the brother great enough that one can state with near certainty that with this defect in the brother, this woman would not have married this man under any circumstances.[41] Indeed, one cannot really find any systemic statement of halachah (in the sense of statement of legal principle) that precludes the application of the principle of "defect" to a case of defect in the man.[42] The exact opposite argument can be found in the writings of both Rabbi Moshe Feinstein and Rabbi Chaim Ozer Grodzinski, who are inclined to rule that since a man can divorce a woman with less difficulty than the reverse, a man is more inclined to marry a woman who might be defective than the reverse, because he is prepared to gamble on a transaction that might not work and from which he can exit of his own free will; she cannot and thus is less inclined to take such a risk.[43]

The obvious question needs to be resolved. How does one understand the rule that "It is better for a woman to be with another [unhappily] than to be alone"[44] and the related phrase "We can attest that she is better with anyone"[45] found in the Talmud.[46] The question is how can one even consider the issue of *kiddushai ta'ut* when the talmudic principle clearly assumes that any given women is better off married than single? This issue requires a direct response: This talmudic principle has not globally changed for all women (throughout the world) but rather creates a refutable presumption that women are better off married, even in less than ideal relationships.[47] By this approach, this principle can be deemed *inapplicable* in any case where it can be shown to be untrue given the facts of a specific man and woman, or indeed any given category of men and women.[48]

This might be the approach halachah takes to many areas where the Gemara creates presumptions that are not applicable in every single case but that cannot be shown to be generally inapplicable. Consider child custody disputes between a man and woman who are divorced. Even though the Talmud provides rules of custody[49] which are quoted in the Shulchan Aruch,[50] the *rishonim* and *acharonim,* almost with one voice, insist that these rules are mere presumptions which a bet din need not follow when it recognizes they are not applicable.[51]

The same is true in the area of *kiddushai ta'ut.* One can show many cases where decisors determined that the presumption that a woman is better off with any husband is rejected, sometimes with the attestation, taken from the *Terumat ha-Deshen*[52] concerning a husband who is an apostate, that this husband is "less than anything!" Indeed, to adopt the posture that these two principles are absolute categorical presumptions is extremely difficult to do, as the Talmud itself recognizes that there are circumstances where it is better for a woman to be divorced than to be married. For example, Yevamot 118b permits one to accept a *get* on behalf of a woman who is categorically better off being divorced from her husband under the principle of *zachen le-adam she-lo be-fanav* ("One can acquire something for another without permission if it is a benefit for that person")[53] when the husband wants to divorce her but she is not present to receive the *get*. This can only be justified by stating the obvious: the principle of "It is better for a woman to be with another [unhappily] than to be alone"[54] is a presumption that, when clearly inapplicable, is also halachically inapplicable.[55]

As an example of this dual approach that the general reality has not changed but is inapplicable, Rabbi Moshe Feinstein,[56] discussing the case of a woman who married a bisexual man who hid that fact from her during their courtship, states:

> even nowadays one should not accept as proper this argument [that women generally are more content not to be married now than in talmudic times] and that, generally, reality has changed.

However, he continues:

> In this case, where the defect is so great, the marriage is a void transaction based on error even for a woman, as I explain in Iggrot Moshe, Even Haezer 1:79 and 80,[57] as this husband is involved in homosexuality which is a particularly great abomination, and greatly repugnant, an embarrassment to the whole family, and even more so to this woman that her husband chooses this disgusting form of sexual relations more than sexual relations with her. *In such a case, the marriage was certainly based on error. It is certain to us that no woman would desire to marry a man as disgusting, repugnant, and embarrassing as this.*[58]

Rabbi Feinstein applied similar analysis to cases where the husband was occasionally a lunatic, or impotent, or suffered heart illness, or was an apostate, or other cases and hid that fact from future spouses.[59]

Indeed, one can find a considerable number of *acharonim* who address cases of possible *kiddushai ta'ut* in this methodology and conclude that the rules of "it is better for a woman to be with another [unhappily] than to be alone"[60] and the related talmudic phrase "we can attest that she is better with anyone"[61] can be determined to be inapplicable within the reality of any given time or place. No less than 15 such cases are cited in note 62, and throughout this appendix another nine *teshuvot* also adopt this view.[62]

The fact that there is a significant dispute about how the application of the principle of *kiddushai ta'ut* derives from a fundamental disagreement about the sociological facts and reality: When does one reach the critical threshold of knowing beyond a doubt[63] certain facts about the intent of the parties in a marriage? As Chazon Ish states, "In the case of defects by the man when there is an unconditional marriage it is clear that the marriage is valid, as there is no categorical presumption[64] that she would not want [to marry him.]"[65] When there is a categorical presumption that had she been aware of his defects she would not have married him, even Chazon Ish would admit that the marriage is void.[66] Reasonable people or rabbis living in different communities, or understanding people's mind-sets differently, might disagree on when that threshold is reached and what such a defect is in the minds of most members of their community. That is a sociological and halachic problem, with results depending on the time and place. The rules remain the same, even as the results might change, a common motif in many halachic areas.

Continuing Marriages Which Started with a Defect

One of the frequent issues in the area of *kiddushai ta'ut* relates to the response of the woman or man upon discovery of the error in the creation of the marriage. Does he or she leave the marriage immediately? Rabbi Feinstein's final comments on the bisexual husband quoted above are worthy of further discussion. He states:

> If as soon as she found out that he was bisexual she left him, it is logical that if one cannot convince him to give a *get,* one should permit her to remarry because of the rule of *kiddushai ta'ut.*

Rabbi Feinstein repeats this:

> But all this[67] is limited to when she leaves him immediately, but if she lives with him (sexually), it is difficult to rule the marriage void.

This factor is significant. Shulchan Aruch, Even Haezer 31:9 rules that if a couple has an improper wedding ceremony for a technical reason (such as the wedding ring being worth only half a *prutah*), when they discover the defect and continue to live together (sexually), that decision creates a valid marriage since both parties were aware of the defect and aware of the fact that they could leave the marriage because of it, and they chose not to.[68] This rule is explicitly described in the context of defects in the woman by the Aruch Hashulchan, who states:

> In the case of defects in the woman which he explicitly stated before the marriage that he does not desire such defects . . . if he lives with her after their sexual relationship for an extended period of time, as a man and woman who are married do, they are certainly married. . . . The marriage was completed with certainty, when he lived with her, as that made it clear that he really does not care about these defects.[69]

This approach is logical. Every pot really does have a lid, and halachah recognizes that a person, even one with glaring defects, can marry someone who understands the virtues and vices of such a marriage. Thus there is little doubt that a woman who cannot have children (an *ilonit*) can validly marry so long as she discloses that fact, and that a man who is impotent can enter into a valid marriage so long as he discloses that fact.[70] The corollary of this is that when this woman or man becomes aware of a significant defect that was hidden, did she or he take steps to leave the relationship, or did he or she decide that they could live with the status quo. If he or she did the latter, even if the marriage was defective at its enactment, a very strong case can be made that this conduct (continuing the sexual[71] relationship with one's spouse with the intent to be married) creates a new and valid marriage.[72] In the case of a relatively insignificant defect, a case could be made that this is a ratification of the previous marriage, and in the case of a significant defect, it creates a new marriage.[73]

It is possible to create a construct in which the woman or man immediately decides to leave, but stays for a short period of time while planning to leave. In order to explain this halachicly, one would have to maintain that the man and woman never intended to have that ongoing sexual relationship create a marriage. Even the words of the Aruch Hashulchan admit the possibility of that construct, since he states, "if he lives with her after their sexual relationship *for an extended period of time, as a man and woman who are married do,* they are certainly married."[74] The rationale, however, is

halachicly complicated, because halachah has a very strong presumption that people who have a sexual relationship and represent
themselves as married actually are, since any known deficiencies in
the marriage ceremony are cured by continuation of the marital
relationship.[75] However, if the woman is unaware that according to
Jewish law her marriage is void and needs re-creation through a sexual act, she can never have the proper requisite halachic intent to
marry through any given sexual act, because the halachah is now
well established that a couple does not become married merely by
living together when they are not aware that their original marriage
ceremony was void.[76]

Conclusion

The problems of *kiddushai ta'ut* have been brought to the forefront
by recent developments, and it is important to grasp how socially
and contextually defined this issue really is. What are the fundamental aspects of a marriage that allow one to assert that deception
about them voids the marriage *ab initio*? Halachah does not have
absolute answers to that question. Halachah recognizes a principle:
defects or conditions that were present at the time of the marriage
but were not revealed, which if the other party to the marriage, as
well as most people in that society, had known about would have
caused that other party to refuse to enter into the marriage, can
make it void *ab initio*. The application of this principle varies from
place to place and time to time, and is affected by the differing
social status given to women, including such issues as how easily a
woman can earn a living without a husband, and (if she is not observant of Jewish law) how easily she can engage in illicit sexual relations outside of marriage,[77] as well as other factors which differ from
society to society.[78]

APPENDIX C

The 1992 New York Get Law: A Less than Ideal Solution that Creates Halachic Problems[1]

Introduction

The 1992 New York State *Get* Law directs the courts of New York to consider the withholding of a Jewish divorce as one of the many factors to be balanced by the courts when it determines the equitable distribution of marital assets in the context of a divorce.[2] This law has been criticized by many halachic decisors, because it improperly diminishes the capacity of the husband and wife to offer and receive a *get* with free will, a requirement of Jewish law.[3] Simply put, the threat of economic penalty undermines the free will needed by Jewish law, and a *get* given without free will can be void according to Jewish law.[4] This criticism stands in contrast to the approval given to the earlier *Get* Law, which merely withheld a civil divorce in certain circumstances until a religious divorce was granted.[5]

The Problems with the 1992 Get Law

In essence, Jewish law mandates that ideally a *get* be given with no coercion present. The 1992 *Get* Law introduces a significant amount of economic coercion in some cases, since the wife can seek to use the penalty provisions of the *Get* Law to impose financial penalties on a recalcitrant husband.

There are three distinct problems with the 1992 *Get* Law:

1. The law permits economic coercion by the secular authorities to induce the issuing of a *get* in cases where Jewish law does not allow coercion.
2. Even in cases where Jewish law directs that a *get* be issued, this law makes no distinction between the various categories of obligation to issue a *get*. In some cases of obligation, coercion is not allowed.
3. The law does not require any participation of a bet din; thus even in cases where perhaps coercion should be ordered, no such order was ever issued by a bet din.[6]

Others have replied to these objections by noting that these allegations are correct, but that the law is still a basically good one because in a situation where illicit coercion exists the bet din will realize that it is present and decline to write the *get*.[7] In other situations, supporters of the *Get* Law argue that the law can be an effective tool to curtail instances where a *get* is improperly withheld.[8]

However, even supporters of the general halachic validity of this *Get* Law must realize that using the instrument of secular law to solve some of the agunah cases (when the secular law's halachic validity and prudence are contested by significant numbers of Jewish law decisors)[9] creates a problematic precedent for the use of secular law to decide internal Jewish law disputes. Coercive secular regulation to enforce Jewish law, in a way that does not allow those who disagree with the secular law's understanding of Jewish law to opt out of it, should be sought to enforce only those Jewish law norms that are accepted by (nearly) all members of the halachic community. This should be true for secular *kashrut* enforcement laws[10] and secular Jewish autopsy laws as well as secular *Get* laws. For this reason alone, in this author's opinion, the 1992 *Get* Law is, at the very least, a bad idea (even if its intentions are laudable and its goals commendable).

It is not the role of the secular authorities to determine whether a particular form of governmental interference is permitted or prohibited according to Jewish law. Indeed, secular interference in the internal workings of Jewish law has been profoundly discouraged throughout Jewish history.[11]

Halachic Considerations

Nevertheless the 1992 *Get* Law remains the law in New York State, and similar laws have been passed in other countries and proposed in other states.[12] Repeal of the law in New York seems extremely unlikely, and retroactive repeal is not even under consideration. Couples are still divorcing and Jewish divorces are still being written. Divorced individuals are seeking to marry again. Thus an examination of the after-the-fact ramifications of the law is needed. This appendix will address whether Jewish divorces issued since 1992 are valid in jurisdictions with such law, and if so, under what circumstances.[13]

Nine different rationales (seven grounded in Jewish law, and two in the reality of America) can be advanced that incline one to rule that a typical *get* given in the shadow of the 1992 law is valid, even if the controlling secular statute is fundamentally unwise.

First, Rabbi Moshe Feinstein states that there is no issue of "coerced divorce" (*get me'useh*) where it is clear that the husband actually wishes to end the marriage and be divorced and is contesting only the fiscal details of the divorce.[14] Similar sentiments are expressed by Rabbi Abraham Isaiah Karelitz (Hazon Ish) when he states that even when there is illicit coercion, if the husband really does want to give the *get* and be divorced, the *get* is still valid, since the true desire of the husband is to be divorced.[15] This point appears to be agreed to, in modified form, by Rabbi Yitzhak Isaac Herzog, who also states that coercion does not invalidate a *get* that is commanded even if it cannot be judicially compelled.[16]

A close examination of Rabbi Feinstein's responsum (*Iggrot Moshe*, Even ha-Ezer 3:44) is in order. That responsum states:

> There is another reason to validate the *get* [in a case of court ordered divorce] even if there was coercion. You [the questioner] asked the husband if he would have divorced his wife anyway without the settlement after the secular divorce, and he answered that he would have, but he would have demanded certain arrangements concerning the children's

education; we see from this that he really wanted to be divorced, and only did not ask for certain things for the children because of the settlement, and gave the *get* immediately. In such a case, even if the settlement is coerced, or even actual force is used to write the *get*, we see that there is no coercion on the giving of the *get*, but only to prevent the *get* from being used to extract other things from her. . . . Every person desires to [support his wife]; however, one who does not wish for this woman to be his wife, or he knows that she will not reside with him in a marital relationship, such a person really does want to be divorced, and it is merely because she desires a *get* that he wishes to extract from her certain things . . . It is not good for a person to be legally married when one lacks any of the marital virtues from one's wife.

Rabbi Feinstein advances two very important insights. The first is that in a situation where the marriage is actually over, there is no halachic problem with using what would otherwise be illicit coercion to compel the giving of a *get*, even if no money is paid to the husband. The second is that where payment is made by the wife to settle this matter and is combined with some coercion placed on the husband (but where the marriage is in fact over) that coercion does not violate halachah and void the *get*. Halachah accepts that the husband is issuing the *get* in return for the payment of money, since the marriage really is over and he derives no real benefit from continuing it.

The first insight, while by no means unique to Rabbi Feinstein, is found in only a small number of authorities (see *T'feret Tzvi*, Even Haezer 102; *Imira Aish*, Even Haezer 57; and *Or Same'ach* on Rambam, *Gerushin* 2:20; *Va-Yishal Shaul*, Even Haezer 2:20; and *Or Zarua*, Teshuva 126). However, the second insight is found in a large number of halachic authorities of the last thousand years and is completely normative. Writing about a case where a husband received payment and was then coerced into writing the *get*, Rabbi Avraham Boorenstein (*Avnei Nezer*, Even Haezer 167) states:

[Those who prohibit this type of coercion] are referring to a case where the husband wishes to live with this woman and represent her as his wife. In such a case halachah never says because of the coercion and the money he divorced her [rather, the *get* is void because illicit force was used]. Certainly, even if one gave a man all the money in the world, he would not divorce his wife [with whom he is living]. But a man such as this who betrayed his wife, and abandoned her for many years, we certainly do say the coercion and the money persuaded him to sell the divorce to an even greater extent than it persuades one to sell a field, since this man desires his wife not at all, and only desires leverage over her so that she cannot marry another without his permission, and he can get money from her for this. Certainly in such a case we say because of the money he divorced her. This is very logical.

Included in the list of *poskim* who accept this rule that payment of money with some coercion, in a case where the marriage is over (and in the case of some of the *poskim*, even if it is not) and the husband does not desire to return to the marital abode, produces a valid *get* are the aforementioned *Avnei Nezer*, Even ha-Ezer 167; *Chatan Sofer* 59; *Tashbetz* 1; *Rabbenu Yosef of Slutzk* 79; *Agudot Azov*, Even Haezer 19(18); *Kuntres Tikun Olam*, Tekun 3, *Teshuva* 1:1, Rashbash 339 (argues with Rama, Even ha-Ezer 134:8); Rashbatz 4:35 and *Nachalat David* 34, as well as perhaps *Shut Oneg Yom Tov* 168. Similar but not identical analysis can be found in *Chemdat Shlomo*, Even Haezer 80(3) and *Na'ot Desha* 144 and is mentioned in *Be'er Yitzchak*, Even ha-Ezer 10:1 and *Berchat Retzay* 118. One can add to this list the above-mentioned *poskim* who accept an even broader rule (*Iggrot Moshe*, Even ha-Ezer 3:44; *T'feret Tzvi*, Even ha-Ezer 102; *Shut Orin T'letai* 61; *Or Same'ach*, Gerushin 2:20, and others). Indeed, no less an authority than the Beit Shmuel (Even ha-Ezer 134:14) notes that there are many circumstances in which one can rely on this approach, even when only a small amount of money is given by the woman. Many other authorities could be cited to support this halachic rule and it appears to be accepted *lechatchelah* by many.

Rabbi Tzvi Gartner, in his recent *Sefer Kefiya ba-Get*, dealing with many aspects of coerced divorce, summarizes the halachah by stating:

> It appears that it is difficult to rely on the approach of *Iggrot Moshe* and Teferet Tzvi in a case where the only benefit which accrues to the husband is removal of the obligation to support his wife, since this is a matter in dispute between Tosafot and Rashba. Nonetheless, their analysis is persuasive at the minimum in the case where the husband does not desire a marital relationship and only desires to extract something from the woman in exchange for a *get*, and she gives him money for the divorce.[17]

Indeed, a plausible reading of Rabbi Feinstein's own words incline one to accept that he was hesitant to rely on his "novel insight" only for the first of them where there was no payment to the husband. The second insight is certainly accepted by many great *poskim* as normative halachah, and validates any *get* given in the process of a settlement where the wife gives anything of value to the husband to which he is not entitled. Nearly all contested secular divorces fit into this category.

Second, the *Get* Law is problematic only if it takes the husband's property away from him in order to induce him to issue a *get*. If halachah recognizes secular law's equitable distribution of marital assets as valid through *dina de-malchuta*, then there is no illicit coercion, since nothing is "taken" from the husband that he owns; rather a "bonus" is withheld from him in order to induce his issuing of a *get*,[18] since secular law rules that equitable distribution assets belong individually to neither partner in the marriage. That withholding is completely permissible. Such an approach is adopted by Rabbi Yitzhak Isaac Leibes.[19] Additional support for the proposition that secular law's rules related to equitable distribution can be incorporated into halachah through *dina de-malchuta* can be found in other authorities.[20]

The theory of equitable distribution is very simple and needs to be understood in this context. Unlike the classical common law, which ruled that whomever title resided in kept the item on divorce, modern American equitable distribution law recognizes that marital property is held in the marital estate which is like a trusteeship, and upon divorce the court divides the property according to the statutory direction. (In communal property states, the division is always even.) One recent hornbook stated:

> In all states today statutes provide that upon divorce the property of the spouses shall, in one way or another, be divided between them, regardless of the state of the title.[21]

An article devoted exclusively to New York family law notes:

> Contrary to the title theory of property, equitable distribution is based upon the premise that marriage should be viewed as a form of economic partnership. This concept reflects the modern awareness that marriage is a

union dependent upon a wide range of non-renumerated services to the partnership, such as homemaking, raising children, and providing emotional and moral support necessary to sustain the other spouse.[22]

This theory is equally valid in secular law for both maintenance payments and marital asset division.[23]

The scope of the halachic duty to follow the law of the land, or the ability of the Jewish community to incorporate the law of the land into Jewish financial dealings through common commercial custom (*minhag hasochrim*), remains one of the fundamental issues in the discussion of the *Get* Law. I believe that the custom of the Orthodox Jewish community, or vast portions of it, is to accept as part of the customary financial law the concept of alimony, post-divorce payments, and very likely equitable distribution. Indeed, for the last number of years, at every wedding at which I am invited to sit at the groom's table (*chatan's tisch*) while the *ketubah* is signed, I ask the husband:

> if the marriage were to end by divorce, does the husband expect to pay his wife the value of the *ketubah* and return to her the assets that she brought to the marriage, or does the couple expect some other form of asset division in cases of divorce?

I am almost always told by the husband and wife that they do not intend for the *ketubah* to control the division of assets. The fact that this is truly the intent of many couples is reflected in the American custom of *not* negotiating the dollar amounts in the *ketubah*, either in terms of how much money the woman actually brings into the marriage or how much the husband shall pay her upon divorce or his death, as is now the practice in Israel and was the custom in Europe centuries ago. Indeed, the standard *ketubah* used in Israel leaves these amounts blank to be filled in for each couple, and the standard American *ketubah* fills in the amount of "200 silver coins," an amount worth considerably less than $10,000. The simple fact is that the community has accepted some sort of equitable distribution and alimony as the *minhag hamakom* to determine the financial rights of each party in a divorce. Indeed, a number of halachic authorities seem amenable to this practice,[24] and many divorces have occurred in the Orthodox community where alimony has been paid without the rabbinic community ruling such payment to be theft.

If one is not prepared to accept this understanding of our *min-hag* in the Orthodox community, what then provides the basis for the common practice of not enforcing the financial provisions of the *ketubah* (which I have never seen done in the many divorces in which I have been involved)? Rather, it is common commercial custom (*minhag hasochrim*) or secular law (*dina de-malkhuta*) that provides the relevant rules.[25] This reality is obvious even to people far removed from America. As Rabbi Avigdor Nevetzal, rabbi of the Jewish Quarter in Jerusalem, states:

> In the laws of oaths, vows, sales and rentals, the intent of most people when they speak nowadays is that the terms "day," "month," and "year" follow the Christian calendar, to our embarrassment and shame, and not the Jewish calendar. So too, in many activities that are dependent on the state of mind of a person, their state of mind follows the secular law and not the Torah law.[26]

It is important to understand that this rationale, standing alone, validates Jewish divorces given in light of the 1992 *Get* Law, since it changes the nature of the penalty imposed by the *Get* Law into either a self-imposed one (valid only *bede'eved*, after the fact) or a denial of benefit to induce the writing of a *get*, which is permitted *lechatchelah*.

In fact, some have argued that the 1992 *Get* Law is merely a maintenance and support law, even in asset division. They contend that the woman who will not receive a *get* will need greater support payments, both alimony and in a larger share of the marital assets for support, since she cannot remarry even after her civil divorce. New York State recognizes this fact in its equitable distribution law: no penalty to give a *get* is intended at all. Although Rabbi Elyashiv clearly disagrees, at least one significant halachic authority (Rabbi Moshe Feinstein, *Iggrot Moshe*, Even Haezer 4:106) clearly states that when a man is ordered to pay higher support provisions until he writes a *get*, even if the higher payments are without any basis in halachah, the resulting *get* is not considered a compelled divorce and is valid.[27] However, many secular legal authorities argue that the asset division provision of the 1992 *Get* Law is in fact a penalty provision, and this approach is thus only half correct.[28]

Third, Rabbi Joseph Kolon (Maharik) rules that there is no problem of a coerced *get* in a case where the husband has the alternative of paying the monetary penalty assuming the penalty is reasonable (as penalties under the *Get* Law normally are). Small economic sanctions of the type typically used in this law are permissible.[29] This position is cited by Rema and other authorities as a significant factor after the fact.[30]

An additional relevant factor is the size of the penalties imposed. I have spoken to a number of practitioners in New York State specializing in Jewish divorce law, and they confirm that the penalties imposed typically are very small, and that it is rare for a penalty ordered under the 1992 *Get* Law to increase the total monthly payments by more than 3 percent, or to shift the distribution of assets by more than 5 percent. While 5 percent of one's assets can be a significant amount of money, Responsa *Beit Efraim* (*Tenyana,* Even ha-Ezer 70) notes that in order to determine whether any particular *get* is void because of financial coercion, the bet din has to investigate whether the amount forfeited is sufficiently great to compel this person to divorce and:

> if it is an amount of money that is sufficiently small that most people would not divorce their wife to avoid this loss, it is obvious that even if this person asserts that he is of those who are weak of mind, and a lover of money and thus they feel compelled to divorce his wife to save the expense, we do not listen to such a person.

A similar approach can be found in *Iggrot Moshe,* Even Haezer 1:137. One is not believed merely when one asserts financial coercion and only a small amount of money is involved. The same should logically be true for a small percentage of the marital estate, even if it is a large amount of money.

This is even truer if one accepts the approach of the authorities cited above who rule that government-ordered support payments (even when lacking any basis in halachah) can never create a situation where the *get* awarded to avoid paying them is invalid. According to this approach, one would have to determine how much of the

court-ordered payments to the wife under the 1992 *Get* Law are
support payments and how much are penalty payments, and then
one must evaluate whether the amount of the penalty alone (independent of the support component) is large enough to be a coercive
amount.

Fourth, it is possible that in any given case under the *Get* Law
coercion is permissible according to halachah because of misconduct by the husband or wife, a situation that would classify the
divorce as either mandatory or a *mitzvah*.[31] According to many
opinions, the resulting *get* (even if coerced) is valid.[32] Certainly in
such a case the presence of coercion does not void the *get* according
to halachah.

Fifth, Rabbenu Yeruchum is of the opinion that economic duress
never creates a situation of a coerced *get*.[33] The 1992 *Get* Law would
thus always be permissible according to this approach. Rabbi Yoab
Weingarten uses this as one side of a multifaceted case of doubt
(*sefek sefeka*) to validate a *get* that might be coerced.[34] More significantly, Rabbi Elijah of Vilna appears to categorically accept the ruling of Rabbenu Yeruchum and rule that whenever physical force is
not threatened or used, there is no problem of a coerced *get*.[35]

Sixth, Rambam rules that coercion is acceptable in any case
where the woman states that her husband is repugnant to her.[36]
Many divorces currently fit that bill; this is even truer for divorces
initiated by the woman, where the *Get* Law is otherwise most problematic. The 1992 *Get* Law would thus be permissible according to
this approach in most cases. Rabbi Isaac Herzog uses this as one
side of a multifaceted case of doubt (*sefek sefeka*) to validate a *get*
that might be coerced.[37] More significantly, in a case where the
woman's claim of repugnancy toward her husband is based on reasonable and provable grounds (*amatla mevu'ert*), many authorities
accept Rambam's rule that coercion is permissible, at least after the
fact; some even rule this way *ab initio* (*lechathelah*).[38] Perhaps most,
and certainly many, divorces fall into this situation.

Seventh, for marriages entered into after the *Get* Law took effect
and with (presumed) knowledge of the law, the penalties found in
the 1992 *Get* Law become a voluntarily pre-agreed penalty for with-

holding a *get*, which are (at least after the fact) permitted by many authorities.[39] The same can perhaps be said for anyone who continues to reside in New York, even if married prior to 1992, and is aware of the *Get* Law, particularly if *dina de-malchuta* appropriately governs the finances of the case.

In addition, even if one considers this a case of illicit coercion because the coercion comes from a secular court, the *get* might not be void. Rabbi Yitzhak Elhanan Spector rules that so long as the illicit coercion from a secular court is not used directly to compel the actual writing of the *get*, but is separated in time and manner from the husband's ordering the *get* to be written, and the husband at the time of the writing of the *get* states to a bet din that his actions are voluntary, it appears that there is no imminent coercion present and the *get* is not void.[40] That is exactly the case of the *Get* Law.

The Reality of Divorce

Added to these many halachic rationales are three empirical observations that also vastly reduce the scope of the problem:

First, there are many Jewish divorces issued where there is no coercion in fact presented by the *Get* Law, since the couple have settled their claims fully independent of any secular law, including the 1992 *Get* Law. These divorces are completely nonproblematic with regard to halachah. Many uncontested divorces are of this type.

Second, even when a penalty is explicitly imposed by the judge under the *Get* Law for withholding a *get*, if the amount is clearly related to the wife's support needs and is comparable to the amount that a bet din could have ordered as maintenance (*mezonot*) for the wife, then there is no halachically improper coercion.[41]

While one can claim that most women who file for divorce are halachically classified as *moredot* (rebellious wives), and thus are not entitled to any support at all, this assertion can readily be questioned.[42] One can imagine many cases where the woman files for divorce, but it is the husband who abandons the wife; indeed, in most cases in which I have been involved it is the husband who moves from the abode and ceases providing support. In those circumstances the wife is not typically a *moredet*[43] although she would be well advised to seek permission from a bet din before filing a request for support in secular court, lest she violate the prohibition of litigating in secular court.[44]

Even in the case of woman who is a *moredet*, a very strong case can be made that a husband has no right to *both* decline to support her *and* decline to divorce her. As Rabbi Eliezer Waldenberg notes:

> [When a woman is a *moredet*], she forfeits her *ketubah* rights and other financial claims against the husband. However, on the other side, the husband must [*chayav*] divorce her and may not keep her connected to him.[45]

Rabbi Waldenberg states that the *psak* of the Israeli Rabbinical Courts, with which he agrees, is to require support payments to be paid even to a *moredet* who is an adulteress when a reasonable time has elapsed and the husband has not ended the marriage by writing a *get*. Indeed, no less an authority than the Pitchai Teshuva (Even Haezer 154:4 and 7) notes that the accepted practice is to make the husband support his wife (until he gives her a *get*) specifically to encourage him to give a *get* and not to compel a woman to remain in a "dead marriage," even if the marriage "died" because of her misconduct. Similar sentiments can be found in the name of many *poskim*, including such luminaries as Noda Beyehuda, Rabbi Akiva Eiger, Chatam Sofer, and Beit Meir; it is the normative halachic posture, even if it is contrary to the assertion of Tosafot.[46]

This well-accepted halachic approach undercuts the *moredet*-based critique of the 1992 *Get* Law. In essence, there is an argument in the alternative that validates the *get* given to an alleged *moredet* who takes court-ordered support payments under the 1992 *Get* Law. If the husband claims that the woman is a *moredet* and the marriage is thus over, the husband should give a *get* because of that fact, and support payments to encourage such are not without significant basis in halachah once the husband makes it clear that he is withholding a *get*: the only time the 1992 *Get* Law would be applicable. If the husband denies that the wife is a *moredet*, there certainly is no problem with ordering him to make support payments.

It is important to add that in any case where the 1992 *Get* Law is applied so that the woman clearly is entitled to financial support, and she receives roughly what she is entitled to according to halachah, there is no problem of illicit coercion in these payments, because she is entitled to the money. If the 1992 *Get* Law is understood as a maintenance and support provision (and not a penalty provision), then a *get* issued to avoid payment of the maintenance would be valid according to at least some authorities, as Rabbi Feinstein (*Iggrot Moshe*, Even Haezer 4:106) explicitly validates a *get* issued to avoid payment of support, even if such support provisions are contrary to the dictates of halachah.

Finally, it is important to note that determining the factual reality is made vastly more complex by the nature of secular divorce law. There are many cases where a husband will consent to the imposition of significant penalty because he knows that he will give (or has already given) the *get* of his own will and thus void the penalty. There are many cases where people agree to such a penalty provision merely to convince their spouse of their genuine desire to issue a *get* and avoid any agunah problems. Thus a significant factual problem is created in determining whether any coercion is present in any given case, since the mere presence of a penalty provision in the judicial divorce decree is not evidence of illicit coercion. So too, the absence of a penalty provision in a judicial divorce decree does not mean no coercion was present, as the mere existence of the law in the legal code can sometimes create coercion in the negotiations that is not reflected in the public record documentation.[47] Indeed, in reality it is nearly impossible for any outside observer to distinguish cases where coercion is present in the settlement negotiations from cases where it is not.

Conclusion

Secular interference in internal matters of Jewish law that are contested within the Jewish community should generally be discouraged and opposed. The 1992 Get Law is not a positive development and raises the possibility of illicit coercion in Jewish divorces. Indeed, it

is possible to create a case of divorce that involves a coercive significant penalty that lacks any of the permissive characteristics mentioned above. Ideally, Jewish law requires that one investigate every
single case of possible coercion to determine the facts on a case-by-
case basis and not rely on generalizations.[48]

However, not all bad ideas lead to *gitten* that are void [*pasul
bede'eved*] and I believe that there are many Jewish divorces issued in
the shadow of the 1992 New York *Get* Law that are valid according
to Jewish law. If one considers the "typical" divorce, one sees how
relevant this point is. In such a case, there is considerable disagreement over the financial terms for dissolving the marriage, but both
sides agree that the marriage is over. Perhaps at some point the husband states that if he does not receive suitable financial terms, he
will consider not writing a *get*. The wife responds that if that occurs,
relief will be sought under the 1992 *Get* Law. The husband drops
that line of negotiation, as his lawyer advises him to do. Before the
civil divorce is completed, the husband goes to a bet din and autho-
rizes the writing of a *get*, which at that time he attests is done under
his own free will and is part of an integrated settlement between the
husband and the wife. Such a *get*, albeit "tainted" by the 1992 *Get*
Law in some way, would appear to be valid.

On the other hand, there is a very strong halachic policy that
considers all Jewish divorces coming from recognized arrangers of
divorce (*mesadrai gitten*) as valid. Few rabbis arrange Jewish
divorces; those who do are experts in the field, and an attestation of
a proper divorce from one of them thus deserves a very strong presumption of validity.[49] This is even truer in the presence of the
numerous halachic rationales and factual realities discussed above.
These factors incline one, post-fact, to validate nearly all Jewish
divorces given under the cloud of the coercion created by the 1992
New York *Get* Law.

Keeping a firm grasp on the facts and the reality is vitally important. During the year I was the director of the Beth Din of America,
I was involved in arranging many *gitten* in New York and found that
most parties were completely unaware of the 1992 *Get* Law or its
implications. Fewer than 10 percent of the parties had heard of the

law or were told by a judge or attorney to participate in a "Jewish divorce"; they came to be divorced according to Jewish law because they wanted to be divorced in God's eyes. It is important to understand how small a percentage of *gitten* the 1992 *Get* Law actually affects, and even in those few cases where it has an effect, how few of these *gitten* are actually invalid because of the 1992 *Get* Law. Other *mesadrim* at other *batai din* can confirm this picture of reality. I have reviewed all of the reported cases in New York since the *Get* Law passed, and cannot find more than ten cases where the law was used or referred to by a judge to address the lack of a *get*. There are more articles about the *Get* Law than cases using it!

Let me repeat my opening conclusions. I believe the 1992 New York *Get* Law is a bad idea, because all coercive secular regulation to enforce Jewish law should be sought to enforce only Jewish law norms that are accepted by (nearly) all members of the halachic community. The 1992 *Get* Law is not; the whole Orthodox community should be against it, because secular regulation of Jewish law should occur only with the consent of the whole Jewish community.[50] However, not all bad laws lead to invalid Jewish divorces, and the 1992 *Get* Law does not lead to void Jewish divorces on a regular basis.

APPENDIX D

Brief History of Secular Marriage and Divorce Law[1]

Secular marriage law has experienced many evolutionary changes over the course of legal history. Several models of marriage have developed, which can be described as (1) sacramental, (2) social, (3) societal, and (4) (Enlightenment) contractarian.

The *sacramental* model incorporated the theological teachings of the Catholic Church, which treated marriage as a natural, contractual, and sacramental unit created by God to enable people to "be fruitful and multiply" and to raise children in the service of love and God. Although marriage was a contractual unit formed by the consent of the parties, the contract could not be altered. The sacramental contract prescribed for couples a life-long[2] relation of love, service, and devotion to each other and proscribed almost any breach (even by mutual consent) of the marital state. From the twelfth to the sixteenth century, the Catholic Church's canon law model dominated marriage law in the West.

By the Reformation, the Lutheran tradition developed a *social* model of marriage, grounded in the Protestant doctrines of the heavenly and earthly jurisdictional kingdoms. As part of the earthly kingdom and its jurisdiction, marriage was subject to the state and not the church. Civil law, not canon law, governed the marriage. Civil courts replaced church courts, and civil marriage statutes replaced canon law rules. Introduced at this time was the idea of

119

public marriage. This change profoundly affected marriage by making it secular.[3]

The *societal* (or commonwealth) model developed soon after. This model embraced the sacramental and social models but went beyond them. In this model the traditional hierarchies of husband over wife, parent over child, and church over family were challenged with a revolutionary new principle of equality between partners in the marriage.

With the eighteenth century, the Enlightenment *contractarian* model of marriage was announced, elaborated on in the nineteenth century and implemented legally in the twentieth. Emphasis was on the contractual model of marriage. The essence of marriage was the voluntary bargain struck between two parties who wanted to come together in an intimate association. The terms of their marriage were set by themselves, in accordance with general rules of contract formation and general norms of civil society.

As the twentieth century arose, many new laws were passed to govern marriage formalities, divorce, alimony, marital property, wife abuse, child abuse, child custody, adoption, juvenile delinquency, and education of minors. These legal changes had many consequences, including making marriage easier to enter into and to dissolve. Additionally, wives received greater independence in their relationships outside of the family. The state eventually replaced the church as the principal external authority governing marriage and family life.

The current marriage system is the logical conclusion of the enlightenment model. With the turn of the twenty-first century marriage law has taken the form of a contractual view. Marriage today is seen as a private bilateral contract to be formed, maintained, and dissolved as the couple wishes. Antenuptial, marital, and separation contracts allow parties to define their own rights and duties. The Uniform Marriage and Divorce Act defines marriage as:

> a personal relationship between a man and a woman arising out of a civil contract to which the consent of the parties is essential.[4]

The Uniform Act requires only the minimal formalities of licensing and registration for all marriages. It makes no provision for voiding a marriage if one is not entered into under these conditions. Only the couple can do this.

Freedom to contract has extended to other areas of marriage. The Uniform Premarital Agreement Act allows parties to contract, in advance of their marriage, all rights pertaining to their individual personal rights and obligations (not in violation of public policy or a statute imposing criminal penalty).[5] Additionally, the Uniform Marriage and Divorce Act allows parties to enter into agreements containing provisions for disposition of property, maintenance of either of them, support, custody, and visitation of their children. These agreements are binding on the courts, absent a finding of unconscionability. In the absence of such agreement with regard to property division, courts will combine all assets and make an equitable distribution between the parties.[6]

As modern marriage law has changed, divorce law has changed too. Until well into the emancipation, divorce remained astonishingly rare or was categorically prohibited. From that period until the mid-1960s secular family law relied heavily on fault-based divorce and thus limited exit from marriage to cases of hard fault (or in some states, mutual consent deviously grounded in pretextual fault). The most that one could observe about marriage law is that:

> Coinciding with the traditional fault ground of "desertion" (when one spouse willfully leaves the other for a set period of time), some colonies (and then states) instituted a set period of absence as a ground for divorce. Beyond these colonial laws, which were of an equitable character to protect wives whose husbands had gone off to sea, were a set of state laws providing for divorce after a set period of separation. By 1955, eighteen states had "living separate and apart" laws; by 1968, twenty-two states had such laws. These laws generally required a longer time for separation than modern no-fault statutes. Such "separate and apart" statutes, with a reduced time period for living separate and apart, still serve as bases for divorce in many states. Even with these variations, the general rule remained that one had to prove fault before a court would grant a divorce. The law presumed that divorce involved a "guilty" party and an "innocent" party.[7]

Pressure mounted on the various state legislatures to change the law, culminating in the famous New York Divorce Reform Law of 1966. This new law allowed for divorce based on adultery or one spouse being sentenced to prison for three or more consecutive years (as opposed to a life sentence). Three additional divorce grounds were added: (1) cruel and inhumane treatment of one spouse by the other, (2) abandonment for two or more years, and (3) living apart for two or more years pursuant to a decree of separation or to a written agreement. The 1966 Reform Act was further modified in 1968 by reducing the two-year separation requirement to one year, which brought the separation ground very close to a no-fault provision (because it was based only on mutual consent).

The reforms in New York foreshadowed more radical changes in California. A reform movement led primarily by academics, judges, and theologians succeeded in pushing through what is commonly thought of as the first "no-fault divorce legislation." Other states soon followed California's lead. Within five years 45 states had some type of no-fault procedure. By 1977 only three states retained fault grounds, and in 1985 South Dakota became the fiftieth state to adopt a no-fault divorce law.

Most recently there has been an additional change in the marriage and divorce laws that is conceptually broader and reflects yet another approach to this problem. The state of Louisiana has introduced a new covenant marriage into marriage law.[8] While the covenant marriage is not a new concept, the idea of allowing couples to choose which marriage to enter into is new. Indeed, the Louisiana act is as much a divorce law as a marriage act in that the "covenantal" components of the law hardly show their teeth until divorce is contemplated.

Jewish law recognizes and understands the approach Louisiana has adopted. In essence, Louisiana and Jewish law recognize that there are any number of valid and proper images of marriage available to people. If the state adopts but one of them, inevitably injustice results. Thus, to fulfill the expectancy needs of the people in a marriage fairly, a state has to have multiple images of marriage available and allow the parties to choose at the time of the marriage the model that fits their needs.

APPENDIX E

Civil Death as a Concept in Public Marriage Jurisdictions Including American Law and Islamic Law

As is noted in American Jurisprudence,[1] civil death (the depriving of one's rights as a citizen) as a punishment for a crime whose sentence is life imprisonment historically included the dissolution of one's marriage, whether or not either spouse wished the marriage to be dissolved. Even if neither spouse wished the marriage to be dissolved, it could still be dissolved.[2] As is stated in American Jurisprudence:

> Some statutes provide that when either spouse is sentenced to life imprisonment the marriage is automatically dissolved, without any judgment or legal process, and that a subsequent pardon will not restore conjugal rights. The same result has been reached under a statute merely declaring such persons civilly dead, where the statutes declaring a marriage of one who has a living spouse to be void, and to constitute the crime of bigamy, expressly except cases in which the living spouse has been sentenced to life imprisonment. *It has been held that dissolution of the marriage takes place without the necessity of any election on the part of the other spouse.*

It is part of the punishment for the crime that causes the marriage to be dissolved. In *State v. Duket*[3] the court held that the marriage was dissolved even if the sentence was subsequently reversed. So too *In re Lindwall's Will*,[4] the New York court held that a husband was not allowed to inherit his wife's estate intestacy, after he had been sentenced to life imprisonment for a crime (not related to her death), since he was civilly dead at the time of his wife's death and thus not legally married to her and thus he could not inherit her estate.

While it is true that in the last twenty years American society has abandoned compelling the end of marriage through the civil death rule in the case of commission of a crime,[5] it is important to understand that there is no such theoretical limit on the power of the state to dissolve marriages.

The use of the regulatory process to dissolve marriages against the wishes of both participants is not limited to the common law tradition; it occurs in Islamic law, which also has a concept of public divorce. "If a Muslim husband, or if a non-Muslim husband refuses to adopt Islam after his wife has done so, the marriage shall be automatically dissolved."[6] This is not some mere abstract provision of Islamic law but remains in effect to this very day. Because the nature of Jewish law's divorce system is private, it cannot encounter this problem.[7]

APPENDIX F

Sample Arbitration and Prenuptial Agreements

The purpose of this appendix is to create prototypes of possible prenuptial agreements, recognizing that part of the theme and thesis of this work is that Jewish law has within it a number of different possible models of marriage, and that individuals who are contemplating marriage should consider which model of marriage they wish to join, and to understand how that model of marriage might affect their rights if there is a divorce. While the Beth Din of America is the listed arbitration organization in these agreements, that can be changed at the discretion of the parties. Care, however, must be taken to choose a bet din wisely.

Each arbitration agreement consists of two distinctly different sections:

1. There is a boiler-plate material which lists the information about the parties and recites the formulaic invocation needed to create either a prenuptial agreement or an arbitration agreement, *and*

2. The substance of the dispute to be arbitrated and the rules to be used by the bet din in the arbitration process.

The first agreement found in this section contains the boiler-plate information in smaller print; the relevant section of each agreement is found in paragraph III, which will be set out with its various possible texts immediately following the opening boiler-plate of the agreement. Following that language which can vary, additional boiler-plate language is reproduced. (In many states

127

prenuptial agreements, but not arbitration agreements, need to be notarized.)

Memorandum of agreement made on:

_____, day of the week, _____ of the month of _____ in the year _____, in the city of _____, State or Province of

_____

between:

Husband-to-be: Wife-to-be:

_____   _____

residing at: residing at:

_____   _____

_____   _____

_____   _____

The parties are shortly going to be married.

I. Should a dispute arise between the parties after they are married, so that they do not live together as husband and wife, they agree to refer their marital dispute to an arbitration panel, namely, the Beth Din of America, Inc., for a binding decision. Each of the parties agrees to appear in person before the Beth Din of America at the demand of the other party.

II. The decision of the Beth Din of America shall be fully enforceable in any court of competent jurisdiction.

Possible paragraph III, and their effect on the rights of the parties at the end of the marriage.

Model A

This type of an agreement assigns to the Beth Din the authority to resolve all disputes between the parties consistent with Jewish law.

III. The parties agree that the Beth Din of America is authorized to decide all issues relating to a *get* (Jewish divorce) as well as any issues arising from premarital agreements (e.g., *ketubah, tena'im*) entered into by the husband and the wife. The parties agree that the Beth Din of America is authorized to decide any other monetary disputes that may arise between them.

Model B

This type of an agreement assigns to the Beth Din the authority to resolve all disputes between the parties consistent with community property laws prevalent in some jurisdictions in the United States.

III. The parties agree that the Beth Din of America is authorized to decide all issues relating to a *get* (Jewish divorce) as well as any issues arising from premarital agreements (e.g., *ketubah, tena'im*) entered into by the husband and the wife. The parties agree that the Beth Din of America is authorized to decide any other monetary disputes that may arise between them based on principles of community property that are the law in the state of California at the date of the wedding.

Model C

This type of an agreement assigns to the Beth Din the authority to resolve all disputes between the parties consistent with Jewish law. It differs from Model A only in that it explicitly grants to the Beth Din the authority to resolve child custody disputes, which are currently reviewed de novo by secular courts, and thus cannot be resolved in a binding way according to secular law in the United States.

III. The parties agree that the Beth Din of America is authorized to decide all issues relating to a *get* (Jewish divorce) as well as any issues arising from premarital agreements (e.g., *ketubah, tena'im*) entered into by the husband and the wife. The parties agree that the Beth Din of America is authorized to decide any other monetary or custodial disputes that may arise between them.

Model D

This type of an agreement assigns to the Beth Din the authority to resolve all disputes between the parties consistent with the law of equitable distribution in force in many states of the United States.

III. The parties agree that the Beth Din of America is authorized to decide all issues relating to a *get* (Jewish divorce) as well as any issues arising from premarital agreements (e.g., *ketubah, tena'im*) entered into by the husband and the wife. The parties agree that the Beth Din of America is authorized to decide any other monetary disputes that may arise between them based on principles of equitable distribution that are the law in the state of New York at the date of the wedding.

Model E

This type of an agreement assigns to the Beth Din the authority to resolve only disputes between the parties that revolve around the giving or receiving of a get.

III. The parties agree that the Beth Din of America is authorized to decide all issues relating to a *get* (Jewish divorce) as well as any issues arising from premarital agreements (e.g., *ketubah, tena'im*), entered into by the husband and the wife.

Additional Paragraph Governing Fault

This additional paragraph governing fault is added by the Beth Din of America so as to grant the Beth Din the authority to penalize one party or the other for conduct that violates Jewish law and which causes the end of the marriage. One could delete this paragraph if one wishes, although such a change would profoundly affect the authority of the Beth Din to reward or penalize proper or improper conduct in ending the marriage.

Notwithstanding any other provision of paragraph III, the Beth Din of America may consider the respective responsibilities of either or both of the parties for the end of the marriage as an additional, but not exclusive, factor in determining the distribution of marital property and support obligations.

Finally, the document ends with standard language:

IV. Failure of either party to perform his or her obligations under this agreement shall make that party liable for all costs awarded by either the Beth Din of America or a court of competent jurisdiction, including reasonable attorney's fees, incurred by one side in order to obtain the other party's performance of the terms of this agreement.

V. The decision of the Beth Din of America shall be made in accordance with Jewish law (*halakha*) and/or the general principles of arbitration and equity customarily employed by the Beth Din of America, unless the parties and the Beth Din of America explicitly agree to some other set of rules. The parties agree to abide by the published Rules and Procedures of the Beth Din of America (which are available at www.bethdin.org, or by calling the Beth Din of America). The Beth Din of America shall follow its rules and procedures, which shall govern this arbitration to the fullest extend permitted by law. Both parties obligate themselves to pay for the services of the Beth Din of America as directed by the Beth Din.

VI. The parties agrees to appear in person before the Beth Din of America at the demand of the other party, and to cooperate with the adjudication of the Beth Din of America in every way and manner. In the event of the failure of either party to appear before the Beth Din of America upon reasonable notice, the Beth Din of America may issue its decision despite the defaulting party's failure to appear, and may impose costs and other penalties legally permitted. Furthermore, husband-to-be hereby obligates himself now (*me'achshav*) to support wife-to-be from the date their domestic residence together shall cease, for whatever reasons at the rate of $100 per day (adjusted by the consumer Price Index All Urban Consumers, calculated as of the date of the parties marriage) in lieu of his Jewish law obligation of support, so long as the parties remain married according to Jewish law, even if wife-to-be has one or more other sources of income or support. Additionally, husband-to-be waives all his claims (to the extent there are any) under Jewish law to his wife's earnings for the period that she is entitled to the above-stipulated sum. However, this support obligation shall terminate retroactively if wife-to-be refuses to appear upon due notice before the Beth Din of America or in the event that wife-to-be fails to abide by the decision or recommendation of the Beth Din of America.

VII. This agreement may be signed in one or more copies each one of which shall be considered an original.

VIII. This agreement constitutes a fully enforceable arbitration agreement. Should any provision of this arbitration agreement be deemed unenforceable, all other surviving provisions shall still be deemed fully enforceable; each and every provision of this agreement shall be severable from the other.

IX. The parties acknowledge that each of them have been given the opportunity prior to signing this agreement to consult with their own rabbinic advisor and legal advisor. The obligations and conditions contained herein are executed according to all legal and halachic requirements. Both parties acknowledge that they have effected the above obligation by means of a *kinyan* (formal Jewish transaction) in an esteemed (*chashuv*) bet din as mandated by Jewish law.

In witness of all the above, the bride and groom have entered into this agreement.

Groom: _____	Bride:_____
Signature: _____	Signature: _____
Name: _____	Name: _____
Witnesses:_____	Witnesses:_____
Acknowledgements	Acknowledgements
State/Province: _____	State/Province: _____
County of _____ ss.:	County of _____ ss.:

On the ___ day of _____, 200__, before me personally came ___, the groom, to me known and known to me to be the individual described in, and who executed the foregoing instrument, and duly acknowledged to me that he executed the same.

On the ___ day of ___, 200__, before me personally came ___, the bride, to me known and known to me to be the individual described in, and who executed the foregoing instrument, and duly acknowledged to me that she executed the same.

_____
Notary Public

_____
Notary Public

Model F
The Prenuptial Agreement Authorized by the Orthodox Caucus

This two part agreement is designed to both compel that all matters be submitted to the bet din chosen by the parties, as well as provide for the support of the wife until such time as a Jewish divorce will be written or the husband is relieved of the obligation to support wife by the bet din chosen by both of them.

A. Husband's Assumption of Obligation

I. I, the undersigned, _____, husband-to-be, hereby obligate myself to support my wife-to-be, _____, in the manner of Jewish husbands who feed and support their wives loyally. If, God forbid, we do not continue domestic residence together for whatever reason, then I now (*meachshav*) obligate myself to pay her $_____ per day, indexed annually to the Consumer Price Index for all Urban Consumers (CPI-U) as published by the US Department of Labor, Bureau of Labor Statistics, beginning as of December 31st following the date of our marriage, for food and support (*parnasah*) from the day we no longer continue domestic residence together, and for the duration of our Jewish marriage, which is payable each week during the time due, under any circumstances, even if she has another source of income or earnings. Furthermore, I waive my halachic rights to my wife's earnings for the period that she is entitled to the above-stipulated sum. However, this obligation (to provide food and support) shall terminate if my wife refuses to appear upon due notice before the Beth Din of America before proceedings commence, for purpose of a hearing concerning any outstanding disputes between us, or in the event that she fails to abide by the decision or recommendation of such bet din.

II. I execute this document as an inducement to the marriage between myself and my wife-to-be. The obligations and conditions contained herein are executed according to all legal and halachic requirements. I acknowledge that I have effected the above obligation by means of a *kinyan* (formal Jewish transaction) in an esteemed (*chashuv*) bet din.

III. I have been given the opportunity, prior to executing this document, of consulting with a rabbinic advisor and a legal advisor.

IV. I, the undersigned wife-to-be, acknowledge the acceptance of this obligation by my husband-to-be, and in partial reliance on it agree to enter into our forthcoming marriage.

B. Arbitration Agreement between Husband and Wife

Memorandum of Agreement made this _____ day of _____, 57__, which is the _____ day of _____, 200__, in the City of ____ _____, State/Province of _____, between _____, the husband-to-be, who presently lives at _____ _____ and _____ the wife-to-be, who presently lives at_____.

The parties are shortly going to be married.

I. Should a dispute arise between the parties after they are married, Heaven forbid, so that they do not live together as husband and wife, they agree to refer their marital dispute to an arbitration panel, namely, the Bet Din of_____ for a binding decision. Each of the parties agrees to appear in person before the bet din at the demand of the other party.

II. The decision of the panel, or a majority of them, shall be fully enforceable in any court of competent jurisdiction.

III. (a) The parties agree that the bet din is authorized to decide all issues relating to a *get* (Jewish divorce) as well as any issues arising from premarital agreements (e.g., *ketubah, tena'im*) entered into by the husband and the wife.

[The following three clauses (b, c, d) are optional, each to be separately included or excluded, by mutual consent, when signing this agreement.]

(b) The parties agree that the bet din is authorized to decide any other monetary disputes that may arise between them.

(c) The parties agree that the bet din is authorized to decide issues of child support, visitation, and custody (if both parties consent to the inclusion of this provision in the arbitration at the time that the arbitration itself begins).

(d) In deciding disputes pursuant to paragraph III b, the parties agree that the bet din shall apply the equitable distribution law of the State/Province of_____, as interpreted as of the date of this agreement, to any property disputes which may arise between them, the division of their property, and questions of support. Notwithstanding any other provision of the equitable distribution law, the bet din may take into account the respective responsibilities of the parties for the end of the marriage, as an additional, but not exclusive factor, in determining the distribution of marital property and support obligations.

IV. Failure of either party to perform his or her obligations under this agreement shall make that party liable for all costs awarded by either a bet din or a court of competent jurisdiction, including reasonable attorneys' fees, incurred by one side in order to obtain the other party's performance of the terms of this agreement.

V. (a) In the event any of the bet din members are unwilling or unable to serve, then their successors shall serve in their place. If there are no successors, the parties will at the time of the arbitration choose a mutually acceptable bet din. If no such bet din can be agreed upon, the parties shall each choose one member of the bet din and the two members selected in this way shall choose the third member. The decision of the bet din shall be made in accordance with Jewish law (*halachah*) and/or the general principles of arbitration and equity (*pesharah*) customarily employed by rabbinical tribunals.

(b) At any time, should there be a division of opinion among the members of the bet din, the decision of a majority of the members of the bet din shall be the decision of the bet din. Should any of the members of the bet din remain in doubt as to the proper decision, resign, withdraw, or refuse or become unable to perform duties, the remaining members shall render a decision. Their decision shall be that of the bet din for the purposes of this agreement.

(c) In the event of the failure of either party to appear before it upon reasonable notice, the bet din may issue its decision despite the defaulting party's failure to appear.

VI. This agreement may be signed in one or more copies, each one of which shall be considered an original.

VII. This agreement constitutes a fully enforceable arbitration agreement.

VIII. The parties acknowledge that each of them has been given the opportunity prior to signing this agreement to consult with his or her own rabbinic advisor and legal advisor.

In witness of all of the above, the bride and groom have entered into this agreement in the City of_____, State/Province of_____.

In witness of all the above, the bride and groom have entered into this agreement.

Groom: _____   Bride:_____
Signature: _____   Signature: _____
Name: _____   Name: _____
Witnesses:_____   Witnesses:_____
Acknowledgements   Acknowledgements
State/Province:_____   State/Province:_____
County of _____ ss.:   County of _____ ss.:

On the ___ day of _____, 200__, before me personally came ___, the groom, to me known and known to me to be the individual described in, and who executed the foregoing instrument, and duly acknowledged to me that he executed the same.

On the ___ day of ____, 200__, before me personally came ___, the bride, to me known and known to me to be the individual described in, and who executed the foregoing instrument, and duly acknowledged to me that she executed the same.

_____   _____
Notary Public   Notary Public

Model G

The arbitration agreement below, written at the request of Rabbi
Haskel Lookstein, is designed to facilitate the giving of a get upon
the conclusion of the civil divorce.[1]

The undersigned hereby agree, promise and represent:

In the event that the covenant of marriage to be entered into this day
200 ( ) by husband ( ) and wife ( ) shall be terminated, dissolved or
annulled in accordance with any civil court having jurisdiction to effectively do so, then in that event husband ( ) and wife ( ) shall voluntarily
and promptly upon demand by either of the parties to this marriage
present themselves at a mutually convenient covenant of marriage in
accordance with Jewish law and custom before the Ecclesiastical Court
(Bet Din) of the Rabbinical Council of America—or before a similarly
recognized Orthodox rabbinical court—by delivery and acceptance,
respectively, of the *get* (Jewish divorce).

This agreement is recognized as a material inducement to this marriage by the parties hereto. Failure of either of the parties to voluntarily
perform his or her obligation hereunder if requested to do so by the
other party shall render the noncomplying party liable for all costs,
including attorneys' fees, reasonably incurred by the requesting party
to secure the noncomplying party's performance, and damages caused
by the demanding party's unwillingness or inability to marry pending
delivery and acceptance of a "get."

The parties hereto recognize that the obligations specified above are
unique and special and they agree that the remedy at law for a breach
of this contract will be inadequate. Accordingly, in the event of any
breach of this contract, in addition to any other legal remedies available, the injured party shall be entitled to injunctive or mandatory
relief directing specific performance of the obligations included herein.

Entered into this day of 200__ .

Groom: _____   Bride:_____
Signature: _____   Signature: _____
Name: _____   Name: _____
Witnesses:_____   Witnesses:_____

Notes

Foreword

1. And indeed, one solution appears to be nakedly inconsistent with the mandates of halachah; see Appendix A.

2. The same is true for the recent attempt to expand the grounds for voiding marriages through the use of error in the creation of the marriage. That topic is dealt with extensively in Appendix B.

Preface

1. This definition stands in sharp contrast to the definition recently advanced by Agunah Inc., an organization that advocates on behalf of women seeking a Jewish divorce. They write that an *agunah* is "a woman who is unable to obtain a *get* despite the fact that her marriage is effectively over" (undated publication entitled *Agunah Inc. Replies to the Beth Din of America*, page 11). This definition is wrong. In order to justify the plight of a woman as an *agunah* entitled to a *get,* and the incorrectness of the man's conduct in withholding a *get,* one must first demonstrate a right to receive and a duty to give. If Agunah Inc.'s definition is correct, every time a person contests a divorce (in either civil court or bet din) the person's conduct in contesting the divorce, rather than cooperating with the spouse's desire to end the marriage legally, is wrong and unethical. For more on this, see Chapters 2 through 4.

2. This is the difference between the 1984 New York *Get* Bill, which prescribes that civil divorce not be given when a *get* is withheld, thus

harmonizing secular law with Jewish law, and at least one understanding of the 1992 New York *Get* Law, whose goal is to insist that a *get* be given when a civil divorce is granted, thus harmonizing Jewish law with secular law.

Chapter One

1. This should not be misunderstood as denying the sacramental parts of marriage (of which there are many); however the contractual view predominates in the beginning-of-marriage and end-of-marriage rites. This is ably demonstrated by Rabbi J. David Bleich, "Jewish Divorce: Judicial Misconceptions and Possible Means of Civil Enforcement," *Connecticut Law Review* 16:201 (1984).

2. Even though such an activity validly marries the couple; *Rav mangid aman de-makadish be-biah*, Yevamot 52a; Shulchan Aruch, Even ha-Ezer 26:4.

3. Shulchan Aruch, Even ha-Ezer 26:4.

4. See Appendix B, "Errors in the Creation of Jewish Marriages."

5. In that the hallmark characteristic of contractarian models is consent.

6. There is a dispute in Jewish law as to whether this requirement is biblical or rabbinic in some cases.

7. For reasons beyond the scope of this book, this agreement was not signed by either the husband or wife, but merely by witnesses. This is so because the Jewish tradition mandated generally that all contracts need not be signed by the parties, but merely by witnesses, so long as the parties assent to the conditions found within them.

8. The Talmud states that the *ketubah* was instituted so that "it will not be easy to divorce her"; Yevamot 89a, Ketubot 11a.

9. Abraham H. Freimann, *Seder Kiddushin ve-Nisu'in Acharai Chatimat ha-Talmud* (Mossad Harav Kook, 1944) and Mordechai Akiva Friedman, "Polygyny in Jewish Tradition and Practices: New Sources from the Cairo Geniza," *PAAJR* 49 (1982), p. 55.

10. On an historical level, one could claim one exception to this model. According to one view expressed, in the time of the post-talmudic Babylonian authorities (approximately 650–900 C.E.), the Jewish law courts engaged in annulment of marriages in cases where mutual agreement could not be reached or under other exigent circumstances. Although what happened during that era will be discussed at some length later, if this view of what actually happened is correct, it is without precedent in Jewish law. For more on this, see Irving Breitowitz, *Between Civil and Religious Law: The Plight of the Agunah in American Society* (Greenwood Press, 1993), pp. 50–55.

11. This work does not address exactly what fault is in the Jewish tradition, a topic worthy of a book of its own. For more on fault, see Dov

Frimer, *Grounds for Divorce Due to Immoral Behavior Other than Adultery According to Jewish Law* (Doctor of Law Thesis, Hebrew University 1980); Benzion Schereschewsky, *D'nei Mishpacha* [3rd ed., 1984], pp. 233–267; Shulchan Aruch, Even ha-Ezer 115 and commentaries, *ad loc.*

12. Although this idea will be elaborated on in Chapter 2, it is important to understand the mechanism of this. In the case of fault by the wife, her post-biblical right to refuse a writ of divorce was denied to her and her *ketubah* was voided, and in the case of fault by the husband, the Jewish court used physical force to coerce his "consent" to divorce his wife. For a discussion of why such was still called consent, see various Commentaries on Maimonides, Divorce 2:20.

13. See Roderick Phillips, *Putting Asunder: A History of Divorce in Western Society* (Cambridge University Press, 1988).

14. This stands in sharp contrast to the power of American law, which can declare people divorced even if neither wishes to be. For more on this, see Appendix E.

15. She might really be widowed, since one can guess that in many such cases the husbands were actually dead. However, since there was no proof of this, these women retained the legal status of a divorcee.

16. This will be addressed in some detail in Chapter 4.

17. Codified in Shulchan Aruch, Even ha-Ezer 17.

18. Shulchan Aruch, Even ha-Ezer 17:56–57.

19. Even Maharsham 9, which is the most far-reaching proposal for using annulments, is predicated not on direct annulment power, but on a decree of Rabbi Gamliel relating to improper conduct in divorce. This technique (which is of great controversy) can be used only with the cooperation of the husband and wife. For a detailed discussion of this issue, see Tzvi Gartner, *Kifiya Beget* (Otzar ha-Poskim 5758), pp. 118–120.

20. Such as not requiring her presence in order to receive the *get* or even authorize receipt, or permitting him to authorize the writing of a *get* through a letter to a bet din rather than appearing in person.

21. Interestingly, the presence of a civil divorce system has gone far toward eliminating this problem in the United States. Its system compels a couple divorcing on the grounds of a change in religious faith to litigate or negotiate a settlement between the two of them. Frequently a *get* will result from that process.

22. Rama, Even ha-Ezer 157:4.

23. This case is markedly easier than all other cases of abandonment, according to halachah, since the death of the husband insures that there is no problem of adultery, perhaps making decisors of Jewish law more lenient (as there is less of a balance between *mitzvah lehatir agunot* [commandment to free agunot] and *chumrah shel eshet ish* when the

husband is dead). It is worth noting that any number of rabbinical authorities limit the validity of conditions imposed in marriages to conditions that are unlikely to happen, rather than conditions that will certainly happen See *Iggrot Moshe,* Even ha-Ezer 1:79–80.

24. See Shulchan Aruch, Even ha-Ezer 17:32–37.

25. Although this technical discussion is beyond the scope of this paper, changes in technology, such as the invention of the telephone or more recent video-conferences have made it extremely rare for a person who actually desires to give a *get* to be unable to contact someone qualified to assist in the writing of such a document, and then arrange for the *get* to be delivered to the wife. This author has participated in Jewish divorces authorized in writing, over the telephone, at a video conference, and in prisons. The technical issues related to giving and receiving a *get* have all but been solved. See generally Rabbi Howard Jachter, "The Use of Video Telephone Conferences for a Get Procedure," *Journal of Halacha and Contemporary Society* 28:5 (1995).

26. The technical procedure can be initiated by the husband over the telephone in less than 10 minutes in a time of urgent need, in a way that requires no further involvement of the husband. I have myself participated in a *get* authorized by the husband in China over the telephone and then followed up with a letter of authorization from him.

27. Shulchan Aruch, Even ha-Ezer 70:1–4.

28. See material found in text accompanying note 20 of Chapter 4.

29. Chapter 4 will elaborate on this point.

30. Much of the material in this section is elaborated on in Irving Breitowitz, *Between Civil and Religious Law: The Plight of the Agunah in American Society* (Greenwood Press, 1993), pp. 77–163.

31. See *Iggrot Moshe,* Even ha-Ezer 1:79–80.

32. See Breitowitz, *Between Civil and Religious Law,* pp. 62–65.

33. *Maharam al-Shakar* 48.

34. Rama, Even ha-Ezer 28:11.

35. For more on this, see Chapter 5 and Appendix C.

36. The withholding of a civil divorce is an even less effective weapon in a society like ours where sexual activity by men or women out of wedlock or even adultery by another is never punished. The absence of a civil divorce no longer prevents much activity other than a second legally valid marriage.

37. Of course, such a person might have to make an end-of-marriage payment as called for in the *ketubah,* but such is markedly less than any ongoing maintenance obligation over time.

38. For examples of these agreements, see Appendix F.

Chapter Two

1. There are a small number of cases where marriage is not discretionary but ethically mandatory; see Deuteronomy 22:19. These cases involve either fault or detrimental reliance by the other. In the case of seduction, the Bible mandates that the seducer is under a religious duty to marry the seduced, should she wish to marry him. That marriage does not require the same type of free will consent to marry, in that the religious and ethical component to the Jewish tradition directs the man to marry this woman; indeed, in certain circumstances he can be punished if he does not marry her.

2. The creation story in Genesis 1 presents the first image of marriage worthy of explanation; God chose to create Adam and Eve, and explicitly endorsed the monogamous marital relationship ("and they shall be one flesh"). Indeed, a small number of classical commentators derive the monogamous ideal from that incident; see *Baal Haturim* and *Chizkuni* on it, and the notes in *Torah Shelama* Genesis 2:24. Indeed, throughout the first book of the Bible, the many characters strive to present monogamy as the ideal, with polygamy as a weak alternative, proper only in the face of divorce. (Thus, while Abraham and Jacob were polygamous, both cases were as an alternative to divorce, one for infertility and one for fraud.) Indeed, the Torah (Bible) contains not a single portrayal of polygamy as ideal or proper, although it is portrayed as legally acceptable. (The situation of Moshe's marital status [whether he was polygamous or not] is the only one that is unclear; while Josephus insists that the Ethiopian woman is not Tziporah, his first wife, most Jewish commentators identify her as such.) While in the Prophets one finds more polygamous individuals, the portrayal of them is not flattering at all.

3. But perhaps synonymous with one year's actual support, in many circumstances.

4. Irving Breitowitz, *Between Civil and Religious Law: The Plight of the Agunah in American Society* (Greenwood Press, 1993), p. 9.

5. This point is implicitly addressed in Shulchan Aruch, Even ha-Ezer 117:11.

6. Unless she had not yet had a child with him, which was a form of fault on his part; *Ta'anat b'eyna hutra le-yada*, see Yevamot 64a, Shulchan Aruch, Even ha-Ezer 154:6–7 and *Aruch ha-Shulchan*, Even ha-Ezer 154:52–53.

7. Yevamot 65a; but see view of Rav Ammi.

8. Through a mechanism called *takanta de-mitivta*, whose exact mechanism is unclear. See Breitowitz, *Between Civil and Religious Law*, pp. 50–53.

9. See Breitowitz, *Between Civil and Religious Law*, pp. 62–65 for a discussion of the circumstances under which annulments were performed. There are five places in the Talmud where a marriage is declared terminated without the need for a *get*, based on the concept that "all Jews who marry do so with the consent of the Sages, and the Sages nullified the marriage." These situations all revolve around marriages under duress or other cases where one of the parties acted improperly.

10. See Eliav Schochetman, "Annulment of Marriages," *Jewish Law Annual* 20 (5757), pp. 349–397, for an extensive review of this issue. The broadest recasting of Jewish law favoring annulments can be found in Menachem Elon, *Jewish Law: History, Sources and Principles* (Jewish Publication Society, 1994), pp. 641–642, and 856–877. Even Justice Elon concedes that in order even to contemplate the use of annulment, one needs a unified rabbinate, something that is far beyond the current contours of our community.

11. Maimonides disagreed with the *geonim* only as to a mechanism: he, and all the authorities who followed him, ruled that annulments were not possible.

12. This insight is generally ascribed to Rabbenu Tam in his view of *meus alay*. In fact it flows logically from the view of Rabbenu Gershom, who not only had to prohibit polygamy and coerced divorce, but divorce for easy fault, as Rambam's concept of repugnancy as a form of fault is the functional equivalent of no fault, identical in result to the *geonim*'s annulment procedure.

13. See *Responsa of Rosh* 43:8, who clearly notes that one of the consequences of this model is that women (and men) will not be able to leave a marriage when they wish.

14. Rabbi Joseph Elijah Henkin writes (in *Adut le-Yisrael* 143–144, reprinted in *Kol Kitvei ha-Rav Henkin* 1:115a–b):

> If a husband and wife separate and he no longer desires to remain married to her and she desires to be divorced from him, in such a case divorce is a mitzvah [obligation] and commanded by Jewish law. . . . One who withholds a Jewish divorce because he desires money for no just cause is a thief, he is worse than a thief as his conduct violates a sub-prohibition (*abizrayu*) related to taking a human life.

15. Rabbi Moshe Feinstein writes (in *Iggrot Moshe*, Yoreh Deah 4:15):

> In the matter of a man and a woman who, for these past years, has not had peace in the house. Since the beit din sees that it is impossible to make peace between them . . . it is compelling that they should be divorced, and it is prohibited for either side to withhold a *get*, not the man to chain the woman to the marriage or the woman to chain the man to the marriage, and certainly not over financial matters.

16. Indeed, one reviewer of this book in manuscript voiced more comfort with the Catholic model (no divorce ever for either spouse) than with the inequality found in the Jewish tradition, as the Catholic model condemns everyone, in every case in which either or even both parties seek to end a marriage, to the status of an agunah, in that one is chained to a "dead" marriage.

17. See Options II and III in this chapter.

18. *Heter meah rabbanim* documents are documents that allow a man to marry a second wife without actually divorcing the first one but merely authorizing the writing of a *get*, which has yet to be delivered. According to Jewish law, such a document can be used only in circumstances of fault by the woman such that were she present, she might be divorced against her will. The *heter meah rabbanim* process is an exception to the decree of Rabbenu Gershom prohibiting polygamy and was designed to prevent a man from being left incapable of marrying anyone.

19. For sources for these statistics, see David Harris, *Jerusalem Post,* September 30, 1997, "Jews will be Israeli majority for foreseeable future," (statistics on marriage and divorce), and Herb Keinon, *Jerusalem Post,* February 8, 1995, "Chief Rabbi lets 24 un-divorced men remarry," (showing that over "the last two years, Chief Rabbi Eliahu Bakshi-Doron has allowed 24 men to take a second wife, in cases where they were unable to deliver a writ of divorce to their first wives.") It is worth noting that the Chief Rabbi's liberalization of the 100 rabbis rite which allowed 12 such men to remarry per year was widely criticized and curtailed by the Israeli Supreme Court; see Herb Keinon, *Jerusalem Post* (April 27, 1995), "Court orders Bakshi-Doron to hear a woman whose husband was allowed second wife," and Herb Keinon, *Jerusalem Post* (February 28, 1995), "Man barred from remarriage without divorce"; ("The High Court of Justice yesterday issued a temporary injunction preventing the Chief Rabbinical Court from allowing a man to take another wife without first divorcing his current wife").

20. For more on this, see Elimelech Westreich, "The Jewish Woman's Status in Israel—Interactions Among the Various Traditions," *Plilim* 7 (1998), pp. 273–347. It might be caused, however, by a host of other inequalities that are not unique to the Jewish divorce problems, such as inequality of resources in divorce litigation, inequality of sexual needs, the presence of the biological clock which ticks more loudly for women than for men, or a host of other issues.

21. Maimonides' model appears on its face to be conceptually inconsistent with talmudic law in how it vastly expands the notion of "fault" in ways that simply appeared to be inconsistent with the talmudic norms. Even Rabbi Karo, whose code (Shulchan Aruch) normally follows

the rule of Maimonides, does not cite him. One is hard-pressed to find sources after the thirteenth century that support Maimonides' view.

22. Rabbi Karo's view has ceased being normative in the last century, as the Israeli rabbinate accepted the decree of Rabbenu Gershom banning polygamy and prohibiting coerced divorce.

23. Outlined in the section on Option I in this chapter.

24. Outlined in the section on Option III in this chapter.

25. This *takkanah*, however, does not render a second marriage invalid according to biblical law, and therefore, if such a marriage does take place, it can be dissolved only by divorce. The criminal law of the State of Israel, however, renders it an offense on pain of imprisonment for a married person to contract another marriage without permission of a rabbinical court (Penal Law Amendment [Bigamy] Law, 5719–1959) Nevertheless, for Jewish citizens no offense is committed if permission to marry a second wife was given by a final judgment of a rabbinical court and approved by the two chief rabbis of Israel. The latter's approval is accepted as conclusive proof that the permission was given according to the law. Special provisions relating to the grant of this permission are laid down in the *Takkanot ha-Diyyun be-Vattai ha-Din ha-Rabbaniyyim be-Yisrael*, 5720–1960.

26. For more on this, see Westreich, "The Jewish Woman's Status in Israel," which notes that there are some Sefardic decisors who do not accept this *takkanah* in a small number of cases.

Chapter Three

1. While such does not appear to be true for marriage, since rabbis, priests, ministers, and imans can all perform marriages in America, in fact such is completely correct even for marriage. The various states have decided that the marriage service (since typically it is performed between two people in love, and without any significant controversy) can be delegated by the state to individuals other than those employed by the judicial branch. However, in order to be civilly married a person needs a state issued marriage license, and whenever a minister performs a marriage, he or she is in fact participating in both a religious and a civil ceremony, leading to a marriage both in the eyes of God and in the eyes of secular government.

Many states appear to restrict the rights of a minister or rabbi to perform a religious ceremony when no civil ceremony is desired, although such restrictions appear on their face to be unconstitutional; see, for example, 45 New York Domestic Relations Law §36, and commentary on same.

2. Indeed, even those people who are married outside America but currently reside in America must be divorced by the civil authorities. For a long discussion of the problems this issue posed in pre-emancipation Russia, see Chearan Y. Freeze, *Making and Unmaking the Jewish Family: Marriage and Divorce in Imperial Russia, 1850–1914* (Ph.D. Dissertation, Brandeis University 1992). This book focuses on the problems the Jewish communities encountered during the beginning of the Enlightenment as the Russian government solidified its control over marriage and divorce law.

3. See Appendix D for an in-depth treatment of shifts in secular marriage and divorce law and Appendix C for a discussion of the New York *Get* Law.

4. Consider the Black's law dictionary definition of extortion: "The obtaining of property from another induced by wrongful use of actual or threatened force, or fear, or under color of official right," and why it is not applicable to the case of a person who withholds money properly due to another, because that person improperly is withholding something belonging to him. That conduct, called "offset," is sanctioned by every legal system, including halachah (see Choshen Mishpat 5:1–4 in the discussion of *avad inish dinah denafshay*, and UCC article 9 in the offset provisions).

5. Consider the case of a secular state that does not allow divorce at all. When is a woman considered an agunah? Or even consider the case of the state that (unlike New York) does not allow unilateral no-fault divorce; either fault must be found or mutual consent must be given. In both of these circumstances, the classical definition of agunah disappears, since the civil system denies the right.

6. One for religious reasons, and one for cultural, social, and secular law reasons.

7. See also Chapter 1.

8. While the Supreme Court has declared that "freedom to marry" is one of the "vital personal rights essential to the orderly pursuit of happiness by all free [persons]" *Loving v. Virginia*, 388 US 1, 12 (1967), it has never asserted a right to divorce as a fundamental right. The Supreme Court has additionally never found a Constitutional right to remarry. If they had done this, a right to divorce could be inferred. In *Zablocki v. Redhail*, 434 US 374 (1978), the Court struck down a statute as unconstitutional where the state could deny a person the right to remarry if he or she had failed to pay child support. This is the closest the Court has come to saying there was a right to remarry.

9. Indeed, for many years divorce was simply illegal in many Western jurisdictions. Even when there was mutual consent and a desire to be

divorced, divorce was not allowed. Some states did not permit divorce at all until the late 1950s, and Ireland did not permit divorce until 1997. (Some of these jurisdictions did permit some form of Jewish divorce ritual; see Alan Reed, "Transnational non-Judicial Divorces: A Comparative Analysis of Recognition under English and RS Jurisprudence," *Loyola Journal of International and Comparative Law* 311:18 (1996).

10. There were only 291 civil divorces in all of England during the 181-year period from 1669 to 1850, an average of 16 divorces every year for the whole country, or less than one divorce per one million individuals. See Susan Dowell, *They Two Shall be One* (London, Flame, 1990) at page 139. The current divorce rate in America is 4,800 per one million individuals, nearly a 5,000-fold increase from the English statistics of 150 years ago. (For statistics for the United States, see *Vital Statistics of the United States*: Marriage and Divorce Table 1–1, at 1–5 and Table 2–1 at 2–5 1987).

11. This is different from, for example, the Jewish law approach to Levirate separation (*chalitzah*) which the codes clearly state is a court function, and cannot be validly done absent a proper Jewish court. Marriage and divorce, on the other hand, do not need a proper court; the role of the rabbi is merely as a resident expert aware of the technical law. This is, indeed reflected in the common Hebrew terms used. One who performs a marriage is referred to as the *mesader kiddushin,* merely the "arranger of the marriage" and one who performs a divorce as the *mesader gittin,* "arranger of the divorce," as a rabbi is not really needed. The participants in a levirate separation (*chalitzah*) are, in contrast, called judges (*dayanim*).

12. As is demonstrated in Rabbi J. David Bleich, "Jewish Divorce: Judicial Misconceptions and Possible Means of Civil Enforcement," *Connecticut Law Review* 16:201 (1984) the term "rite" is a misnomer; "contract" would be more accurate.

13. See Appendix E for a discussion of civil death and involuntary divorce.

14. Consider the simplest private divorce system I can find: the law in the Soviet Union in the 1920s that allowed for postcard marriages and divorces (All one had to do to register one's marriage was send in a postcard to the marriage bureau, and all that one had to do to register one's divorce was mail in a postcard of divorce); See Michael J. Bazyler, "The Rights of Women in the Soviet Union," *Whittier Law Review* 9 (1987), pp. 423–24, which states:

> The Russian Revolutionaries, upon taking power, sought to create full legal equality for women. [B]eginning in 1918, some revolutionary legislation was passed. Divorce laws were liberalized extensively, and a couple could obtain a

divorce merely by applying for it by mail. To obtain this "postcard divorce," no grounds for the divorce needed to be stated.

15. See "34 Months and Still No Divorce," *New York Times* (August 3, 1996), sec. A, p. 19.

> I was not expecting my divorce proceedings to be pleasant, but I wasn't expecting them to turn into a nightmare. When I filed for divorce 34 months ago after four years of marriage, it took every bit of courage and money. I could muster. I was prepared for a judicial process that was reputed to be slow. I was expecting delays. Indeed, my case was delayed from the beginning, although no children were involved and the marital property issue was simple. A spouse can control the pace of a divorce action by filing interminable motions, delaying conferences, fighting disclosure of financial records and not appearing in court for a scheduled trial (If my husband were not contesting the divorce, there would be no trial).
>
> After my husband did not show up for the trial in August of last year, the presiding judge rescheduled the trial for September. It was later delayed until March 1996, because my husband's lawyers were preparing an appeal. Then one of those lawyers had an operation, and the new judge delayed it further, until late June, marking it "final" on the court calendar. Later, the judge, in the midst of a trial that might not have finished by then, extended the "final" date until October.
>
> I am back to square one. October will mark the third anniversary of when I filed for divorce.
>
> Neither law nor logic offers a plausible reason why a case as straightforward as mine should not have been resolved long ago. Since I filed for divorce, a friend has gotten married and has had two children. She jokes that she will be a grandmother by the time I get divorced.
>
> I, who would have loved to be free to remarry and have children, am left to ponder: What a waste. What sadness. What now?

16. See Appendix E for a longer discussion of these issues.

17. It is important to understand how this differs from the halachic model, in that a bet din can never grant a divorce. In a limited number of circumstances it can attempt to compel the husband to participate in the divorce process. However, the will of the husband must be at least present, and at least appear to be voluntary.

18. For a discussion of civil death, and involuntary divorce in Islam, see Appendix E.

For a discussion of whether Jewish law permits a court to compel divorce when neither side wishes to be divorced, see Shulchan Aruch, Even Haezer 1:3 for the dispute between Rabbi Karo and Rama as to whether a bet din should prevent the marriage of a young man who has not had children to a postmenopausal woman, and other cases where the marriage itself is permissible but leads to other violations. Indeed, the same set of issues can be raised in the context of marriage counseling of couples who are not observant; see Rabbi Yosef regarding the role of a therapist; see Rabbi Ova-

dia Yosef, *Yabia Omer* 3:21, where he discusses numerous issues that relate
to counseling. See also Rabbi Moshe Sternbuch, *Teshuvot ve-Hanhagot*
1:730. Rabbi Yehudah Amital notes, in J. J. Schachter, ed., "Rebuking a
Jew: Theory and Practice," *Jewish Tradition and the Non-Traditional Jew*
(Northvale, NJ: Jason Aronson, 1992), pp. 119–138, that such is the practice of the rabbinical courts in Israel on a daily basis.

A clear distinction can be found (based on the Rama referred to
above) between a prohibited marriage and a marriage in which the couple
do not observe Jewish law, but are permitted to marry each other. Encouraging the former is prohibited and the latter is permitted, although perhaps
based only on the reality that the rabbinical courts lack the practical
authority to separate them, and have, in fact, always lacked that "political"
authority, although it is clearly granted to them by Jewish law, and that the
exercise of such authority is vastly disruptive of community tranquility.

19. At some level this is analogous to the difference between a
corporation and a partnership. Corporations are created by the state and
dissolved by the state. Private parties can never create or destroy
corporations, as they are a product of public law. Partnerships are created
by private agreements and ended by private agreements. Law, while it will
adjudicate disputes between partners can neither create partnerships nor
dissolve them.

20. See Appendix C for an in-depth treatment of the 1992 New York *Get*
Law.

21. See Edward S. Nadel, "New York's Get Laws: A Constitutional
Analysis," *Columbia Journal of Social Problems* 27:55 (1998); Patti A. Scott,
"New York Divorce law and the Religion Clauses: An Unconstitutional
Exorcism of the Jewish Get Laws," *Seton Hall Constitutional Law Journal*
6:1117 (1996).

22. New York Domestic Relations Law §253 (McKinney, 1986).

23. New York Domestic Relations Law §236 (b) (McKinney, 1992).

24. In that an agunah is a woman who is "entitled" to a divorce, and the
secular system creates an entitlement.

The difficulties that the Catholic Church specifically, and Canon law
generally, have had with this dual system problem are symptomatic of the
sociological challenges facing the Jewish tradition. According to Canon
law, there is no right of divorce, and no right ever to remarry when there is
a first valid marriage. There is, however, a concept of annulment in Canon
law, which is limited in scope to cases of defective consent. Sociologically,
it has proven very difficult for Canon law to function in a secular society
where divorce on demand is the norm, and yet Canon law provides no
right to divorce at all. The "solution" that appears to have taken hold in
many Catholic dioceses is to allow for annulments in many cases where by

tradition annulments were not granted. This "solution" to the dual hoop problem is unique to the American Catholic diocese, and while only 6% of the world's Catholics live in the United States, 78% of the annulments granted were granted in the United States; See Robert H. Vasoli, *What God Has Joined Together: The Annulment Crisis in American Catholicism* (Oxford Press, 1998), p. 5.

25. Chaim Malinowitz in an exchange with Michael Broyde, "The 1992 NewYork *Get* Law: An Exchange," *Tradition* 31:3 (1997), pp. 23–41, and Michael Broyde, "The NewYork State *Get* [Jewish Divorce] Law," *Tradition* 29:4 (1995), pp. 3–14.

26. See Malinowitz, *supra* note 25. Consider also the following remark by Rabbi Malinowitz in "The 1992 NewYork *Get* Law," *Journal of Halacha and Contemporary Society* 27:5–26 (1994), pp. 10–11:

> Action taken by anyone to facilitate a *get* for a man/woman if the *get* is halachically unjustified, even if that action does not halachically invalidate the *get*, is anti-halachic.

27. See Tosafot, Ketubot 63b *Aval amra*, and Ketubot 63a *ve-hamar Rav.*

28. Indeed, a number of halachic authorities seem amenable to this practice; see R. Yehuda Leib Grauburt, *Ha-Valim ba-Neimim*, Even ha-Ezer 55 which rules, in the alternative, that secular law provides a woman with financial rights against her husband (or his estate); R. Joseph Trani, *Mabit* 1:309, is another such responsa. For a similar type of claim, see R. Yitzhak Isaac Liebes, *Bet Avi* 4:169. Similar reasoning can be implied from R. Moshe Feinstein's ruling (*Iggrot Moshe*, Even ha-Ezer 1:137) that the wife's waiver of past-due support payments mandated by secular law, in return for the husband's issuing a *get*, is a form of permissible coercion which does not invalidate the *get* (create a *get me'useh* situation). This waiver of a financial claim is valid coercion only in a case where the woman's claim to the money is halachically valid, as the wife is entitled to these payments through *dina de-malchuta*. Indeed, Rabbi Feinstein implies that this is the more likely result in his analysis found in *Iggrot Moshe*, Even ha-Ezer 1:137; see also *Pitchai Teshuva*, Even ha-Ezer 134:9–10.

If one is not prepared to accept this understanding of the common practice of the Orthodox community, what then provides the basis for the common practice of not enforcing the financial provisions of the *ketubah*? Rather, it is common commercial custom (*minhag ha-sochrim*) or secular law (*dina de-malchuta*) that provides the relevant rules. This reality is obvious even to people far removed from America and its modern Orthodox Jews.

29. Shulchan Aruch, Choshen Mishpat 331:1. See also Jerusalem Talmud, Bava Metzia ′ 7b (statement of Rav Hoshea, "Custom supersedes

halachah"); Joseph Kolon, *Maharik*, 102 and Shlomo Shwadron, *Maharashdam*, no 108.

30. Moshe Feinstein, *Iggrot Moshe*, Choshen Mishpat 1:72. See also Yeheil Mekheil Epstein, *Aruch ha-Shulchan*, Choshen Mishpat 73:20.

31. See, e.g., Moshe Feinstein, *Iggrot Moshe*, Choshen Mishpat 1:72; David Chazan, *Nidiv Lev* 12–13; Isaac Aaron Ettinger, *Maharyah ha-Levi* 2:111; Avraham Dov Baer Shapiro, *D'var Avraham* 1:1; Israel Landau, *Beit Yisroel*, 172; Yitzhak Blau, *Pischa Choshen*, *D'nei Halva'ah*, chapter 2, halachah 29, note 82. For example, *Yosef Iggeret*, *Divrei Yosef*, 21, states:

> One cannot cast doubt upon the validity of this custom on the basis that it became established through a decree of the King that required people to so act. Since people always act this way, even though they do so only because of the King's decree, we still properly say that everyone who does business without specifying otherwise does business according to the custom.

32. Letter of Approbation to R. Neharia Moshe Gotel, *Hishtanut ha-Tevaim be-Halachah* (5755), p. 15. (It is important to note, however, that the practice of resolving these disputes in secular court remains a clear violation of halachah, which requires that these types of disputes be resolved in a bet din. See Choshen Mishpat 26:2. However, the fact that these disputes should be resolved in bet din does not in any way cause one to assert that bet din cannot accept the common commercial custom of using secular law as the basis to resolve this dispute. Indeed, one of the prenuptial agreements explicitly lists that possibility as one of its options).

33. Of course, there remains a separate and self-standing prohibition of litigating in secular court, which has absolutely nothing to do with what rules are followed. Jewish law can be enforced in a secular court and the prohibition is in place, and secular law can be enforced in a bet din (or through arbitration) and the prohibition not violated. For more on this, see Michael Broyde, *The Pursuit of Justice and Jewish Law* (Yeshiva University, 1996), Chapters 3–5, 27–43.

34. For examples of these agreements, see Appendix F.

Chapter Four

1. Shulchan Aruch, Even ha-Ezer 1:3. While it is true that normative Jewish law no longer invokes its coercive power to prevent such marriages, as practical experience has taught that such coercive interference is extremely disruptive, it is still quite clear that the theoretical shape of the bet din's power includes such review. For example, Dr. Chearan Freeze of Brandeis University shared with me part of the record book of the Vilna bet

din, which notes 138 Jewish divorces. In addition to the names of the husband and wife, the *mesader gittin,* and the witnesses, the document notes which bet din authorized the divorce and why the couple was getting divorced.

2. One could ponder why this is truer in the area of marriage and divorce than in the area of *kashrut,* which has for the last 25 years seen a vast, and ongoing, raising of standards. Among the possible answers is that as food production centralized in America in the hands of large companies, the supervision process was forced to do the same to demonstrate the value of its "hashgacha" (*kashrut* certification). Marriage and divorce, while they have impact on the community, are fundamentally private activities and thus less well set up for communal regulation absent a governmental grant of jurisdiction, as is the case in Israel. Indeed, even in America the government has been repeatedly enlisted by *kashrut* agencies, and it is unclear how much of the advances are attributable solely to governmental regulation. For more on this, see Karen Ruth Lavy Lindsay, "Can Kosher Fraud Statutes Pass the Lemon Test?" *University of Dayton Law Review* 65:337 (1998); Stephen F. Rosenthal, "Food for Thought: Kosher Fraud Laws and the Religion Clauses of the First Amendment," *George Washington Law Review* 65:951 (1997).

3. See Gittin 89a–b.

4. For more on this generally, see Michael Broyde, *The Pursuit of Justice and Jewish Law* (Yeshiva University Press, 1996).

5. See Johnson v. Rockefeller, 58 FRD 42 (SDNY, Dec. 18, 1972), where New York sought to void the marriage of a prisoner (by the prison chaplain) on the basis of the fact that one who is incarcerated loses the ability to marry.

6. This depends on whether the jurisdiction is a fault or no-fault jurisdiction.

7. For more on this, see Benzion Schareschevsky, *D'nei Mishpacha* (3rd ed., Jerusalem, 1983), pp. 348–375.

8. In determining the rights of the parties, there are models that require only that bet din implement the formal structure that requires little independent thought (such as the unilateral no-fault divorce regime). Consider the case of mutual consent to be divorced, with an agreement by the parties to divide the assets and no children in the marriage. In such a case, the bet din serves an essentially procedural role, and not a substantive one.

9. Indeed, even the significant number of these cases resulting from the tragic circumstances of the *Shoah* seem to have been addressed effectively.

10. Thus the rabbinical courts of Israel maintain that there are 21 current cases of agunah in Israel in 1997; see *Jerusalem Post,* February 16,

1997. (Rabbi Ben Dahan said there was an improvement in the situation of agunot, whose number stands at 21 today compared to 450 some years ago.) Indeed, the rabbinical courts in Israel have, besides the right to imprison a person, the right to strip him of his driver's license, freeze his bank accounts, and impose other penalties.

While it is true that even these measures will not stop the occasional husband who would rather spend his life in prison than divorce his wife (like one man, who recently died in prison after 32 years), these cases represent profound anomalies.

11. For more on this, see Obadiah Yosef, *Yabia Omer,* Even ha-Ezer 7:23, a *teshuvah* co-signed by Rabbi Eliezer Yehuda Waldenberg and Rabbi Yitzhak Kolitz.

The first recording of these "separations" can be found in Rabbenu Tam's *Sefer ha-Yashar* (Chelek ha-Teshuvot §24), which states:

> Decree by force of oath on every Jewish man and woman under your jurisdiction that they not be allowed to speak to him, to host him in their homes, to feed him or give him to drink, to accompany him or to visit him when he is ill. In the event that he refuses to divorce his wife, you may add further restrictions upon him.

It is endorsed by Rama in a gloss on Even ha-Ezer 154:21, citing a responsum of Mahari Colon (*shoresh* 102). While it is true that *Pitchai Teshuva* (Even ha-Ezer 154:30) cites *Gevurat Anashim* 72 (this work was written by Rabbi Shabtai ben Meir ha-Kohein, the author of the *Shach*) who asserts that "today" the sanctions described by Rama are the equivalent of *nidui* (excommunication) and would constitute improper coercion to give or receive a *get*, except in cases where there is a legal obligation to do so. It can be argued, however, that *Gevurat Anashim*'s stringent ruling applies to an insular and thoroughly intertwined Jewish community which was the norm in the pre-emancipation communities of Eastern Europe at that time. In such a community, withholding favors from an individual would have a devastating effect upon him.

This result, it is claimed, is the equivalent of *nidui*. In the typical Orthodox community in America where most people earn their living through economic interactions with the secular world, withdrawing favors from an individual would of course not have nearly the same impact as it would in those communities. Hence it appears reasonable to conclude that even Shach would rule that, in today's circumstances, imposing *harchakot de-Rabbenu Tam* in America on a recalcitrant spouse would not constitute improper coercion.

Moreover, none of the commentaries on the Shulchan Aruch other than Pitchai Teshuva express dissent to Rama's acceptance of *harchakot de-Rabbenu Tam*. In fact, *Aruch ha-Shulchan* (Even Haezer 154:63), as well as

other authorities (*Maharam M'Lublin* 1 and 39, *Eliyahu Rabbah* 1–3, Rabbi
Betzalel Ashkenazi 6 and 10, Chief Rabbi Yitzchak Isaac Halevi Herzog,
Techuka le-Yisrael al pi ha-Torah III:202 and 209) cite Rama's ruling as nor-
mative. Rabbi Eliyahu Ben-Dahan, director of the rabbinical courts in
Israel, stated at the Zwillenberg International Conference for Dayanut (in
New York on 6 Kislev 5753, December 1, 1992) that the practice of the
Rabbinical Courts in Israel is to impose *harchakot de-Rabbenu Tam* upon
recalcitrant spouses upon whom halachah does not permit coercion to be
employed. Rabbi Dahan's report is substantiated by Rabbi Chagai Izirar
who writes (*Be'erurim be-Halachot Hara'ayah* [R. Kook], p. 243) that "the
harchakot de-Rabbenu Tam are accepted as the halachic norm, and it is well
known that rabbinical courts implement it." Rabbi Izivar writes that *harchakot de-Rabbenu Tam* may be utilized even in a case where a woman has
unilaterally decided to end the marriage (*to'enet maos alai*), if she provides a
reasonable basis (*amatla mevu'eret*) for her actions.

12. Historically it appears that the more powerful the bet din system is
generally, the fewer the number of agunot there will be, since all but the
intractable cases will be resolved.

13. See, for example, Nadine Brozan, "Women Allege Betrayal by
Rabbis' Talk: Rare Lawsuits Complain Reputations as Jews Were
Damaged," *New York Times*, (December 14, 1998), sec. B, p. 1:

> Mrs. Sieger, who is a nursing home administrator, filed suit last month in
> Supreme Court in Manhattan against the Union of Orthodox Rabbis of the
> United States and Canada, the Bet Din Zedek of America, a rabbinical court,
> and five individual rabbis for libel and slander. She is seeking $13 million in
> damages.
>
> Her lawsuit revolves around an unusual instrument of Jewish divorce, called
> a Heter Meah Rabonim, that the defendants got for her husband, Chaim
> Sieger, on the grounds that she had repeatedly refused to accept a routine *get*.

Another example is found in the case *Rakoszynski v. Rakoszynski,*
reported in *New York Law Journal* (November 6, 1997).

14. The *Jerusalem Post* (February 16, 1997), p. 12, reports:

> He [Rabbi Ben-Dahan] said there was an improvement in the situation of
> *agunot*, whose number stands at 21 today compared to 450 some years ago. This
> was due to dispatching detectives abroad to locate recalcitrant husbands.

15. Witness, for example, the recent problems in America with bogus or
invalid *heter meah rabbanim* documentation. Essentially, while there have
been a number of decrees by the various Jewish law courts (*batai din*)
throughout the United States to prevent this practice from continuing,
there seems to be little that actually can be done to prevent this practice.
However, when a person with such documentation entered Israel, he was

swiftly incarcerated by the rabbinical courts; the *Jerusalem Post* (February 22, 1997), wrote:

> The Israeli parliament has passed legislation to punish men who refuse to divorce their wives. Judaism gives the husband the final say, but now civil courts have a battery of sanctions to help women who want to end their marriages. They include taking away cheque-books, passports and driving licenses, preventing the husband from running a business or occupying public positions. If all that fails, the courts will be able to jail husbands for up to 10 years. Left-wing Meretz Party MP Dedi Zucker said the new law on divorce, passed Tuesday night, "modernized legislation that is a thousand years old." The bill was presented after rabbis had kept a husband in jail for 32 years for refusing to grant his wife a divorce.

16. Sometimes one gets a sense that the rabbinical courts can do no right in the eyes of some. Consider the following case, reported by Haim Shapiro, "Haredi family fears for future after father is excommunicated," *Jerusalem Post*, July 17, 1996:

> The story of one Tel Aviv-area family began about four years ago, when a brother of the excommunicated man became involved in divorce proceedings. After a rabbinical court levied a monthly support payment which was more than the brother could pay, the brother disappeared. The rabbinical court appears convinced that the rest of the family knows where the brother is.
>
> What followed, according to the wife of the excommunicated man, was a series of orders to appear at various rabbinical courts around the country. Whenever a family member failed to appear, the court would order them arrested. Family members also found that the rabbinical courts had imposed liens on their homes.
>
> "My mother-in-law is eighty years old. She's a survivor of Auschwitz. After she was arrested, she had a heart attack," the wife said.
>
> Her husband, in an effort to keep from being arrested, filed a petition with the High Court of Justice against the rabbinical court. It was, she admitted, a very serious step for a haredi man to take, but it resulted in an end to the arrest and lien orders from the rabbinical courts.
>
> Last week, however, the family was shocked to find huge posters hanging in their neighborhood and other haredi neighborhoods with what appeared to be a copy of a herem (excommunication order) issued by the Jerusalem Rabbinical Court. The herem was signed by Rabbi Ezra Basri, president of the Jerusalem Rabbinical Court, and Rabbinical Court judges Shlomo Fisher and Nehemia Goldberg.
>
> The herem warns all Jews not to come within four cubits of the man involved, not to have any dealings with him, talk to him or count him for a minyan in the synagogue. This past Shabbat, she said, the family went elsewhere, and the husband attended the synagogue of his hasidic community.
>
> The husband has also refrained from riding the bus or shopping in any neighborhood stores, she said, adding that she has gotten the cold shoulder from a few of her neighbors.

"This thing could easily destroy my marriage, but I respect my husband for his courage. Can they destroy my life because of another woman's life? You'd think this was the Middle Ages," the wife said.

17. United States Department of State, "Travel Advisory Warning for Israel," January 22, 1997.

18. Of course, the rabbinical courts would allow couples to write prenuptial agreements that change the default rules, if that is what the couple wishes. For example:

> The rabbinical establishment has agreed in principle to offer couples the option of signing a prenuptial agreement, which could help many women trapped in broken marriages to obtain divorces more quickly. In a meeting yesterday with representatives of several women's organizations, Sephardi Chief Rabbi Eliahu Bakshi-Doron and Rabbi Eli Ben-Dahan, administrative director of the rabbinical courts, said the rabbinate would offer couples registering for marriage the option of signing a prenuptial agreement. Under the agreement, should the marriage sour, the husband would be obligated to pay his wife a daily sum from the moment they separated to the day he granted a *get* (writ of divorce), unless the rabbinical court decreed otherwise.

See *Jerusalem Post* (June 17, 1996), p. 12, "Chief rabbi agrees to act on prenuptial agreements, " by Esther Hecht.

19. This point is important to note, because it clearly distinguishes the normative policy of the rabbinical court, which is to impose support payments for the benefit of a spouse who is entitled to be supported by the terms of the *ketubah*, from the policy of imposing a payment obligation, whether or not directly mandated by halachah, in each case of separation, even if the woman is working and thus not entitled to support. This kind of policy is designed to create incentives for writing a *get* rather than fulfilling the halachic obligation of support. Proof to that fact can be found in that Jewish law mandates that in return for support payments, income earned by the woman goes to her husband, and these prenuptial agreements all require the waiver of that provision, since absent such a waiver, this agreement accomplishes the halachic obligation to support one's estranged wife but does not provide a firm enough incentive to encourage divorce. This fact is not trivial, as the Rabbi Willig prenuptial agreement indicates its purpose (to encourage the issuing of a *get*) with its dual requirement of support by the husband in cases of separation, and its waiver by the husband of his reciprocal right to collect his wife's wages in return for his support, as he is entitled to according to halachah. (See Even ha-Ezer 70 and 77.) In Israel, if the wife works, she is not entitled to support upon separation.

20. *Tzitz Eliezer* 18:58. This *psak* can also be found in *Peskai Din Rabaniyin* 1:238 and 9:171 as the *psak* of the rabbinical courts of Israel and

is defended by Rabbi Herzog and others in the appendix to volume 2 of *Otzar ha-Poskim*. Particularly, the analysis found in 9:171 supports the contention that the *moredet* issue is not significant, since a *get* should be given even to a *moredet*.

21. Even ha-Ezer 154:4, 7.

22. Tosafot, Zevachim 2b s.v. *stam*. The approach of Tosafot is rejected, or limited to a case where the woman does not want to be divorced, by a breadth of authorities, including *Noda Beyehuda*, Tenyana, Even ha-Ezer 12, Rabbi Akiva Eiger, *Derush ve-Chedish, teshuvah* at the end of the *Ketavim* section, Chatam Sofer, Nedarim 89a, s.v. *be-rishona* (cited in the preface), *Beit Meir,* Even ha-Ezer 117, *Pitchai Teshuva* 154 (4 and 7) and it can be implied from *Aruch ha-Shulchan*, Even ha-Ezer 178:25–26. See the short article by Rabbi Yaakov Moshe Toledano in the appendix to *Otzar ha-Poskim* (2:16); he avers that the approach that requires a husband to support his wife who is a *moredet,* and thus not technically entitled to support, in order to encourage the writing of a *get* by the husband, is the normative halachah without a doubt.

23. *Jerusalem Post,* February 22, 1997.

24. This point requires some elaboration, because I appear to be claiming that a certain amount of agunot are acceptable to the system. While such is not the ideal at all, in fact every system of justice has its occasional failures; while I would prefer a system with no agunot at all, the presence of some crime is not proof that the criminal justice system does not work, and the existence of some agunot is not proof that the halachic system has failed.

25. Posted on Mail-Jewish, vol 25, issue 45. See www.shamash.org.

26. This lack of authority has led some to grasp at straws for solutions. In the absence of any "authority," the only type of solutions that can work in the face of recalcitrance are those that can be imposed unilaterally by a bet din, such as annulment. This is, putting aside any technical halachic concerns, of which there are many, a reflection of the fundamental impotence of the bet din in America to impose solutions to agunah problems that require the cooperation of those who do not wish to cooperate.

27. Indeed, except for very insular hasidic communities, it is lacking in all communities residing in North America. Some have analogized the current status of the Jewish court system to the chaos that reigned in the *kashrut* field 75 years ago, which led to lower rather than higher standards and a general lack of esteem in the field. For more on this subject, see Harold Gastwort, *Corruption and Holiness: The Controversy over the Supervision of Jewish Dietary Practice in New York City, 1881–1940* (Kenikat Press, 1974).

28. One bet din wrote:

Mr. Seymour Klagsbrun has taken up residence in the Monsey/Spring Valley community. After numerous conversations with Mr. Klagsbrun the following facts are clear to us:

1. Mr. Klagsbrun has never given a Jewish divorce to his wife Shulamith Klagsbrun.

2. Mr. Klagsbrun has since remarried, claiming that he has the necessary permission from a rabbinical court to do so.

3. Seymour Klagsbrun has refused to tell us the name of the rabbi who performed the marriage with his second wife.

4. Mr. Klagsbrun has refused to show us the claimed written rabbinical permission allowing him to remarry.

5 . The issues between Mr. and Mrs. Klagsbrun were addressed by a reputable Bet Din which ordered Mr. Klagsbrun to give a Jewish divorce to his wife. Mr. Klagsbrun has not complied with the order of that Bet Din.

6. Mr. Klagsbrun has refused to inform us of the name of his designated representative to a new Bet Din to adjudicate any outstanding property issues between him and Mrs. Shulamith Klagsbrun.

7. Mr. Klagsbrun has repeatedly threatened the Vaad Harabonim with the bringing of legal actions in a civil secular court.

In light of all the above it is obvious that Seymour Klagsbrun is not entitled to any honors or participation in synagogue services and that all possible social sanctions should be placed against him until he complies with the orders of the Bet Din and grants a Jewish divorce to his wife, Shulamith Klagsbrun.

Another bet din wrote:

A. Since it is known and established in our city of Monsey and its vicinity that the man Mr. Shimon Klagsbrun married a second wife on top of his first wife (Shulamith) [and he has admitted as such in front of our Bet Din].

Behold, in light of the above and in light of the investigation and examination and clarification of the issues, it is the opinion of the Bet Din that this man mentioned above is banned under the Cherem of Rabbenu Gershom Me'or HaGolah and his Bet Din [with all the laws and outcome that spring from this—Yoreh Deah 334:22]; and all of this despite his screaming at the top of his lungs "that he has a Heter of 100 Rabbis." Clarification of all the details and our reasoning is on file in our Bet Din.

B. And as regards his second wife [Mrs. Judith Klagsbrun (Oshry)] it comes out that she may also be under ban (*Otzar ha-Poskim* 1:61:4), and in any event she is surely violating the Torah violation of "in front of the blind" [for as regards her it is surely a situation of two banks of a river according to all opinions] and besides which, she has applied to her, as well as anyone else who helps the man mentioned above in any way, the law of someone who aides the hands of transgressional sinners, who are caught by his sin. (Tractate Shevuot, Chap. 5 Mishnah 6–9; Tractate Shabbat 54b–55a; Tractate Shavuot 39a–39b).

C. It also became clear that in the year 5748 [1988], a few years prior to all of the above (meaning prior to his marrying a second wife), there had already been an order (*psak din*) from the Bet Din of Bet Yosef Navarodek to divorce his wife Shulamith and he refused to comply with the *psak din* mentioned above, and a written seruv was issued and permission was granted to her to press her complaints against him in secular court.

D. Again, in the year 5752 [1992], the above mentioned Bet Din proclaimed against him the distancing of Rabbenu Tam (that it will not be permissible for anyone to have any dealings with him or to provide him with comfort in any way, or even to talk with him (Levush EH end of section 134, who brings a few other matters, and also Ramah 154:21).

E. And what comes out from all that is mentioned above is that besides that Mr. Shimon Klagsbrun is keeping his wife Shulamith an Agunah in the chains and agony of Agunahood from the year 5748 [1988] until this time, now he has added transgression upon crime in marrying a second wife upon her, which is prohibited, that due to all of this, he is distanced by the Bet Din of Rabbenu Tam and under ban by the Bet Din of Rabbenu Gershom

29. Essentially a system of private divorce law, even when it has the possibility of coercion, cannot "resolve" ever case of *igun,* since there will be certain cases where one party is precluded from participating in the writing of the *get* because of mental incapacity or simple stubbornness (even after coercion). *Heter mea rabbanim* fixes this matter when the recalcitrant spouse is the wife and there is fault, not by issuing a divorce, but by permitting nominal polygamy when the woman is at fault and will not receive a *get.* The fundamental problem (that Jewish law has no procedure that allows for a valid divorce in the case of mental incapacity of either spouse) remains unsolved. The modern common law of America has fixed this problem by allowing one to divorce one's spouse against his or her will in a case of mental incapacity. Upon reflection, it is unclear if that solution is any more ethical than the halachic posture, although it certain does solve the agunah problem.

30. For an example, as is noted in footnote 28, it is alleged that Seymour Klagsbrun has a letter from a charlatan Jewish law court representing itself as permitting him to remarry according to Jewish law, even though he has not yet divorced his wife. Needless to say, normative Jewish law courts view such documentation as a nullity.

31. For example, the Beth Din of America enforces this imposition of duty on the husband in one of three ways:

A. By requiring the husband to state in the arbitration agreement that he agrees to give a *get* upon the wife's signing of the arbitration agreement

B. By requiring that the husband authorize the writing of a *get,* to be delivered to the wife at the discretion of the Beth Din of America.

C. By requiring that the husband authorize the writing of a *get,* which is immediately to be delivered to the wife.

All of these methods are employed contextually to ensure that if the husband appeals to the Beth Din of America to conduct a din torah about the financial matters related to the *get* that he cannot withhold a *get* forever.

32. *Harchakot Shel Rabbenu Tam* can never lead to *get me'useh*; for more on this point, see note 11. It is important to note that even though one cannot contractually agree to use the civil courts according to Jewish law, there is no doubt such an agreement is identical to a choice of law provision, and would cause even a Jewish court to refer to secular law for the rules of decision.

33. *Seruv* is a writ of excommunication written by a Jewish court indicating that a particular person's conduct violates Jewish law.

34. See Rules and Procedures of the Beth Din of America as found at: www.bethdin.org/rules.htm.

35. See Chapter 2, note 30.

36. See Chapter 4, note 31. One final comment about this matter is important. There are a host of situations where any bet din would, on an informal basis, encourage or even urge the husband to give a *get* immediately, even though *al pi din* halachah cannot mandate that a *get* be given immediately in the context of that situation, or even that sanctions are proper. Thus, for example, the Beth Din of America strongly advises husbands that it is better to give a *get* prior to a civil divorce even though it is our sense that on a formal level, sanction of a person who will not give a *get* until the civil divorce is rarely proper.

37. For more on this, see Gastwort, *Corruption and Holiness*.

38. One cannot require that a person go to bet din in every case when the other side will go only if he or she cannot triumph in secular court. R. Moshe Sternbuch (*Teshuvot ve-Hanhagot* 1:795, rev. ed.) advances this same rationale. He explores the possibility that a litigant who is not generally observant of Jewish law and would not accept it when it is to his detriment is not entitled to accept Jewish law's legal rules selectively when they are to his benefit. According to this principle, even if a bet din were to hear the case, it is possible that secular law would actually provide the legal rules of decision. He bases his analysis of this topic on whether the rule that an apostate has the same status as a gentile is to be applied even in financial situations that are to the detriment of the apostate. For more on this subject, see R. Yehudah Amichai, "A Gentile Who Summons a Jew to Bet Din," *Tehumin* 12 (1991), pp. 259–265.

39. There is quite a literature on building subcommunities in the United States as well as the tools needed to enforce their community structure. In addition to a piece I wrote ("Forming Religious Communities and Respecting Dissenters' Rights" in M. Broyde and J. Witte, eds, *Human Rights in Judaism: Cultural, Religious, and Political Perspectives* ([Northvale,

NJ: Jason Aronson, 1998], pp. 35–76), there is a rather extensive literature on community formation and the use of arbitration agreements in communities whose values are far distant from that of the Jewish community.

For an example of this phenomenon, see Clark Freshman, "Privatizing Same-Sex `Marriage' Through Alternative Dispute Resolution," 44 *UCLA L Rev* 1687 (1997) and Nicole Berner, "Child Custody Disputes Between Lesbians: Legal Strategies and their Limitations," *Berkeley Women's Law Journal* 10:31 (1995). For a more general discussion of the role of ADR in rule creation, see Jack B. Weinstein, "Some Benefits and Risks of Privatization of Justice through ADR," *Ohio St. Journal on Dispute Resolution* 11:241 (1996), and Robert G. Bone, "Lon Fuller's Theory of Adjudication and the False Dichotomy Between Dispute Resolution and Public Law Models of Litigation, 75 *Boston University Law Review* 1273 (1995).

Chapter Five

1. Literally: "Afterwards the rabbis can take the marriage away from him." This is the term used for annulment.

2. Found at www.mail-jewish.org/rav/talmud-torah.

3. Consider annulment of marriage. From the perspective of this chapter, annulment cannot be posed as a solution without one's addressing the issue of when one uses it. The decision to annul only in situations where Rabbenu Tam maintains that there is a duty to divorce leads to a completely different result than the decision to annul whenever the woman cannot get a *get,* as Rosh understands the ruling of the geonim. Annulment is a tool; when it is used is the crucial issue that needs to be addressed. Indeed, what is surprising is how little any clear discussion about when annulment is appropriate takes place in those denominations where it is advocated. There is absolutely no discussion of the proper circumstances for annulment in the whole literature of the (Conservative) Rabbinical Assembly, which endorsed it in 1968 as a valid solution to the agunah problem. For a paper that elaborates on the Conservative Movement's understanding of when to end a marriage, see Mayer E. Rabinowitz, "Agunot Conference" at http://www.learn.jtsa.edu/topics/luminaries/monograph/agunot.html. The essential point of that paper is that the Joint Bet Din of the Conservative Movement is prepared to end the marriage of any person after the civil divorce is granted, whether the person wishes to be divorced according to Jewish law or not. This is a search for a mechanism, rather than a discussion of whether the result is good. In this case, even the mechanism is faulty.

4. See *Seder Kiddushin ve-Nisuin Achar Chatimat ha-Talmud*. For more on this, see responsa *Maharam Al-shakar* 48, who makes this point explicitly. The broadest recasting of Jewish law favoring annulments can be found in Menachem Elon, *Jewish Law: History, Sources and Principles*, (Jewish Publication Society, 1994) pp. 641–642 and 856–877. Even Justice Elon concedes that in order to even contemplate the use of annulment, one needs a unified rabbinate, something that is far beyond the current contours of the community. Even this solution is profoundly difficult and has been subject to criticism from many; see Eliav Schochetman, "Annulment of Marriages," *Jewish Law Annual* 20:349–397 (5757), for an extensive review of this issue; he demonstrates that most authorities accept that annulment is limited to the talmudic cases.

5. See "Marriage and Divorce Law," from Allen Parkman, *No Fault Divorce: What Went Wrong* (1993), pp. 12–23.

6. Ibid.

7. Cited by Irving Breitowitz in *Between Civil and Religious Law: The Plight of the Agunah in American Society* (Greenwood Press, 1993), with no reference at p. 58. This is the prenuptial agreement used by Rabbi Haskel Lookstein which can be found in appendix F of this book.

8. Even clearer on this point is the proposal of Rabbi Louis Epstein that the wife be appointed the agent for the writing of the bill of divorce by the husband at the beginning of the marriage, so that she can write her own bill of divorce at any time she wishes. Besides the devastating criticism voiced as to the technical problems with Epstein's proposal (Breitowitz, at pp. 64–68), in my opinion the most significant proposal is the complete reversal of the essence of both *Cherem de Rabbenu Gershom* and the near unanimous stand against unilateral no-fault divorce. Were Epstein's proposal adopted, the woman would have the right to be divorced whenever she wished but the husband would be bound by *Cherem de Rabbenu Gershom* not to divorce his wife without her consent. This complete reversal of the general talmudic law (unilateral no-fault divorce initiated by the woman, but only fault divorce for the man) seems difficult to accept as grounded at all in the Jewish notion of marriage.

9. One other notation needs to be made in this area. Some have claimed that the basic problem is that a dual system issue exists. According to this view, it is not that halachah should not be independent and autonomous, but requiring that two distinctly different systems each adjudicate any given dispute is deeply unwise and can be very unfair. This objection is quite correct; there are significant systemic problems associated with such a structure of divorce, as multiple legal systems rarely coordinate activities and significant problems of forum shopping that are nearly unsolvable without the functional abandonment of one system or another are created.

However, this argument is of little merit from an indigenous halachic view, since Jewish law asserts jurisdiction in these areas in such a way that those who are religiously loyal to Jewish law can hardly avoid complying. In such circumstances, Jewish law would require that people adopt mechanisms (such as a prenuptial agreement or an arbitration agreement) which strengthen Jewish law. For more on this, see Chapter 3.

10. The term "concubinage" is not exactly correct, since it seems to denote a slavery type of ownership, which is not at all found in the rabbinic term *peligesh*.

11. Breitowitz, *Between Civil and Religious Law*, p. 70.

12. Ibid., pp. 78–96 See Appendix F for sample documents.

13. For more on this, see Michael Broyde, "The 1992 New York *Get* Law: An Exchange," *Tradition* 31:3 23–41 (1997) and Appendix C.

14. Jewish law maintains as the normative (*lechatchila*) rule that even a "pre-agreed upon penalty" constitutes coercion according to halachah when the husband changes his mind and declares that he does not want to give the *get*. Thus an agreement by the husband at the time of his marriage that he will give his wife a *get* anytime she asks for one or will pay one million dollars, would be improper. While it is true that Rama (Even ha-Ezer 134:5), after citing the various opinions, rules that "it is better (*lechatchila*) to be fearful of the strict opinions and to nullify the penalty, but if already divorced because of this the *get* is valid," normative Jewish law would never permit itself to be structured in a way that relies on this *bede'eved* rule as the ideal. This is particularly true given the fact that *Mishkanot Yaakov* 38 argues with the Rama and voids such *gittin*. In truth, a clear consensus agrees with the Rama in this regard, at least *bede'eved*. Certainly in a case where the husband does not categorically state at the time of the *seder haget* that he is being coerced, which is a very rare circumstance, the *get* is valid; *Levush* 134 and Chazon Ish, Even ha-Ezer 99:5, but see *Aruch ha-Shulchan*, Even ha-Ezer 134:26–29 (Were the husband to state that he was coerced, without a doubt the bet din would not write the *get*, although many *poskim* would permit such a *get* to be written).

15. Even child support rights are different in out-of-wedlock births.

16. In a technical sense, assuming that the couple went before a Jewish law court every day and announced that even though they expected to have a sexual relationship that day, that sexual relationship should not be understood as an implied waiver of their prior conditions.

17. There has been some opposition to the use of even these prenuptial agreements based on pastoral concerns that addressing issues of divorce prior to marriage will weaken the marriage. See *Iggrot Moshe*, Even ha-Ezer 4:107, in the large edition. For reasons that have never been explained, the

text of this responsa was changed in the small edition. Among the changes were an affirmative recommendation that such agreements not be used for pastoral reasons absent special needs (the original edition simply indicates that the officiating rabbi should get to know the parties before using this agreement). In addition, there were insertions made to address the withholding of a civil divorce that were not found in the first edition. These matters have never been explained properly.

18. Technically referred to as *yotzee* cases which are not *kofin*.

19. Truth be told, the pastoral concerns seem contrary to the Jewish tradition in that the *ketubah* clearly discusses these issues with no hesitation and difficulty. Why should we not do so also?

20. Taken from http://www.jlaw.com/forms/prenuptial.html. For a collection of arbitration agreements, see Appendix F.

21. Shulchan Aruch, Even ha-Ezer 80:1–3.

22. For a detailed listing of who has endorsed such an agreement and who has acknowledged that such an agreement is permitted by Jewish law (even if they have not endorsed actually using such an agreement for pastoral reasons), see http://www.orthodox.caucus.org. In this writer's opinion, there have been no successful critiques of this type of prenuptial agreement grounded in Jewish law.

23. Simply deleting the clause that follows accomplishes this task:

> However, this obligation (to provide food and support, *parnasah*) shall terminate if my wife refuses to appear upon due notice before the Bet Din of __ _____ or any other bet din specified in writing by that bet din before proceedings commence, for purpose of a hearing concerning any outstanding disputes between us, or in the event that she fails to abide by the decision or recommendation of such bet din.

24. These last two forms of agreement accomplish one other significant activity not generally addressed. Talmudic law establishes that in the absence of a designated bet din, parties may establish a "one-time" bet din through a mechanism of each side picking a judge and then the two judges picking a third judge to hear a case (in Hebrew, *zabla*). There is a well-discussed problem with such a system in that one side could pick as "judge" one who is unethical or corrupt or who profoundly deviates from normative Jewish law, and who will not accept as a third anyone whom he senses disagrees with him. An agreement to arbitrate, in order to be valid in American law, must specify which bet din one will go to, thus vastly reducing this problem. It could also allow a certain amount of forum shopping, in which the parties negotiate prior to the marriage over which bet din one would go to, perhaps reflecting the different perspectives the parties have to the nature of marriage and the financial duties one spouse has to the other.

25. There have been no less than seven draft agreements proposed that focus on the reciprocal obligation, anti-nuptial support agreement, conditional release, or the trading chip process. To survey them, see Breitowitz, *Between Civil and Religious Law*, pp. 150–162.

26. One could use the structure of a Rabbi Willig prenuptial in a variety of ways that are designed to create paradigms for marriage other than unilateral no-fault divorce. For example, one of these authors has seen reverse R. Willig agreements, in which the woman agrees to forfeit her earnings without any right to support if she permanently leaves the marital abode without the consent of her husband or the decision of an agreed-upon bet din that such conduct was proper. Such an agreement would be written in an attempt to impose financial penalties on a woman who exercises her right to walk out of the marriage and end the marital unit with neither consent nor fault.

27. This is a simplification, in that a bet din could order that she is entitled to a divorce, but it is not a case of *kofin* (where actual force is permitted), but merely of *mitzvah/yotzee* (where Jewish law rules it proper to be divorced). However, even in cases of *yotzee* or *mitzvah*, or even merely rabbinic encouragement to get divorced, a well-run bet din with proper secular legal authority will develop methods to nearly mandate the *get* in most circumstances. Thus in modern day Israel, even where there is no halachic right or duty to give a *get* at all *al pi din*, when the bet din wishes to compel the *get* it invokes *harchakot de-Rabbenu Tam*, explained in the previous chapter, and can use that tool to suspend a person's driver's license, right to electricity, use of a passport, and a variety of other needs. Given authority, those cases that can be solved normally will be.

28. This is not the place to explain the rules related to coerced divorces (see Appendix C). Jewish law does not rule that any coercion, no matter how minor or indirect, invalidates a Jewish divorce, and the precise boundaries of this coercion are part of a variety of exchanges that have occurred in various Jewish law journals. See, e.g., Michael Broyde, "The 1992 New York State *Get* Law" (*Tradition*, Summer 1995); Rabbi Chaim Malinowitz, "The 1992 New York *Get* Law," *Journal of Halacha and Contemporary Society* 27 (1994), pp. 5–26; Rabbi Gedalia Dov Schwartz, ibid., pp. 26–34 ; Rabbi Chaim Malinowitz and Rabbi Michael Broyde, "The 1992 New York *Get* Law: An Exchange," in *Tradition* 31:3 (1997), pp. 23–41.

29. For a discussion of the various cases, see Breitowitz, *Between Civil and Religious Law*, pp. 239–250.

Chapter Six

1. Consider these two cases:
Husband disappears and

    A. Is presumed dead, but such is unproven; wife prefers husband's return, or divorce.
    B. Abandons wife, whereabouts unknown.

2. Consider this case:
Husband is known to be alive and is unable to arrange a divorce.
3. Consider these cases:
Wife abandons marriage; husband denies marriage is over, and:

    A. will not issue *get*.
    B. will issue *get* after civil divorce.
    C. will issue *get* only after going to bet din, both parties agreeing to abide by its decisions (no prenuptial agreement).
    D. will issue *get* only after going to bet din as stipulated in prenuptial agreement, both parties agreeing to abide by its decisions.

4. Consider these cases:
Both agree marriage is over; husband makes issuance of a *get* conditional on:

    A. sum of money he admits he has no claim to.
    B. sum of money that he claims wife owes him.
    C. sum of money wife clearly owes him.
    D. settlement of all financial claims by one party against the other.
    E. going to a bet din to settle all matters; couple has no prenuptial agreement.
    F. going to the bet din designated in the couple's prenuptial agreement.

5. Consider these cases:
Both agree marriage is over, and husband withholds *get* because of:

    A. wife's perceived impropriety.
    B. wife's halachic impropriety.
    C. wife's refusal of the husband's visitation request before civil decision.
    D. wife's refusal of husband's visitation rights granted by civil decision.
    E. wife no longer observant, living with another man; seeks *get* for future children's sake.

F. wife no longer observant, living with another man; doesn't care whether she receives *get* or not, but rabbi requests it.

6. Consider these cases:

A. Couple marries religiously, husband abandons Judaism; both agree mariage is over, but husband refuses to perform religious rituals to end the marriage.
B. Couple marries civilly; marriage ends, but husband refuses to perform religious rituals.
C. Couple marries in a Reform Jewish ceremony; husband declines to participate in Jewish divorce rite because Reform Jewish law does not require such.

7. This third case is a particularly troubling example of the failures of practical Jewish ethics of our times. Consider the following responsa addressing this issue in *Current Reform Responsa* (1973), pp. 218–219.

Q. A man divorced his wife in a civil suit but turned down her request for a *get*, thereby interfering with her chances to marry again, inasmuch as the Orthodox man to whom she was engaged would not marry her until she received a *get*. The divorced husband now wishes to marry another woman and has asked a Reform rabbi to officiate at his second wedding. The rabbi is well aware of the circumstances surrounding the dissolving of the man's first marriage and had, indeed, urged that he give his divorced wife a *get*. Under these circumstances, should the rabbi officiate at the man's second marriage?

A. Since Reform (in America, at least) accepts the full validity of the civil divorce, there is no impediment to the man's remarriage. I do not see how a Reform rabbi in America can refuse to marry him. He is, however, a mean fellow who refuses to allow his former wife, since he refuses to give her a *get*, to be married to the man of her choice. It is certainly our moral duty to persuade him to be considerate and to urge him to go through the ceremony of a *get*, even though to him as a Reform Jew it will have little meaning. We may even go so far as to speak to him and his new intended bride and say that unless he gives the *get*, the Orthodox rabbinate would consider this intended marriage invalid, though of course we do not. If after all pleading he refuses to be of help to his former wife, I do not see how we can refuse to officiate at his marriage.

Thus, the official Reform view is that a Reform rabbi may perform a marriage for a man who is withholding a *get* from his first wife, whether or not the first marriage is Orthodox, Conservative, or Reform.

8. Consider this case:

A wife is legally mentally incapacitated (insanity, illness) and because of such illness abandons marriage.

9. Although classical Jewish law certainly would direct such to the community. See Michael Broyde, "Forming Religious Communities and

Respecting Dissenters' Rights" in M. Broyde and J. Witte, eds., *Human Rights in Judaism: Cultural, Religious, and Political Perspectives* (Jason Aronson, 1998), pp. 35–76

10. New Jersey Statutes §2C:21–7.

Chapter Seven

1. See Chaim David Zweibel, "Accommodating Religious Objections to Brain Death: Legal Issues," *Journal of Halacha and Contemporary Society* 17:49 (Spring 1989), pp. 49–63.

2. This is completely consistent with the empirical theory related to methods of alternative dispute resolution. Theoreticians of alternative dispute resolutions insist that the only situation in which parties can agree on a system of law that governs their dispute different from the rules provided by secular law, which is the default law in society, is prior to the dispute arising. After a dispute has arisen, one party or another will decline to accept the jurisdiction of a third party resolution (including bet din) as such a forum will not be to his or her advantage. Precisely because prior to a dispute no one is certain whether switching forum will be advantageous, a choice of law and choice of forum agreement is possible. After the dispute has already arisen, the only type of agreement that is in fact possible is one that is purely efficient, providing benefits to each party. Consider the case of a simple Jewish divorce, in which the couple had assets of $100 and two children. Assuming that secular law would divide the assets and children equally, so that each party got $40 and one child, and $20 went to legal fees, neither party would ever consent to appearing in front of a bet din that was likely to award them less than $40 and one child. The bet din would be allowed to hear the case only if it were more efficient than the secular court, so that neither party would be "hurt," either financially or in terms of the custody arrangement. If the bet din could not do that, each party will invoke its halachic right to *zebla* and prevent the bet din from resolving the matter. However, before the dispute arose, each party would have the ability to craft rules or make choices concerning forum unaware of the direct consequences to his or her case, since the person would have no idea what the particular dispute (if one ever arose) would look like.

For more on this matter from a law and economics view, see Steven Shavell, "Alternative Dispute Resolution: An Economic Analysis," *Journal of Legal Studies* 1:24 (1994), p. 33.

3. Indeed, as is widely known in rabbinic circles, there is significant, albeit sometimes understated, halachic opposition to the use of the

assumption of obligation agreement emanating out of Rabbi Elyashiv's chambers in Israel, which, although it has never been published and is thus hard to evaluate technically, provides considerable "safe harbor" for people who wish not to sign such an agreement.

4. In response to my view, others have said that we should have only one prenuptial agreement, which we will encourage people to sign, since our view of marriage is "better." This agreement would encourage the giving and receiving of a *get* when only one party wishes to be divorced, as the current Orthodox Caucus agreement does. While I think that this is a good approach in theory, in fact I suspect that it will not work. Many couples will simply sign nothing, since the limits of rabbinic authority, particularly within our community, are well known.

5. Appendix F contains sample agreements.

6. Some will respond that this policy is unfair, because who says that the innocent spouse did not want a prenuptial agreement and the other one declined to sign. Let me respond by saying that if we really want to send a message that one should not marry *anyone* without a prenuptial agreement, then even this "innocent" spouse is in error. Indeed, it is precisely because we need to teach the Jewish public that everyone should sign a prenuptial that I raise this issue. I am not really advocating this draconian policy, and I write it only as something to think about. However, if we really wish to push prenuptial in a way that makes it clear that all *really* must use them, this is the only way that such a system will work.

Chapter Eight

1. Not only will the two normative models of marriage and divorce (no-fault and fault) be codifiable to a couple through these types of prenuptial agreements, but even prenuptial agreements that specify alternative models completely can be crafted. Let me give two extreme examples:

> A. A couple agrees to be married and both of them accept that the ground rules for their marriage shall be those found in the Jewish communities of Iran and Iraq, which include polygamy and unilateral divorce initiated only by the husband, as an option. They could write such a prenuptial agreement accepting this as proper, and it would be enforceable according to Jewish law, assuming it was consistent with American law in the state in which the final arbitration occurred.

> B. A couple agrees to be married and both of them accept that the ground rules for their marriage shall be those enunciated by Bet Din Leba'ayot ha-Agunot in the advertisement found in the *Jewish Week* (August 28, 1998), which include that the couple does not intend that their marriage ceremony be valid according to Jewish law, that the woman and man do not consent to the halachic formulation of *kinyan* needed to create a valid marriage according to Jewish law,

and that the woman does not wish to be married to a man according to Jewish law if she cannot leave the marriage except when she wishes. They could write such a prenuptial agreement (actually closer to a declaration of principles) accepting this as proper, and it would be enforceable according to Jewish law.

A Jewish law court would enforce the declarations of the parties governing their marriage.

(While the rationale for accepting the second case is not obvious, a very strong case could be made that the parties, by signing such an agreement, have indicated that they themselves did not intend to be married according to Jewish law, and thus there is no requirement for a *get*. When there is no genuine intent to enter into a valid marriage according to Jewish law, even when there is an apparently proper wedding ceremony with the requisite exchange of value, the intent of the parties to deny the presence of a formal *kinyan* causes one to recognize that there is not a valid marriage ceremony according to Jewish law. This situation is perhaps closely analogous to the case of a couple that deliberately chooses to be married in a civil marriage ceremony when a halachic wedding ceremony is readily available and neither party wants one; in such a case, most halachic authorities agree that according to technical Jewish law, no *get* is required [even as our practice is to seek one when possible]).

Appendix B

1. See Chapter Eight, note 1.

2. Indeed, one of the first systemic discussions related to *kiddushai ta'ut* focuses on whether or not one assumes *kiddushai ta'ut* when a couple marries unaware of the fact that Jewish law prohibits them from marrying. This topic is discussed at great length in *Otzar ha-Poskim* 39:12–13, (pp. 210–216). Indeed, as noted by *Chelkat Ya'akov*, infra note 61, the proper resolution of this matter might depend on the religiosity of the parties. See also Acheizer 1:27, which discusses the case of a divorced woman who married a *kohein*.

3. For a detailed review of this issue, see Shulchan Aruch, Even ha-Ezer 39:1, and the commentaries on this. It is clear that the formulation in the Shulchan Aruch regarding *pesulai cohanim* is not fully accurate, as left-handed individuals are ineligible for service as *cohanim*; see *Otzar ha-Poskim* 13, p. 91. More generally, as noted in *Otzar ha-Poskim* 39:31:2, the vast consensus of halachic authorities notes that this determination is social and not strictly halachic (in the sense of independent of the social reality; for example, the definition of chametz is objective).

4. The technical term used for transfer of title or status.

5. See Tosafot, Ketubot 47b s.v. *shelo,* as well as Tosafot Ketubot 72b s.v. *al,* and 73a s.v. *lo.* For reasons beyond the discussion in this appendix, in such cases normally a *get* would be given when it possibly can.

6. When exactly one is in one category or the other remains a significant dispute among contemporary decisors; see *Achiezer* 1:27 and compare it with Iggrot Moshe, Even ha-Ezer 1:79. A close read of the three Tosafot referred to in the previous note indicates that Tosafot too disagreed on this point. However, Shulchan Aruch, Even ha-Ezer 39 indicates quite clearly that the Shulchan Aruch thought that in the case of a serious hidden defect, *mum gadol,* no *get* was needed, although that rule is stated only in reference to a defect found in the man, not in the woman. The stakes, however, are the same, because the defect in the woman permits her to marry another man without a *get* from her first husband.

7. Shulchan Aruch, Even ha-Ezer 26.

8. Shulchan Aruch, Even ha-Ezer 37. The case of *kiddushai ketana* is a special one in that the Torah directed that the father is the one authorized to accept a marriage proposal.

9. See *Aruch ha-Shulchan,* Even ha-Ezer 26:1–6. This appendix notes, without directly commenting on, the famous view of R. Eziekeil Abromsky that in the areas of both family law and contract law, requirement 1 is significant, and requirements 2 and 3 are mere manifestations of 1; he avers that, at least as a matter of theory, valid transactions can occur without requirement 3. See Y. Abromsky, *Dinai Mamonut.*

10. See Shulchan Aruch, Even ha-Ezer 38 and 39. Even ha-Ezer 38 addresses explicit conditions (*tenaim*) and 39 addresses implicit or explicit states of mind (*al manat*).

11. The consensus of most decisors is that civil marriages do not create valid marriages according to Jewish law, as they are deficient in fundamental elements of point 3, even if the couple subsequently cohabitate based on their reasonable belief that they are married. See R. Moses Feinstein, *Iggrot Moshe,* Even ha-Ezer 1:73–76; 2:19; R. Yitzchak Isaac Herzog, *Hechal Yitzchak* 2:31; R. Eliezer Waldenberg, *Tzitz Eliezer* 2:19; *Piskai Din Rabaniyaim* 7:36. For a dissenting view, see R. Yosef Henkin, *Perushai Ibra* 1:4.

12. See Shulchan Aruch 44:4 (first opinion). Indeed, many authorities aver that there is no dispute between the two opinions; one is aware of the fact, and one is not. *Kiddushin she-lo nimsaru le-bi'ah* is a halachic concept and not a factual one.

13. For a discussion of this, see *Iggrot Moshe* 1:79.

14. This is the talmudic discussion of an *iylonit*; for a lengthy review of this issue, see *Seredai Aish* 3:33, which concludes that it is possible that a *get* is not needed.

15. A *ma'ase kinyan.*
16. See Shulchan Aruch, Choshen Mishpat 232:3–9. Choshen Mishpat 232:6 reads:

> Anything which is agreed by the members of the city (state) as a defect that one must return the item for, one must return the item when that defect is found. Anything which all agree is not a defect, one need not return the item for as it is not a defect, one need not return the item unless one made it explicit [that such was a condition]. Anyone who does business unconditionally does so in reliance on common commercial custom.

17. Chulin 50a. "Kosher" here refers to a physiological defect in the cow that prevents it from ever being kosher, rather than a defect in the slaughtering process.
18. Many *trefa*s cannot be detected until after slaughter.
19. As noted by Tosafot (Bava Kama 110a), this does not apply to the case where a person purchased a cow and then it became *teref*; even though it is true that when he purchased it he desired that it neither be *teref* nor become *teref*, the latter is not subject to disclosure, and thus cannot be an implied condition in the deal. Of course, as per note 77 below, this could be a formal *tenai*, but formal *tenai'im* require very specific formulas, and cannot be implicitly created. For more on this, see *Bet Halevi* 3:3, who explicitly discusses this issue.
20. In the sense of intentional misrepresentation.
21. Of course it is easier to prove the lack of agreement when there was actual intent to defraud. However, that is merely evidentiary in nature and not directly relevant. Consider the discussion found in *Avnei Chafetz* 30 about one who contracts marriages with the intent to defraud the woman, or *Mari ha-Kohein Tenyana* 13. The same approach can be found in the discussion of one who marries a woman and does not inform her that he is already married to another.
22. Consider, for example, the discussion found in *Yabia Omer*, Even ha-Ezer 2:9 concerning the case of a woman who represents herself as a virgin but is not. He concludes that the marriage remains valid and a *get* would be needed if they chose to separate over that issue.
23. It might not apply to the *yibum* relationship, in that *yibum*, like divorce according to Torah law, does not require the consent of the woman in order to be valid. Thus the position of those *rishonim* concerning the apostate brother's not voiding the marriage is not inconsistent with this.
24. Rama, Even ha-Ezer 39:4.
25. Ibid.
26. Shulchan Aruch, Even ha-Ezer 39:3.

27. For examples, see *Otzar ha-Poskim* 39:17–27, which discusses a variety of hypothetical cases.

28. Shulchan Aruch, Even ha-Ezer 39:1–8.

29. *Iggrot Moshe,* Even ha-Ezer 4:83 (2) in the last sentence of that section.

30. Rambam, Ishut 6:1–5; for an excellent short essay on this topic, see "Me-Pi ha-Shmu'a," *Mesorah* 2 (5744), pp. 39–42.

31. Consider the case of a couple who go through a perfectly proper Jewish wedding ceremony for the sake of allowing one of the two parties to acquire a residency permit ("green card" in America) based on the citizenship of the spouse. As Rabbi Moshe Feinstein notes in *Iggrot Moshe,* Even ha-Ezer 4:112, even in a case where the ceremony was completely proper in form (*chupah kedin*), if neither party had any intent to enter into a valid wedding, even if the putative couple takes up residence, commences a sexual relationship, and acts as husband and wife after the ceremony, they are not married, since they both agreed that they would not be married by this ceremony. (Of course, as a matter of proof to this proposition, they would have to demonstrate that they had informed others before the ceremony took place that it was bogus.)

32. Even ha-Ezer 38–39 (*en passant*); but see Rema, Even Ha-Ezer 157:4.

33. Even ha-Ezer 157:4.

34. See the extensive analysis of this topic in *Pitchai Teshuva*, Even ha-Ezer 157:4.

35. Either through a formal ceremony or through living together sexually with the intent to marry; see Even ha-Ezer 31:8–9.

36. When exactly does one assert that there is an implicit *tenai* and when is there a mistake (*ta'ut*) is, at the margins, a matter in dispute. Rambam, cited above in note 30, limits *tenai* to cases of explicit invocation of the conditions, following the explicit doubling formulations (the doubling formulation requires that one mention what happens both if the condition is fulfilled, and if it is not); all other cases fall under the rules of *ta'ut*. Ra'avad (*Ishut* 6:1) disagrees, and allowing for cases of implicit condition in all matters other than marriage and divorce. Ramban (Gitten 45b and other places) categorizes all prospective stipulations as *tenai* and all retrospective conditions as *ta'ut*. Tosafot (Kiddushin 45b) avers that all implicit conditions are really cases of *ta'ut* when the conditions are the normative ones expected in any transaction, and the only time one can have a condition is if it is made explicit as a *tenai*. Rabbi Chaim Soloveitchik (*Chidushim*) argues that Rambam actually distinguishes between those conditions that are designed to prevent the marriage from taking effect immediately (*me-achshav*) and those stipulations that are immediately fulfillable at the time of the marriage are merely a form or

ta'ut; Rabbi Moshe Feinstein (*Iggrot Moshe*, Even ha-Ezer 1:79–80) rejects this view, and accepts the formulation of the Rambam mentioned above. For more on this, see note 19, which discusses the matter in the context of commercial norms.

37. Why that should be so can be readily explained on a social level and should not be understood to mean that the absence of this discussion indicates anything halachicly. Indeed, one can explicitly find such a discussion among the *rishonim*, who discuss *ach mumar*. I will leave an explanation of why the Shulchan Aruch does not address that problem in the context of husbands, and only brothers of husbands, for another time.

38. Even ha-Ezer 154:2.

39. Beit Meir on *id.* stands alone in arguing with this approach conceptually and is inclined to accept that there can be no concept of *kiddushai ta'ut* for a woman for defects found in a man. He argues that the talmudic language seems to be limited to defects in the woman. One could respond to this objection by noting that the linguistic reference in the Gemara is to the typical case.

40. See for example, *Terumat ha-Deshen* 223. It is important to read closely Rashi's explanation of the Bava Kama 110b case, as Rashi indicates quite clearly that a social judgment is being rendered. Indeed, the language of *annan sadi* ("we attest") is consistent with a statement of social reality and not rabbinic decree.

41. Consider the case of the man who is deathly ill, hides this fact from his fiancee, dies soon after the wedding, and leaves only a brother who is six months old to do *chalitzah*. As was noted by Rabbi Chaim Berlin (*Even Shoham, Kuntres ha-Agunot*), this states a strong case in that in such a circumstance one is fairly certain that this woman would not agree to marry this man.

42. The strongest such statement by a modern *posek* can be found in Rabbi Henken's *Perush Ibra*, p. 41, which clearly is discussing the facts of marriage and not the halachah.

43. *Iggrot Moshe*, Even ha-Ezer 1:80 and *Achiezer* 1:27.

44. *Tav lemativ tan du, melemativ armelo.*

45. *Anan sa'adi de-minach necha la be-kol de-ho.*

46. Bava Kama 110b–111a and Ketubot 75a.

47. See for example, *Iggrot Moshe*, Even ha-Ezer 4:113 or Even ha-Ezer 4:83 or Acheizer 1:27, each of whom reaches this result, which is fully consistent with the discussion found in the various *rishonim* about the *ach mumar* problem.

48. For example, *Iggrot Moshe* is inclined to state that the principle is completely inapplicable to people who are not religious; *Iggrot Moshe*, Even ha-Ezer 4:83.

49. See Eruvin 82a, Ketubot 59b, 65b, 122b–123a.

50. Even ha-Ezer 82:7.

51. The facts of this case indicate that a child is better off being placed with the mother or father in any particular case, even if the talmudic presumptions might not place this child with this parent at this time. For more on this topic, see Eliav Shochatman, "The Essence of the Principles Used in Child Custody in Jewish Law," *Shenaton le-Mishpat ha-Ivri* 5:285 (5738) and Michael Broyde, "Child Custody in Jewish Law: A Conceptual Analysis of the Issues," *J. Halacha and Contemporary Society* 37 (1999), p. 21–46.

52. *Terumat ha-Deshen* 223.

53. That one can take possession of something for a person when it is an unmitigated benefit for them.

54. *Tav lemativ tan du, melemativ armelo.*

55. Such can also be implied from the view of Rava in Ketubot 75a. This is also consistent with the practices of *batai din* throughout the world who permit the use of the *get zekui* procedure where it clearly is of benefit for the woman to be divorced.

A number of readers have referred me to a recorded lecture Rabbi Soloveitchik gave in which he indicated that the principle of *tav lemativ tan du, melemativ armelo* is an immutable presumption that cannot change and is applicable to every person and every marriage under every circumstance. As has been noted throughout this appendix, that view cannot be correct; there is a wealth of halachic literature to suggest that even if this presumption is immutable on a general level, it is not applicable to every marriage and under every circumstance. Indeed, I suspect that Rabbi Soloveitchik's formulation at that lecture is limited to opposing the wholesale abandonment of the principle rather than merely asserting that it did not apply in any given case or set of cases.

56. *Iggrot Moshe*, Even ha-Ezer 4:113.

57. 1:79 concerns *kiddushai ta'ut* in the case of impotence and 1:80 insanity. In both cases, Iggrot Moshe concludes that the marriages are void, since no one would marry a person who is an occasional lunatic or is impotent.

58. Ibid. Emphasis added.

59. See *Iggrot Moshe*, Even ha-Ezer 4:73 and 4:13 for the cases of heart disease and sterility (or even perhaps compelled abortion). Rabbi Feinstein, surprisingly enough, does not consider *kiddushai ta'ut* the case where a 20-year-old woman was seeking to marry and did not wish to reveal that she had not yet begun to menstruate. See *Iggrot Moshe*, Even ha-Ezer 3:27, where he argues that such conduct can be explained as within the framework of normal. However, I believe that Rabbi Feinstein is

less inclined to consider defects in the woman to be relevant for *kiddushai ta'ut* than defects in the man, since defects in the woman can be grounds to compel her to receive a *get*, thus reducing the need for this rationale. This important and logical insight was first noted by R. Chaim Ozer Grodzinski in *Achiezer* 1:27.

60. *Tav le-mativ tan du, me-le-mativ armelo.*

61. *Anan sa'adi de-minach necha la be-kol de-ho.*

62. Besides the many halachic authorities cited throughout this appendix, one can see a discussion of the relationship between the state of mind of the parties, the intent to marry only a person of a particular character, and the rules of *tav le-mativ tan du, me-le-mativ armelo* and *anan sa'adi de-minach necha la be-kol de-ho.* The following list is not intended to be complete and should not be taken to indicate that each *teshuvah* permits each woman to leave each marriage without a *get.* Rather these *poskim* discuss whether one assumes that, given the social reality of the couple and the society, one can consider whether there was enough of a failure in understanding the agreement that the marriage was not validly entered into when any particular defect is present. They are as follows: *Ain Yitzchak* 24, who discusses impotence as grounds for hidden error; *Avnei Chefetz* 30, who discusses marriage to a criminal as grounds for hidden error; *Berchat Retzai* 107, who discusses epilepsy and what perhaps is polio as grounds for hidden error; *Beit ha-Levi* 3:3, who discusses serious defects generally as grounds for hidden error; *Chayim Shel Shalom* 2:81, who discusses apostasy as grounds for hidden error; *Chavat Ya'ir* 221, who discusses impotence as grounds for hidden error; *Chelkat Ya'akov* 3:114, who discusses apostasy by the husband when the wife is secular as grounds for hidden error; *Divrei Malkeil* 1:86, who discusses whether there is a difference between intentional fraud and accidental misleading information as grounds for hidden error; *Even Yekara* 53, who discusses epilepsy as grounds for hidden error; *Hari Besamim Mahadura* 2, Even ha-Ezer 147, who discusses insanity as grounds for hidden error; *Mahari ha-Kohein Tenyana* 13, who discusses marriage to a criminal as grounds for hidden error; *Melu'ai Even* 29, who discusses insanity as grounds for hidden error (he is *makil* for a reason that is astonishing, and beyond the scope of this appendix); *Noda Beyehuda*, Even ha-Ezer 1:88, who discusses apostasy as grounds for hidden error (this is at tension with his *Tenyana* 80); *Seredai Aish* 3:33, who discusses impotence and apostasy as grounds for hidden error; *Sha'arit Yosef* 44, who discusses apostasy as grounds for hidden error; *Tashbetz* 1:1, who discusses impotence as grounds for hidden error; *Yad David (Piskai Halachot)* 186:3, who advances a general rule that any illness that would be grounds for compelled divorce after marriage, if

hidden would be grounds for *kiddushai ta'ut* if hidden; *Yeriyot Shlomo* 1:8, who discusses what appears to be syphilis as grounds for hidden error.

63. The reason that one would have to know beyond a doubt, rather than by some lower standard, is that after what appears to be a valid and proper wedding ceremony the couple is presumed married and the woman *bechezkat eshet ish*. Halachah would not allow one in that presumptive status to remarry without a near certain insistence that the presumptive status is wrong. For more on this, see *Perushai Abira* (Rabbi Henkin), p. 41.

64. *Umdana de-muchach.*

65. Chazon Ish, Even ha-Ezer, Ketubot 69:23. He immediately thereafter makes reference to the difference between a diseased person and an apostate, and how the presumption is that she would not desire the second but perhaps would the first.

66. How exactly one demonstrates the presence of an categorical presumption is a significant halachic dispute among the poskim as to the relationship between presumption, categorical presumptions, and near certain knowledge that has no witnesses. It is generally accepted that an *umdana de-muchach* is somewhat more than 90 percent, with some halachic authorities asserting the percent to be 95 percent and some to 98 percent.

67. Her ability to leave without a *get.*

68. Such is our practice, for example, when individuals who are married in a civil ceremony become religious. When they realize that their civil marriage was void in the eyes of halachah and yet continue to stay married, they are married.

69. *Aruch ha-Shulchan*, Even ha-Ezer 39:13.

70. *Seredai Aish* 3:33.

71. A sexual relationship being one of the three ways the couple can create a valid *kinyan*. In the alternative, the couple could actually have another wedding ceremony. For more on this, see *Yabia Omer* 2:9.

72. *Aruch ha-Shulchan*, Even ha-Ezer 39:13 quoted above, and others. It is for this reason that there is a greater consensus that *kiddushai ta'ut* in cases of impotence is easier than any other case, since there is no possibility of post-discovery ratification of the marriage through a sexual relationship, which, given the nature of the *ta'ut* here, cannot happen.

73. In the case of a relatively insignificant defect, there is a dispute about whether the first marriage continues or a second marriage is created; compare the views of Beit Shmuel (Even ha-Ezer 68:6) and the Beit Meir (Even ha-Ezer 68). However, a strong case can be made concerning Rama's argument in Even ha-Ezer 67, based on his ruling in the case of a "marriage" to a lunatic who recovers. For more on this issue, see Yabia Omer, Even ha-Ezer 2:9.

74. *Aruch ha-Shulchan*, Even ha-Ezer 39:13.

75. The word "known" is vitally important, because a consensus has developed that when the couple does not know that the marriage is deficient, they do not cure the defect by continuing to live together as husband and wife, since they lack any intent to ratify the marriage or create a new one. One cannot ratify that which one does not think is deficient. A similar concept is present in the conversion of minors.

76. This is the dispute between Rabbi Moshe Feinstein and Rabbi Yosef Henkin and has been explained well by others. The near unanimous practice in America is to rule like Rabbi Feinstein, at least in the case where a *get* cannot be procured.

77. The first is important because it goes to the question of whether a woman would accept a marriage proposal from one who is sexually unfit for purely economic reasons; the second is relevant because it goes to the question of whether a woman would accept a marriage proposal from one who is unfit for other reasons so as to have a licit sexual outlet. The first of these factors is considered in *Iggrot Moshe,* Even ha-Ezer 1:79, and the second in Even ha-Ezer 4:83. Rabbi Moshe Feinstein is prepared to consider the possibility that the principles used by halachah in these circumstances differ significantly when the couple is not generally religious, and even more so when they are promiscuous.

78. Consider these five cases:

A. A physically normal man represents, while dating a woman, that he is a partner in a large law firm and earning $400,000 per year. In fact, he works in the copy department earning $17,000. Indeed, he actively perpetuated this fraud by bringing his fiancee to see "his" large office in the law firm one early Sunday morning. The moment the woman found out these facts, but after the marriage, she left him. She claims *kiddushai ta'ut.*

B. A woman has a physical defect present from birth that prevents both of her breasts from lactating. The man and woman are both modern professionals and did intend that their children would be breast-fed. The marriage ended unrelated to this problem, and he claims *kiddushai ta'ut.*

C. A man deceives a woman regarding three different issues; he tells her that he is a partner in a business in which he is really an employee; that he is a citizen when he really needs to marry her so that he can get a green card; and that he is 27 when he is really 30. She discovers each of these defects after the couple has separated because of incompatibility; he will not give her a *get.*

D. A man is impotent and hides that fact from his wife (he might not have been aware of it, in fact). After he tries to fix this problem medically for a number of years, the woman wishes to leave the marriage without a *get,* because she does not wish to be considered a divorcee and she has never had a sexual relationship with her husband.

E. A man states that he will not marry a woman who does not cover her hair. The man and woman agree, while courting, that his wife will cover her hair when she marries him. Immediately after the wedding she announces that she will not and never intended to.

The purpose of these five cases is not to provide normative answers to these questions, but rather to insist that categorical answers to each can be found only in a sociological review of the halachah. Each of these cases could be *kiddushai ta'ut* (although in each there is no doubt that a *get* should be given if possible). One is required to undertake a social determination of what the categorical presumption is in each case, and whether each of these defects rises to the level of a significant defect. Only when there is either a categorical presumption present in our society, or an explicit discussion of ground rule norms by the couple *and* a categorical rejection of the marriage once the deviation from the norm or agreement is made clear, might the marriage be void. Determining when that happens requires both a fluency with halachah and a familiarity with social norms.

Appendix C

1. This appendix derives from a number of articles and exchanges I have had in *Tradition*. See "The New York State *Get* Law," *Tradition* 29:4 (1995), pp. 3–14 and "The 1992 New York *Get* Law: An Exchange" *Tradition* 31:3 (1997), pp. 23–41, as well as letters to the editor in *Tradition* 32:1 (1997), pp. 99–100 and *Tradition* 32:3 (1998), pp. 91–97.

2. Domestic Relations Law §236B(5) formally states:

> In any decision made pursuant to this subdivision the court shall, where appropriate, consider the effect of a barrier to remarriage, as defined in subsection six of section two hundred and fifty three of this article, on the factors enumerated in paragraph (d) of this sub-division.

Section 253(6) limits "barriers to remarriage" to situations where a *get* is withheld.

3. For a review of this area, and of the various criticism of the law, see Irving Breitowitz, *Between Civil and Religious Law: The Plight of the Agunah in American Society* (Greenwood Press, 1993), pp. 209–238 as well as various articles and letters to the editor in the pages of *Tradition*.

4. The crucial words are "illicit coercion." Not all coercion is illicit; *Pitchai Teshuva*, Even ha-Ezer 134 and many commentators, both before and after, devised many perfectly legal forms of coercion to encourage the giving of a *get*. This includes social ostracization, dismissal from one's job,

denouncement, withholding of benefits, and many other actions. Even in circumstances where there is no halachic reason to give a *get*, such coercion or persuasion is still permitted.

5. For more on this, see Breitowitz, *Between Civil and Religious Law*, pp. 179–209.

6. See Responsa of Rabbi Yosef Shalom Elyashiv, 1 Elul 5752, and Breitowitz, *Between Civil and Religious Law*, pp. 230–236.

7. In addition there are those who argue that the law as written itself exempts from its application those cases where Jewish law would not allow an economic penalty. For more on this line of reasoning, and an extremely thorough reply, see Breitowitz, *Between Civil and Religious Law*, pp. 233–238.

8. Rabbi Gedalia Dov Schwartz, "The 1992 New York *Get* Law," *Journal of Halacha and Contemporary Society* 27 (1994), pp. 26–34 .

9. See, e.g., Rabbi Yosef Shalom Elyashiv, as cited in Breitowitz, *Between Civil and Religious Law*, pp. 230–231.

10. See, e.g., *Ran-Dav's County Kosher, Inc., v. New Jersey*, 608 A.2d 1353 (N.J., 1992) (stating that New Jersey may not, as a matter of constitutional law, permit only one standard of kosher and prohibit other, tenably kosher, institutions that adhere to a lower standard to claim to be kosher).

11. See, e.g., Menachem Elon, *Jewish Law: History, Sources, Principles, 1914–1917* (Jewish Publication Society, 1994), pp. 50–51.

12. See Breitowitz, *Between Civil and Religious Law*, pp. 163–179.

13. Who should determine when and if an apparently valid *get* is actually invalid is answered simply: before one asserts that a validly written *get*, given by recognized *mesader* which comes with a strong presumption of validity, is not valid, one should investigate to determine what the facts were. The burden should be on those who question the *patur* of a recognized bet din, which attests to the validity of the *get*. As Rabbi Feinstein (*Iggrot Moshe*, Even ha-Ezer 1:137) states: "We should not contemplate that invalidity of a *get* arranged by a rabbi appointed for this process, and claim perhaps a *get* was written in violation of *halachah*."

14. Rabbi Moshe Feinstein, *Iggrot Moshe*, Even ha-Ezer 3:44. Rabbi Feinstein, however, is hesitant to rely on this rationale absent other lenient factors. The rationale for his ruling is very simple. He argues that the prohibition of a compelled *get* is limited to situations where the compulsion is used to divorce a couple who actually wish to remain married. Compulsion in a case where divorce is truly desired does not create a *get me'useh*.

15. Rabbi Abraham Isaiah Karelitz, *Chazon Ish*, Even ha-Ezer 99:2.

16. Rabbi Yitzhak Isaac Herzog, *Otzar ha-Poskim* 2:11–12 (appendix) and *Hechal Yitzchak* 2. The ruling that coercion does not invalidate a *get* when divorce is genuinely desired can perhaps be also explained by combining the rulings of Rabbi Henkin and Herzog discussed above. First, one must realize that there is an obligation to have a Jewish divorce once there is an irreconcilable separation and that this is commanded by Jewish law, as Rabbi Henkin states above. Second, Rabbi Herzog rules that coercion does not invalidate a Jewish divorce that is an obligation (*mitzvah*) even if not judicially mandated (*kofin*). Thus, since all cases where the husband genuinely desires divorce are irreconcilable separations, one comes to the conclusion that once there is a desire to end the marriage, and the only disagreement concerns terms, coercion does not invalidate the *get*, since the *get* is obligatory.

17. Rabbi Tzvi Gartner, *Sefer Kefiya ba-Get*, p. 244.

18. For a full discussion of these issues, see Rabbi J. David Bleich, *Contemporary Halakhic Problems* II (Hoboken, NJ: KTAV, 1986), pp. 94–103 and *Piskai Din Rabaniyim* 10:300–308.

19. Rabbi Yitzhak Isaac Leibes, *Beit Avi* 4:169.

20. See Rabbi Yehuda Leib Grauburt, *Ha-Valim be-Neimim*, Even ha-Ezer 55, which rules, in the alternative, that secular law provides a woman with financial rights against her husband (or his estate). Such can also be found in Rabbi Joseph Trani (*Mabit*), Responsa 1:309.

21. Homer Clark and Carol Glowinsky, *Domestic Relations*, 5th ed., p. 809.

22. David Kaufman, "The New York Equitable Distribution Statute," *Brooklyn Law Review* 53:845 (1987).

23. One commentator who sought to claim that any situation where the secular law recognizes that the parties "are free to reach any agreement they want" precludes an application of *dina de-malchuta* misunderstands the relevant issue here. The question is "does the husband own the assets according to secular law," and the answer is that assets in the marital estate are owned by neither party, and can be distributed only by mutual consent or judicial declaration. This type of ownership can certainly be accepted by halachah and is even more legitimate under a theory of common commercial practice (*minhag ha-sochrim*) than under *dina de-malchuta*.

24. See R. Yehuda Leib Grauburt, *Ha-Valim ba-Neimim*, Even ha-Ezer 55, which rules, in the alternative, that secular law provides a woman with financial rights against her husband (or his estate); R. Joseph Trani, *Mabit* 1:309, is yet another such responsa. For a similar type of claim, see R. Yitzhak Isaac Liebes, *Beit Avi* 4:169. Similar reasoning can be implied from R. Moshe Feinstein's ruling (*Iggrot Moshe*, Even ha-Ezer 1:137) that the wife's waiver of past-due support payments mandated by secular law, in

return for the husband's issuing a *get*, is a form of permissible coercion which does not invalidate the *get*. This waiver of a financial claim is valid coercion only in a case where the woman's claim to the money is halachically valid, since the wife is entitled to these payments through *dina de-malchuta*. Indeed, Rabbi Feinstein implies that this is the more likely result in his analysis found in *Iggrot Moshe*, Even ha-Ezer 1:137; see also *Pitchai Teshuva*, Even ha-Ezer 134:9–10.

25. It is important to note, however, that the practice of resolving these disputes in secular court remains a clear violation of halachah, which requires that these types of disputes be resolved in beit din. See Choshen Mishpat 26:2. However, the fact that these disputes should be resolved in bet din does not in any way lead one to assert that bet din cannot accept the common commercial custom of using secular law as the basis to resolve this dispute. Indeed, Rabbi Mordechai Willig's prenuptial agreement explicitly lists that possibility as an option.

26. Letter of Approbation to R. Neharia Moshe Gotel, *Heshtanut Hatevaim Behalacha* (5755), p. 15.

27. See Breitowitz, *Between Civil and Religious Law*, pp. 228–229. One can add that there certainly were *poskim* who ruled that even property illicitly taken from the husband may be used as leverage to induce the writing of a *get* where the property was not originally taken for the purpose of inducing the issuing of a *get*. As was noted by Professor Irving Breitowitz in his extraordinary book (n. 637 and pp. 214–217), many *acharonim* accepted this rationale. This viewpoint would validate the use of equitable distribution penalties even according to those who rule that the wife has no claim on the jointly held assets. This rationale is particularly proper if the 1992 *Get* Law is merely a support bill and not a penalty law.

28. Indeed, the strongest rationale for supporting the 1992 *Get* Law as a before-the-fact rule would be to label it as a support and maintenance law, which many aver can never lead to coerced divorce. However, the secular purpose of the 1992 *Get* Law remains unclear, and we all wait for some clarification from the New York Court of Appeals.

29. Rabbi Joseph Kolon (Maharik), Responsa 63.

30. See Rema, Even ha-Ezer 134:5 and *Pitchai Teshuva* 134:11–12.

31. Either a *kofin* or *yotzi* situation; see Shulchan Aruch, Even ha-Ezer 119 for more on this.

32. See Rabbis Herzog and Leibes, cited in notes 16 and 19.

33. Rabbenu Yeruchum, *Sefer Toledot Adam ve-Chava*, Netiv 24, Chelek 1.

34. Rabbi Yoab Weingarten, *Chelkat Yoav*, D'nei Ones 5.

35. Rabbi Elijah of Vilna, *Bi'ur ha-Gra*, Even ha-Ezer 154:67.

It is important to note that this view does not rise to the level of normative halachah, and I want to note explicitly that they should be used only as one side of a multisided *sefek sefeka,* as numerous *acharonim* have done. While my reading of the Gra (as supporting the concept that economic duress does not create coercion) would put the Gra in tension with most *acharonim* and *rishonim,* such a reading of the Gra is not unique to me (see Rabbi Ovadia Yosef's comments in *Yabia Omer,* Even ha-Ezer 7:23 and 8:25). While the Gra is ambiguous on this issue in Choshen Mishpat 205:18, in *Bi'ur ha-Gra,* Even ha-Ezer 154:67, he states:

> Since he can flee to another city and *any situation where they do not do violence to his body is not called force.*

36. Rambam, Ishut 14:8.

37. Rabbi Herzog, as in note 16.

38. See the many sources cited in Rabbi Ovadia Yosef, *Yabia Omer,* Even ha-Ezer 3:18, where he cites many authorities who accept that economic coercion may be used in a case of reasonable and provable repugnancy (either *post facto* [*bedeeved*] or *ab initio* [*lechathila*]), including Rabbi Yosef himself.

39. Rabbi Shimon Duran, *Tashbetz* 2:168, Rabbi Yom Tom Ishbili (Ritva) as quoted in Rabbi Joseph Karo, *Beit Yosef,* Even ha-Ezer 154, Rema, Even ha-Ezer 134:5. While it is true that *Mishkanot Yaakov* 38 is strict on this matter and argues with the Rama, a clear consensus agrees with the Rama in this regard, at least *bede'eved.* Certainly in a case where the husband does not categorically state at the time of the *seder ha-get* that he is being coerced, which is a very rare circumstance, the *get* is valid; *Levush* 134 and Chazon Ish, Even ha-Ezer 99:5, but see *Aruch ha-Shulchan,* Even ha-Ezer 134:26–29. (Were the husband to state that he was coerced, without a doubt the bet din would not write the *get,* although many *poskim* would permit such a *get* to be written.)

40. Rabbi Yitzhak Elhanan Spector, *Be'er Yitzchak* 10(8).

41. See Rabbi Moshe Feinstein, *Iggrot Moshe,* Even ha-Ezer 4:106 (at the end) and 1:137. It is important to realize that Rabbi Feinstein (in 4:106) does not require that the secular award be lower than that mandated by Jewish law, only comparable. This assumes that the support provisions of the 1992 *Get* Law are truly support provisions and not merely penalty clauses in the guise of support. Their proper understanding is disputed by various secular legal scholars; see Breitowitz, *Between Civil and Religious Law,* pp. 213–229, esp. n. 634, 636, 640, 643 and 662.

42. More significantly, in a case where the woman's claim of repugnancy toward her husband is based on reasonable and provable grounds (*amatla mevu'eret*), many authorities accept Rambam's rule that coercion is permissible as correct either *lechathilah* or *bede'eved.* (See the many sources cited in Rabbi Ovadia Yosef, *Yabia Omer,* Even ha-Ezer 3:18).

43. See Even ha-Ezer 77.

44. If my argument above is correct and, in fact, the common custom in our community is to determine separation agreements on the basis of secular law, a strong claim could be made that the custom is to pay support even in a situation where the woman might halachically be classified as a *moredet*, so long as secular law and custom are to provide support. This approach would validate the *Get* Law, even if the woman is a *moredet*. (My thanks to Professor Breitowitz, who first pointed this out.)

45. *Tzitz Eliezer* 18:58. This *psak* can also be found in *Piskai Din Rabaniyin* 1:238 and 9:171 as the *psak* of the rabbinical courts of Israel and is defended by Rabbi Herzog and others in the appendix to volume 2 of *Otzar ha-Poskim*. Particularly the analysis found in 9:171 supports the contention that the *moredet* issue is not significant, because a *get* should be given even to a *moredet*.

46. Tosafot, Zevachim 2b s.v. *stam*. The approach of Tosafot is rejected, or limited to a case where the woman does not want to be divorced, by a breadth of authorities, including *Noda be-Yehuda*, Tenyana, Even ha-Ezer 12; Rabbi Akiva Eiger, *Derush ve-Chedish, teshuvah* at the end of the *ketavim* section; Chatam Sofer, Nedarim 89a s.v. *be-rishona* (cited in the preface), *Beit Meir*, Even ha-Ezer 117, *Pitchai Teshuva* 154 (4, 7) and can be implied from *Aruch ha-Shulchan*, Even ha-Ezer 178:25–26. See the short article by Rabbi Yaakov Moshe Toledano in the appendix to *Otzar ha-Poskim* (2:16) who avers that the approach which requires a husband to support his wife who is a *moredet,* and thus not technically entitled to support, in order to encourage the writing of a *get* by the husband, is the normative halachah without a doubt. Consider the simple remarks of Rabbi Moshe Sofer, in *Chidushei Chatam Sofer*, Nedarim 89a, s.v. *be-rishona*:

> But, when a woman demands a *get*, since he cannot fulfill his obligation of marital relations, why should he gratuitously withhold a *get*? Even if she sinned and committed deliberate adultery, and is prohibited to return to the marriage, nonetheless, we should not let him withhold a *get* from her.

47. In the economic literature this situation is referred to as "negotiating in the shadow of the law."

48. See Rabbi Shabtai ben Meir ha-Kohein (Shach), Yoreh Deah 98:9, who states that correctable gaps in one's factual knowledge do not create legally significant "doubt" in Jewish law.

49. Rabbi Moshe Isserles (Rama), Even ha-Ezer 154 (*seder ha-get*) in the introduction to the appendix.

50. One additional point needs to be considered in discussing the 1992 Get Law. The possible relationship between the rule *sha'at hadechak kemo*

bede'evad ("a time of urgency is to be treated as if it is after the fact") and the 1992 *Get* Law also requires some exploration. Given the reality of the agunah problems in America, and the fact that not solving the problem in any given case can also lead to *mamzerut* (due either to women abandoning Orthodox Judaism and marrying anyway, or receiving a "Jewish divorce" from a "bet din" that claims to be releasing many agunot without a *get*), perhaps a less than ideal, but minimally acceptable solution is all that we can realistically aspire to, and the 1992 *Get* Law is such. Maybe it is halachically better to rely on the many leniencies advanced by many *poskim* in support of validating *gittin* issued in light of the 1992 *Get* Law as *sha'at ha-dechak kemo be-di'avad*, rather than maintaining the none-too-pleasant or successful status quo, which also leads to *mamzerut*. This is even truer given the recent public desecrations of God's Name that have occurred relating to the use of physical force to address the agunah problem. That calculus would require the approval of the foremost halachic authorities of our times.

Appendix D

1. Much of the material in this appendix is derived from the fine work of my colleague at Emory, John Witte, and is expanded upon in his book *From Sacrament to Contract: Marriage, Religion and Law in the Western Tradition* (Westminster John Knox Press, 1997).

2. "What God has joined, let no man put asunder" (Mark 10:7).

3. With the sixteenth century came the covenantal model of marriage, which modified the social model of marriage in that marriage was now seen as an association of the entire community, grounded in the order of creation and governed by the law of God for the benefit of humankind.

4. Uniform Marriage and Divorce §201

5. Uniform Premarital Agreement Act §3.

6. Uniform Marriage and Divorce §306.

7. Joel A. Nichols, "Note Louisiana's Covenant Marriage Law: A First Step Toward a More Robust Pluralism in Marriage and Divorce Law?" *Emory Law Journal* 47:929 (1998), pp. 934–935.

8. Louisiana Covenant Marriage Act, 1997 LA Acts 1380.

Appendix E

1. American Jurisprudence 2d Criminal Law, 21A §1034.

2. In the classical common law, even the act of marriage itself was a form of civil death for the woman. The famous Lawes Resolution of Women's Rights of 1632 described marriage as follows:

Wedlock is a locking together. It is true that man and wife are one person; but understand in what manner. When a small brook or little river incorporates with the Thames the poor river loses her name. . . . A woman, as soon as she is married is called covert . . . she has lost her stream.

In the common law, one commentator noted that "man and wife are one—but the man is the one." Granville L. Williams, "The Legal Unity of Husband and Wife," *Modern Law Review* 10:16,18 (1947).

3. 63 NW 83 (1895).

4. 287 NY 347 (1942)

5. See NY Matrimonial and Family Law §1.06 (McKinney 1998)

6. Jamal L. Nasir, *The Status of Women Under Islamic Law and Under Modern Islamic Legislation* 28 (1990).

7. See "New Tack for Egypt's Islamic Militants: Imposing Divorce," *New York Times,* (December 28, 1996), sec. 1, p. 22, which reads in part:

Governments have ways of silencing troublesome writers: assassination, imprisonment, torture, harassment, isolation. But Islamic militants in Egypt have pioneered a new method: lawsuits. In the last three years, religious zealots inspired by Sheik Yusuf el-Badry, an Egyptian who preached in 1992 in a mosque in Paterson, New Jersey, have filed more than 50 suits in Egyptian courts against writers and other intellectuals whose work they consider heretical or insulting to Islam.

No case has attracted more attention or indignation than that of Nasr Hamid Abu-Zaid, an Egyptian intellectual whom Egypt's courts branded a religious heretic last year. His legal problems, which involved fleeing Egypt rather than accept a court-mandated divorce from his wife, have outraged American and Arab scholars, feminists and human rights groups. The case has also embarrassed the Egyptian Government.

In June 1993, a group of such guardians of religious orthodoxy, led by Sheik Badry, filed suit against Mr. Abu-Zaid. They charged that his "perverse" and "atheistic" ideas proved that he was an "apostate," a traitor to Islam. Under Egyptian religious law, they argued, his marriage to a Muslim woman, a believer, was illegal and had to be dissolved.

In the first ruling on the case, in January 1994, a Personal Status court dismissed the Islamists' suit, finding that the plaintiffs lacked judicial standing. But the militants appealed. In June 1995, an appellate court ruled in their favor. Based on his academic writing, the court concluded, Mr. Abu-Zaid was, in fact, an apostate and therefore could not legally be married to Ms. Yunis. Since some interpretations of Islam say that Muslims should kill apostates who do not recant, or at least expel them from Muslim society, the ruling alarmed Arab and Western intellectuals.

Appendix F

1. A similar such agreement, written consistent with the laws of the state of Israel (and in Hebrew) was written by Professor Ariel Rosen-Tzvi of Tel Aviv Law School.

Table of References to the Bible, Talmud, Post-Talmudic Codes, Commentators, Responsa, Articles and Books

This section contains a table of reference to most of the works cited in this volume. I owe thanks to Avi Wagner of Georgetown Law School for preparing this material.

✳ ✳ ✳

Bible

Deuteronomy 22:19	141
Torah Shelemah, Genesis 2:24	141

Jerusalem Talmud

Bava Metzia 27b	148

Babylonian Talmud

Chulin 50a	170
Eruvin 82a	173
Gittin 89ab	149
Ketubot 11a	138
59b	173
65b	173
75a	173
123a	173
Yevamot 52a	138
64a	142
89a	138
118b	98

Talmudic Commentaries

Abromsky, Y. *Dinai Mamonot*	169
Chatam Sofer, Nedarim 89a, s.v. *berishona*	182
Rabbi Akiva Eiger, *Derush ve-Chidush*	182
Ramban, Gittin 45b	171
Rashi, Bava Kama 110b	173
Takanat ha-Geonim, p. 112	28
Tosafot, Bava Kama 110a	170
Kiddushin 45b	171
Ketubot 47b s.v. *shelo*	28
63a s.v. *aval*	28
72b s.v. *al*	169
73a s.v. *lo*	169

63a *vehamar Rav* — 149
63b *aval amra* — 149
Zevachim 2b s.v. *stam* — 182

Rambam and Commentators

Or Same'ach, Rambam,
  Gerushin 2:20 — 106–107
Rabbi Chaim Soloveitchik
  (Chiddushim) — 171
Rabbenu Yeruchum
  Sefer Toledot Adam ve-Chava
    Netiv 24, Chelek 1 — 182
Ra'avad, *Ishut* 6:1 — 171
Rambam, *Ishut* 6:15 — 171
  14:8 — 28, 182

Shulchan Aruch

Rama
  Even ha-Ezer 28:11 — 141
  39:4 — 171
  67 — 176
  134:5 — 162, 182
  134:8 — 107
  154 — 183
  154:21 — 150
  157:4 — 171
Shulchan Aruch
  Choshen Mishpat 5:14 — 144
  26:2 — 148, 180
  232:39 — 170
  331:1 — 148
  Even ha-Ezer 1:3 (with Rama) — 147
  1:9 — 28
  17:32–37 — 139
  17:56–57 — 139
  26, 37, 39, 39:1 — 169
  26:4 — 138
  31:89, 38, 39, 39:18, 39:3 — 171
  31:9 — 100
  38, 39, 44:4 (first opinion) — 170
  39 — 94, 97
  70, 77 — 156
  70:14 — 141
  77:2 — 28
  77 — 182
  80:13 — 163
  82:7, 154:2 — 173
  115 — 138
  117:11, 154:67. — 142
  119 — 182

Commentators on Shulchan Aruch

Aruch ha-Shulchan
  Even ha-Ezer 26:16 — 169
  39:13 — 173, 176
  134:26–29 — 163, 182
  154:52–53 — 142
  154:63 — 150
  178:25–26 — 182
Beit Meir
  Even ha-Ezer 82:7 — 173
  117 — 182
  154:2 — 173
Beit Shmuel
  Even ha-Ezer 68:6 — 176
  134:14 — 107
Biur ha-Gra
  Choshen Mishpat 205:18 — 182
  Even ha-Ezer 154:67 — 182
Chazon Ish
  Even ha-Ezer 99:2 — 179
  69:23 — 173
  99:5 — 163, 181
Pitchai Teshuva,
  Even ha-Ezer 134 — 179
  134:9–10 — 149, 180
  134:11–12 — 182
  Even ha-Ezer 154:41 — 82
  154:7 — 182
  154:30 — 150
  157:4 — 171
Shach
  Yoreh Deah 98:9 — 183

Modern Halacha Codes

Blau, Yitzchak, *Pischa Choshen*
  D'nei Halva'ah, II:29, n. 82 — 148
Gartner, Tzvi, *Sefer Kefiya ba-Get*
  (*Otzar ha-Poskim*, 5758) — 107
  pp. 118–120 — 139, 180
Henkin, Yoseph Eliahu
  Edut le-Yisrael 143–144 (reprinted in *Kol Kitvei ha-Rav Henkin*)
    1:115a–b — 142
  Perush Ibra 1:4 — 170
  p. 41 — 173
  p. 1107 — 71
  Kol Kitvei ha-Rav Henkin
    1:115a–b — 28

TABLE OF REFERENCES   189

Herzog, Yitzchak Isaac Halevi
Techuka le-Yisrael al pi ha-Torah
3:202, 209 ... 150
Izirar, Hagiz
Be'erurim be-Halachot ha-Ra'ayah
[R. Kook], p. 243 ... 150
Klein, Isaac
A Guide to Jewish Religious Practices
p. 293 ... 71
Toledano, Yaakov Moshe
Otzar ha-Poskim
2:16 (appendix) ... 182
39:12–13 ... 182
39:31:2 ... 169
39:17–27 ... 171
Schereschewsky, Benzion
D'nei Mis pacha [3rd. ed. 1984]
pp. 233–267 ... 138
*Seder Kiddushin ve-Nisuin Achar
Chatimat ha-Talmud* ... 161
Tn'ai be-N'suin ve-Get ... 71

Responsa

Achiezer 1:27 ... 169, 173
Agudot Azov
Even ha-Ezer 19(18) ... 107
Ain Yitzchak 24 ... 173
Ashkenazi, Betzalel, Responsa 6 ... 150
Responsa 10 ... 150
Avnei Chafetz 30 ... 170, 173
Avnei Nezer 171 ... 106, 107
Beer Yitzchak 10(8) ... 182
Even ha-Ezer 10:1 ... 107
Beit Avi 4:169 ... 149, 180, 182
Beit Efrayim, Tenyana
Even ha-Ezer 70 ... 111
Beit ha-Levi 3:3 ... 173
Beit Yisrael 164 ... 148
Berchat Retzai 107 ... 173
118 ... 107
Chatan Sofer 59 ... 107
Chavat Yair 221 ... 173
Chelkat Yaakov 3:114–165 ... 173
Chelkat Yoav, D'nei Ones 5 ... 182
Chemdat Shlomo
Even ha-Ezer 80(3) ... 107
Divrei Malkeil 1:86 ... 173
D'var Avraham 1:1 ... 148
Eliyahu Rabbah 13 ... 150

Even Shoham
Kuntres ha-Agunot ... 173
Even Yekara 53 ... 173
Hari Besamim Mahadura 2
Even ha-Ezer 147 ... 173
Ha-Valim ba-Neimim
Even ha-Ezer 55 ... 149, 180
Hechal Yitzchak 2:31 ... 170
Iggerot Moshe
Choshen Mishpat 1:72 ... 148
Even ha-Ezer 1:73–76 ... 170
1:79–80 ... 99, 141
1:79 ... 139, 169, 173, 176
1:80 ... 139, 173
1:137 ... 111, 149, 179, 180, 182
3:27 ... 173
3:44 ... 28, 105, 107, 179
4:73 ... 173
4:83 ... 173, 176
4:106 ... 110, 115, 182
4:107 ... 71, 163
4:112 ... 171
4:113 ... 173
79 ... 66
Yoreh Deah 4:15 ... 28, 143
Imira Aish, Even ha-Ezer 57 ... 106
Kuntres Tikkun Olam 3, Teshuva 1 ... 107
Mabit 1:309 ... 149, 180
Maharam al-Ashkar 48 ... 141, 161
Maharam me-Lublin 1 ... 150
39 ... 150
Mari ha-Kohein
Tenyana 13 ... 170, 173
Maharik, Responsa 63 ... 181
102 ... 148
Maharsham 9 ... 139
Maharashdam 108 ... 148
Maharyah ha-Levi 2:111 ... 148
Melunai Even 29 ... 173
Mishkanot Yaakov 3 ... 182
38 ... 163
Nachalat David 34 ... 107
Na'ot Desha 144 ... 107
Nidiv Lev 1213 ... 148
Noda be-Yehuda, Even ha-Ezer 1:88 ... 173
2:14 ... 182
2:80 ... 173
Oneg Yom Tov 173 ... 107
Or Zarua, Teshuva 126 ... 106
Orin T'letai 61 ... 107

Otzar ha-Chayim 209   71
Peskai Din Rabanayim 1:238   28, 156, 182
  7:36   170
  9:171   28, 156, 17
  10:300–308   180
Rabbenu Tam, *Sefer ha-Yashar*
  Chelek ha-Teshuvot 24   150
R. Chaim, *Or Zarua*, Teshuva 126   28
Rabbenu Yosef of Slutzk 79   107
Rashbash 339   107
Rashbatz 4:35   107
Responsa of Rabbi Yosef S.
  Elyashiv, 1 Elul 5752   179
Responsa of Rosh 43:8   142
Seredai Aish 3:33   170, 173
Sha'arit Yosef 44   173
Teshuvot ve-Hanhagot 1:730   147
  1:795 (rev. ed.)   160
Tashbetz 1:11   68
  2:168   182
  107   107
Terumat ha-Deshen 223   173, 98, 173
Teshuvot ha-Rosh 43:8   28
T'feret Tzvi, Even Ha-ezer 102   106, 107
Tzitz Eliezer 2:19   170
  18:58   28, 156, 182
Yabia Omer 2:9   170, 176
  3:2   147
Va-Yishal Shaul, Even Ha-ezer 2:20   106
  3:18   182
  7:23   149, 182
  8:25   182
Yad David (Piskai Halachot) 186:3   173
Yam shel Shalom 2:81   173
Yeri'ot Shlomo 1:8   173
Yosef Iggeret, *Divrei Yosef* 21   148

Miscellaneous Works

Amichai, Yehuda, "A Gentile Who Sum-
  mons a Jew to Bet Din"   160
Amital, Yehudah, "Rebuking a Jew: Theory
  and Practice"   147
Baard, Anne T., "34 Months and Still No
  Divorce"   146
Bazyler, Michael J., "The Rights of Women
  in the Soviet Union"   146
Berner, Nicole, "Child Custody Disputes
  Between Lesbians: Legal Strategies and
  Their Limitations"   161

Bleich, J. David, *Contemporary Halachic
  Problems II*   180
———., "Jewish Divorce: Judicial Miscon-
  ceptions and Possible Means of Civil
  Enforcement"   138, 146
Bone, Robert G., "Lon Fuller's Theory of
  Ajudication and the False Dichotomy
  Between Dispute Resolution and Public
  Law Models of Litigation,"   161
Breitowitz, Irving, *Between Civil and Reli-
  gious: The Plight of the Agunah in American
  Society*   xv, 71, 138, 141, 142, 162,
  164–65, 177–78, 181–82
Broyde, Michael J., "Child Custody in Jew-
  ish Law: A Conceptual Analysis of the
  Issues"   173
———., "Forming Religious Communities
  and Respecting Dissenters' Rights" in M.
  Broyde and J. Witte, eds. *Human Rights in
  Judaism: Cultural, Religious and Political
  Perspectives*   160, 166
———., "The New York State Get Law,"
                                        149, 164, 177
———., "The 1992 New York Get Law: An
  Exchange"   162, 177
———., *The Pursuit of Justice and Jewish
  Law*   148–49
Brozan, Nadine, "Women Allege Betrayal
  by Rabbis' Talk: Rare Lawsuits Complain
  Reputation as Jews Were Damaged," 153
Current Reform Responsa   166
Clark, Homer and Glowinsky, Carol,
  Domestic Relations   180
Dowell, Susan, *They Two Shall be One* 144
Elon, Menachem, *Jewish Law: History,
  Sources, Principles 1914–1917*
                                        41, 162, 179
Freeze, Chearan Y., *Making and Unmaking
  the Jewish Family: Marriage and Divorce in
  Imperial Russia, 1850–1914*   143
Freimann, Abraham H., *Seder Kiddushin ve-
  Nisu'in Acharai Chatimat ha-Talmud*
                                                  138
Freshman, Clark, "Privatizing Same Sex
  Marriage Through Alternative Dispute
  Resolution"   161
Friedman, Mordechai A., "Polygyny in Jew-
  ish Tradition and Practices: New Sources
  from the Cairo Geniza"   138

Frimer, Dov, *Grounds for Divorce Due to Immoral Behavior Other than Adultery According to Jewish Law* 138

Gastwort, Harold, *Corruption and Holiness: The Controversy over the Supervision of Jewish Dietary Practice in New York City* 156, 160

Harris, David, "Jews Will Be Israeli Majority for Foreseeable Future" 143

Hecht, Esther, "Chief Rabbi Agrees to Act on Prenuptial Agreement" 155

Jachter, Howard, "The Use of Video Telephone Conferences for a *Get* Procedure" 141

Kaufman, David, "The New York Equitable Distribution Statute" 180

Keinon, Herb, "Chief Rabbi Lets 24 Undivorced Men Remarry" 143

———., "Court Orders Bakshi Doron to Hear a Woman Whose Husband Was Allowed Second Wife" 143

———., "Man Barred from Remarriage Without Divorce" 143

Lindsay, Karen Ruth, "Can Kosher Fraud Statutes Pass the Lemon Test?" 149

Malinowitz, Chaim, "The 1992 New York Get Law," *Journal of Halacha and Contemporary Society* 27 (1994), pp. 526 149, 164

———. "The 1992 New York Get Law: An Exchange" 149, 165

Miller, Judith, "New Tack for Egypt's Islamic Militants: Imposing Divorce" 184

Nadel, Edward S., "New York's Get Laws: A Constitutional Analysis" 147

Nasir, Jamal L., *The Status of Women Under Islamic Law and Under Modern Islamic Legislation* 28 (1990) 184

Nevantzal, Avigdor, "Letter of Approbation to R. Neharia Moshe Gotel" 148, 181

Nichols, Joel A., "Note Louisiana's Covenant Marriage Law: A First Step Toward a More Robust Pluralism in Marriage and Divorce Law? 183

Parkman, Allen, *Marriage and Divorce Law, No Fault Divorce: What Went Wrong* (1993), pp. 12–23 162

Phillips, Roderick, *Putting Asunder: A History of Divorce in Western Society* 139

Reed, Allan, "Transnational Non-Judicial Divorces: A Comparative Analysis of Recognition under English and RS Jurisprudence" 144

Rosenthal, Stephen F., "Food for Thought: Kosher Food Laws and the Religion Clauses of the First Amendment" 149

Schochetman, Eliav, "Annulment of Marriages" 173

———., "The Essence of the Principles Used in Child Custody in Jewish Law" 173

Schwartz, Gedalia D., "The 1992 New York Get Law" 179

Scott, Patti A., "New York Divorce law and the Religion Clauses: An Unconstitutional Exorcism of the Jewish Get Laws" 147

Shapiro, Haim, "Haredi Family Fears for Future After Father is Excommunicated" 153

Shavell, Steven, "Alternative Dispute Resolution: An Economic Analysis" 167

US Department of State, "Travel Advisory Warning for Israel" 155

Vasoli, Robert H., *What God Has Joined Together: The Annulment Crisis in American Catholicism* 149

Vital Statistics of the United States: Marriage and Divorce 144

Weinstein, Jack B., "Some Benefits and Risks of Privatization of Justice through ADR" 161

Westreich, Elimelech "The Jewish Woman's Status in Israel Interactions Among the Various Traditions" 143–144

Willaims, Granville L "The Legal Unity of Husbands and Wife" 184

Willig, Mordechai, *The Prenuptial Agreement* 71

Witte, John, *From Sacrament to Contract: Marriage, Religion and Law in the Western Tradition* 183

Zweibel, Chaim D., "Accomodating Religious Objections to Brain Death: Legal Issues" 167

Cases, Statutes, and Model Codes

American Jurisprudence 2d, Criminal Law
21A §1034   184
In re Lindwall's Will, 287 NY 347 (1942) 184
Johnson v. Rockefeller, 58 FRD
SDNY (Dec. 18, 1972)   149
Laws Resolution of Women's Rights
of 1632   184
Louisiana Covenant Marriage Act
1997 *LA Acts* 1380   183
Loving v. Virginia 388 US 1, 12 (1967) 144
NJ Statutes §2C:217   166
NY Domestic Relations Law §36   143
§236B   147
§236B (5)   177
§253   147
§253 (6)   177

NY Matrimonial and Family Law
§1.06   184
Rakozynski v. Rakozynski
reported in *New York Law Journal*
(November 6, 1997)   153
RanDav's County Kosher, Inc. v. New Jersey
(1992) 608 A.2d 1353   179
State v. Duket, 63 NW (1895)   184
State of Israel, Penal Law Amendment
[Bigamy] Law, 5719 (1959)   143
Uniform Criminal Code
Article 9   144
Uniform Marriage and Divorce Act
§201   183
§306   183
Uniform Premarital Agreement Act
§3   183
Zablocki v. Redhail, 434 US 374 (1978) 144

Subject Index

Listings for rabbinic authorities can be found either according to the authority's last name, the name of the classical work, the personal acronym used by the authority, or, in the case of Talmudic Sages, by first name.

✳ ✳ ✳

Abromsky, R. Ezekiel 169
Agun de-gavra 74
Agunah xvi, 3, 10, 35, 37, 47, 137, 145, 147
  conversion of 5
  in America 8
  in Israel 9–10, 151
  in medieval times 5
  solutions for xi–xii, 60–71, 75, 86
  problems xi, xiii, xv, 40, 59, 73–5, 79, 85–6, 156, 158
Alternative dispute resolution 167
Annulment xii, 4–5, 10–11, 19, 59–61, 138–39, 142, 149, 161
Arbitration agreements 65
Ben-Dahan, R. Eliyahu 152

Bet din (Jewish court) xii, 25, 31, 37, 41, 43–4, 57–8, 77, 82, 86, 104, 128, 147, 151, 150, 163
  in America 127, 128, 129, 130, 131, 158–60
  corruption 52, 55
  fidelity to 53
  integrity of 53, 55, 77
  jurisdiction of 46–7, 49, 156–57
  role of 28 (chart), 45, 55, 71 (chart)
Betrothal (of a minor) 169
Blau, R. Joseph 52
Breitowitz, R. Irving xv, 63–64, 71 (chart), 182

Chalitzah, see Levirate separation
Cherem de Rabbenu Gershom
  (*see* Rabbenu Gershom)
Cherem, see Excommunication
Child custody   98
Civil divorce   29–31, 36, 37
  statistics   145
Civil death   125–126, 139
Civil marriage   xii, 30, 139, 144,
  168, 170, 175
Coercion (to give *get*)   10, 179
Coercive penalties   69, 162–163
Communal Practice   39
Community property laws   129
Concubine   63, 162
Conditions, *see also Tenai*   169
Conditional divorce   xii, 4
Conditional marriage   xii, 10, 12,
  64–65
Conditional promise
  (to give a *get*)   10, 12
Consent to marriage   2, 15–16, 141
Covenant marriage
  (Louisiana)   122–123
Custom   109, 110
  Common Commercial   38–9, 109,
  149, 170, 180

Death, evidence of   4
Din Torah   11
Dina de-malchuta   108, 110,
  113, 149, 180
Distancing of Rabbenu Tam   48, 56,
  57, 150, 160
Divorce
  authorization to   6, 8, 56,
  139–140, 162
  coerced   184
  compelled   147
  contractual model of   1, 2, 3 ,7,
  31, 91–94, 138
  dual system of   32, 39, 40,
  73, 162
  fault   10, 17, 18, 24, 28 (chart),
  121, 142, 143
  and the Jewish community   7

  mandatory   45, 47–8
  mutual consent to   21, 23
  pluralistic images of   81
  private law model of   32–3, 45, 54
  public law model of   32–3, 45
  and Reform Judaism   166
  refusal of   2
  religiously required   45, 48
  right to   xvi, xvii, 36–7,
  49, 80, 145
  in the Soviet Union   146
  technology   7–8, 73, 139
  unilateral exit rights   xii, 2, 14,
  16, 17, 18–23, 26–7, 28 (chart),
  60–61
  unilateral no-fault   38, 40,
  75, 168
  wife as agent   162

Eiger, R. Akiva   51, 114
Elyashiv, R. Shalom Yosef   110, 167,
  179
Engagement   2
Equitable distribution   108–109,
  129, 181
Error in the marriage
  bisexual man and   99, 100
  conditions of   90, 169
  continuing a marriage with   100–1
  economic reasons   176
  heart disease   174
  impotence   174
  menstruation   174
  prohibited marriage and   169
  promiscuity   176
  taut   11, 89–102, 137, 169,
  171, 174, 175, 176, 177
  sterility   174
Excommunication   10, 53, 150–52
Extortion   30, 145

Fault, penalty   130
Feinstein, R. Moshe   23, 28 (chart),
  39, 71 (chart), 89, 95, 97, 99, 100,
  105, 107, 108, 110, 115, 143, 176
Freeze, Chearan   150

Gender equality 23–5, 74, 85, 143, 146
Geonim 19–20, 23, 60, 87, 142
get me'useh, see Improperly coerced divorce
Get (writ of divorce) xi, 23, 24, 30, 45, 51, 130, 137, 179
  zekui 174
  presumption of validity 179

Harchakot shel Rabbenu Tam
  see Distancing of Rabbenu Tam
Henkin, R. Yosef Eliahu 23, 28 (chart), 71 (chart), 176, 179
Herzog, R Yitzchak Isaac 105, 112, 179–180
Heter meah rabbanim
  see Permission from 100 Rabbis
Husband, disappearing 3–4, 47, 73

Ilonit 101, 170
Improperly coerced divorce
  (get me'useh) 10, 13, 64, 104, 105–108, 111, 150, 160, 162, 164–165, 179, 181
  misconduct 112
  Rabbenu Yeruchum position 112
  repugnancy and 112
  size of penalties 111
  small economic sanctions 111
Islamic Law 126, 184
Israeli Rabbinical courts 9–10, 53–4, 88, 151, 153–54
  jurisdiction of 46–7, 49, 51
Isserless, R. Moshe 96, 111
"It is better for a woman to be with another (husband) unhappily than to be alone" 98, 99, 173, 174

Jewish family structure xiii
Jewish marriage models vi, 10

Karelitz, R. Abraham Isaiah 100, 105
Karo, R. Joseph 25, 143, 144, 147

Ketubah (dower) 2, 9, 17, 18, 20, 22, 38, 64, 109, 128, 129, 130, 134, 138, 141, 149, 153–54, 163
Kiddushin she-lo nimsaru leb'iah 170
Kinyan meshicha 93
Kinyan 131, 133, 170, 176
Kofin 163, 164, 180, 181
Kolitz, R. Yitzchak 151
Kashrut (kosher food laws) 75–6, 104, 151, 157, 177

Landau, R. Eziekeil 51, 114
Leibes, R. Yitzchak Isaac 108
Levirate marriage (yibum) 5–6, 96, 97, 171
Levirate separation (chalitzah) 97, 145–146, 173
Lookstein, R. Haskel 136, 162

Ma'os alai1 50
Maimonides 20, 21, 22, 24, 26–7, 28 (chart), 60, 71 (chart), 76, 112, 142–43
Malinowitz, R. Chaim 37
Marital stability 61
Marital Abode 23, 26, 28 (chart)
Marriage
  common law view 1, 126
  Catholic view 1, 119, 143, 149
  contractual model 1, 2, 3, 7, 31, 91–94, 138
  covenental model of 183
  Enlightenment model of 120
  European view 1
  intent to defraud upon entry 170
  intent to marry 171
  pluralistic images of 81
  in Russia 144–45
  private law model of 32–33, 45, 54
  prohibited 147
  public law model of 32–33, 45
  right to marry 145, 151
  social model of 119
  societal model of 120
  support obligations 9, 50

Mesader gittin   146, 150
Mesader kiddushin   146, 150
Minhag hasochrim, see Custom
Monogamy   141
Moredet   50–1, 113–14, 156, 182

Nachalat Shiva   13, 71 (chart)
Negotiation
  economic theory of   183
Neventzal, R. Avigdor   39, 110
New York Get Laws   12–13, 35–36,
  103–117, 137, 181–83
New York Divorce Reform
  Law (1966)   122
New Jersey   76
No-fault divorce legislation   122

Offset   145
Or Zarua, Rebbenu Chaim   23, 24,
  27, 28 (chart)
Oriental Jewry   22

Peligesh, see concubine
Permission from 100 Rabbis   24–25,
  143 , 153, 158
Polygamy   2, 18, 19, 23, 24, 25,
  52, 141, 143–44, 158
Prenuptial agreement   xii, 2, 29, 40
  54, 57, 58, 66–8, 71 (chart), 75, 79,
  82, 86, 127–136, 155–56, 162–63,
  164, 164–67
  of Orthodox Caucus   132–33
  pastoral concerns   163
Presumption   112, 152, 175, 182

Rabbenu Tam   24, 26–27, 28 (chart),
  48, 50, 67, 142, 161
Rabbenu Yeruchum   112
Rabbenu Gershom   2, 21, 22, 23,
  24–25, 26, 28 (chart), 48, 49, 50, 67,
  76, 141, 143–44, 162
Rabbinical Council of America   136
Rambam, *see* Maimonides
Recalcitrant husband   8, 34, 51,
  52, 73

Retaliation   73
Rosen, Ariel   185

Sanhedrin   43
Schreiber, R. Moshe   51, 114,
  182–83
Secular court   150, 180–81
Secular legal system   xii, xiii, xvi, 39,
  41, 44, 62, 79–80, 119–123, 139
Secular legislation   xvii, 10, 12,
  68–70, 104–105, 115–17
Seruv   56, 160
Shulchan Aruch   39, 88, 94,
  97, 100
Soloveitchik, R. Joseph   59, 174
State intervention in Jewish
  legal affairs   xvii, 10, 12, 68–70,
  104–105, 115–17
Submission to Rabbinical jurisdiction
  10, 14
Support   113
  agreements   10, 13, 66–7, 156
  payments   50–1, 156

Tav le mativ tan hu, melemativ armelo,
  see "It is better . . ."
Tenai   95–97, 170, 171
Toledano, R. Moshe   71 (chart)

Uniform Marriage and Divorce Act
                                 120–21
Uniform Premarital Agreement Act
                                     121
US Department of State
  advisory on travel   49–50

Waldenberg, R. Eliezer   28 (chart),
  51, 114, 151
Willig, R. Mordechai   66, 71 (chart),
  156, 164, 181

Yibum, see Levirate marriage
Yotzee   163–64

Zabla   164

About the Author

Michael Jay Broyde is an Associate Professor of Law at Emory University School of Law and the Academic Director of the Law and Religion Program at Emory University. His primary areas of interest are Jewish law and ethics, law and religion, and comparative religious law. In addition to Jewish law, he has taught courses on Federal Courts, Alternative Dispute Resolution, Secured Credit, and other subjects. He received a *juris doctor* from New York University and published a note in the *Law Review*.

Broyde clerked for Judge Leonard I. Garth of the United States Court of Appeals, Third Circuit. In addition, he was ordained as a rabbi by Yeshiva University (*yoreh-yoreh veyadin-yadin*) and is a member (*dayan*) of the Beth Din of America, the largest Jewish law court in America. He served as director of that court during the 1997–98 academic year while on leave from Emory. He is also the rabbi of Young Israel of Toco Hills, Atlanta.

His first book, *The Pursuit of Justice and Jewish Law*, was published by Yeshiva University Press and his second, *Human Rights and Judaism*, by Jason Aronson. He recently authored an article in the *Connecticut Law Review* entitled "Cloning People: A Jewish View."

Broyde has published more than fifty articles in various aspects of law and religion and Jewish law, including several in the area of federal courts, including an article in the *Harvard Journal of Law and Public Policy* on the impeachment process.